Illness as Many Narratives

Πονόμετρο δε βρίσκεται για να μετρά τον πόνο
τον πόνο τον κατέχουνε όσοι τον έχουν μόνο.

There is no instrument to measure pain
it can only be measured by those who experience it.

(Cretan *mantináda*)

Illness as Many Narratives

Arts, Medicine and Culture

Stella Bolaki

EDINBURGH
University Press

Edinburgh University Press is one of the leading university presses in the UK. We publish academic books and journals in our selected subject areas across the humanities and social sciences, combining cutting-edge scholarship with high editorial and production values to produce academic works of lasting importance. For more information visit our website: www.edinburghuniversitypress.com

© Stella Bolaki, 2016

Edinburgh University Press Ltd
The Tun – Holyrood Road, 12(2f) Jackson's Entry, Edinburgh EH8 8PJ

Typeset in 11/13 Adobe Sabon by
IDSUK (DataConnection) Ltd

A CIP record for this book is available from the British Library

ISBN 978 1 4744 0242 2 (hardback)
ISBN 978 1 4744 0243 9 (webready PDF)
ISBN 978 1 4744 1151 6 (epub)

The right of Stella Bolaki to be identified as the author of this work has been asserted in accordance with the Copyright, Designs and Patents Act 1988, and the Copyright and Related Rights Regulations 2003 (SI No. 2498).

Contents

Acknowledgements	vi
Introduction: Illness as Many Narratives	1
1. Re-Covering Scarred Bodies: Reading Photography	26
2. Artists' Books in the Medical Community	51
3. Performance Medicine and Radical Pedagogy	88
4. Collaborative Film as Terminal Care	125
5. Messy Confrontations: Theatre and Expert Knowledge	152
6. Animated Documentary and Mental Health	177
Afterword: #Illness	211
Bibliography	223
Index	244

Acknowledgements

Illness as Many Narratives is about the many narratives of illness, but the development of the ideas and the process of writing it contain a multitude of other narratives and encounters too. First and foremost, I owe a great debt to the anonymous reviewers for their insights and direction as the project was taking shape and to Jackie Jones, as well as to the editorial team, at Edinburgh University Press for their support at different stages. The book has been enriched by conversations with, and inspiration from, a number of friends, colleagues and scholars of illness narratives, medical humanities and disability studies over many years. I am especially thankful to Clare Best, Alan Radley, Angela Woods, David Bolt, Véronique Plesch, Harry Newman, Ariane Mildenberg, David Stirrup, Donna Landry, Stefanos Pavlakis, Maria Vaccarella, David Shuttleton, Chris Gair, Patricia Novillo-Corvalán and Shahd Alshammari. My gratitude goes to Cally Gurley, Jennifer S. Tuttle and Cathleen Miller for their generous help with material pertaining to the Martha Hall collection at the University of New England, as well as to Alan Hall, who kindly gave me permission to use images and quote from Martha Hall's artists' books. I would also like to acknowledge the financial assistance of the Institute for Advanced Studies in the Humanities (IASH) for a postdoctoral fellowship that helped me to develop my interest in illness narratives long before I conceived this project.

An earlier version of Chapter 1 entitled 'Re-Covering the Scarred Body: Textual and Photographic Narratives of Breast Cancer' appeared in *Mosaic, a Journal for the Interdisciplinary Study of Literature*, Volume 44, issue 2 (2011): 1–17. Portions of Chapter 2 appeared as '"What the Book Told": Illness, Witnessing, and Patient-Doctor Encounters in Martha Hall's Artists' Books' in *Gender Forum*, Volume 26 (2009), Special Issue on Literature and Medicine: 'Women in the Medical Profession Part II: Personal Narratives', guest edited by Carmen Birkle. I am grateful that this material could be reprinted with permission from these publications as well as to all the artists, institutions and organisations who allowed me to reproduce the images contained in this book, for which they hold copyright: Terry Dennett, Sam Taylor-Johnson and the White Cube, Bowdoin College Library, the Maine Women Writers Collection at the University of New England, Guillermo Gómez-Peña and La Pocha Nostra, Wim Wenders Stiftung and Andy Glynne at Mosaic Films.

My research has been energised by several fascinating conferences and workshops that I was fortunate to attend in the last few years, in particular: 'Global Medical Humanities' (University of Aberdeen, 2013); 'Attentive Writers: Healthcare, Authorship and Authority' (University of Glasgow, 2013); 'Malady and Mortality' (University of Falmouth, 2013); 'Concepts of Health and Illness' (University of the West of England, Bristol, 2010); 'The Boundaries of Illness: An Integrative Meeting' (King's College London, 2014); and 'Avoidance in/and the Academy: The International Conference on Disability, Culture, and Education' (Liverpool Hope University, 2013).

Many thanks to the students of the MA in Medical Humanities and the MA in the Contemporary programmes at Kent who participated in my illness narrative seminars, as well as to my students at the universities of Glasgow and Kent who chose my course on illness and disability in American culture. Finally, a very special thank you to my family for their love and support and to Derek for generously giving time to share insights, read and comment on numerous drafts, and for his trust that it would all come together in the end.

Introduction

Illness as Many Narratives

This book starts from the premise that illness narratives are characterised by multiplicity. Among the texts and artworks I encountered in my research, few have driven this idea home (in all its different senses) to me more than my father's own cancer narrative. His untitled story is unfinished and remains unpublished, handwritten in a language that would not be accessible to an Anglophone audience without translation. Reading it a couple of years after his death in 2009, as two kinds of readers inhabiting the same body – a daughter and an academic equipped with various critical tools – I found myself being moved and intellectually intrigued by several of its features.

My father was trained as a mathematician, acquiring expertise in what I considered to be the ultimate discipline of abstraction, and never hid his admiration for numbers. Yet, with the exception of one mathematical equation he devises to explore the relationship between finite life and the concept of infinity (often treated as if it were a number in mathematics), the tools he uses to endow his experiences with meaning are narrative tools. This is not to say that his is a straightforward or single narrative. In its multiplicity of styles, it refuses easy categorisation: one can find diary sections with medical facts and details, but these are integrated into a larger life narrative, and the latter, in turn, into what has been described in literary studies as 'narrative of community'.[1] My father's story was, consciously or not, documenting not only the everyday rituals of illness and a body in crisis but also details of the rich local life of a Cretan village, where he grew up: the lives of its few remaining inhabitants (improvised stories that emerge, as his narrative indicates, as these people pass by the porch where he sat to write on their way to their daily business), small and large events, traditions under threat by a range of social and cultural changes in Greece; in short, a collective story with the ability to 're-enchant' his illness narrative by investing in other stories and encounters outside of the clinical framework of patients and doctors.² These narratives, personal and collective, are often interrupted by interpolated drawings (of his garden and the view of the sky's horizon from where he sat to write), signalling the need to turn to a visual medium to communicate aspects of his story better, as well as by what is known as *mantináda* (μαντινάδα in Greek), an oral tradition associated with poetry, music and performance.³ Especially prominent on the island of Crete, *mantináda* refers to a compressed narrative or short poem that typically consists of rhyming couplets. It is often improvised and recited in the rhythm of accompanying music at feasts and other singing events. When composed and performed in this way, a verse elicits a response by another person and this in turn leads to another response – the dialogue continues until the end of the song. *Mantinádes* are much more than a means of entertainment. Many Cretans, especially the older generation, approach them as a fundamental way of expressing feelings such as love, pain, fear and loneliness and even as an *ars vivendi*, a Cretan 'art of living', which in the case of my father's illness experience was also a kind of alternative or complementary treatment.

In opening *Illness as Many Narratives* with my father's story, my aim is not simply to account for my personal interest in illness narratives (though scholarship in this area often still invites autobiographical justifications), but rather to raise a set of broader questions with which this book is also concerned: in (re)reading my father's story I knew that, as a representation, it did not offer unmediated access to his lived experience during the years of his illness. However, this does not lessen the work's expressive power; neither does the fragmentation, discontinuity or the switches to alternative genres, noted earlier, even as they draw attention to the contingent nature and inadequacy of verbal forms of communication, and the affective excess that cannot be contained by them. In gathering together the many different strands of his narrative performance, I wondered which of the stories or components in my father's account would be considered more relevant or 'fitting' for an illness narrative. Would a medical practitioner or educator skip the sections from his 'narrative of community' or try to establish connections across distinct narratives? What would critics of self-indulgent memoirs make of these vignettes that populate the narrative with the stories of the villagers, or of the *mantinádes*? How relevant is my father's national/cultural/professional background to the structure and the forms he chose for his narrative, and what kind of response do they call out in other people? What demands, if any, does his narrative make for anyone who encounters it, and how can these demands be met? What are the ethical and other potential questions raised by my particular mode of responding to this narrative here, or my responsibility in the future (for example, if I were to fulfil my father's wish to make his story available to others)?

Responding to the criticisms that narrative has received in the last decade or so after a period of enthusiastic reception within the growing field of the medical humanities,[4] *Illness as Many Narratives* offers ways to open up the category of illness narrative and the limited methods employed so as to produce more sophisticated and interdisciplinary readings of health, illness and medicine. It draws on important work that has been done in literary and cultural studies on the illness memoir but expands current understandings of illness narrative by adopting a comparative approach in its juxtaposition of arts/media and illnesses across and within chapters. I focus on a wide range of artistic and cultural representations – both autobiographical and collaborative projects, including mixed media forms – to create a more inclusive illness narrative canon that decentres the literary form as the paradigm for understandings of this genre and draws connections between different illness experiences. The works I discuss include photographic portraits, artists' books, performance art, theatre, film, animation and online narratives, many of which have yet to receive sustained attention, and treat breast cancer, liver disease, lung cancer, chronic fatigue syndrome and mental health. In enlarging the field's scope beyond canonical works and those bound by the context of biomedicine or merely the doctor-patient encounter, the following case studies challenge instrumental or reductive applications of the arts within the medical humanities, establish important links between medical and the broader culture and demonstrate how the arts/humanities and medicine can critically interact with each other. It is in all these ways that 'illness as many narratives' can be seen as furthering the work of the *critical* medical humanities.[5]

Illness narratives and the critical medical humanities

Illness narrative as a term is used across disciplines that inform the medical humanities, including medical sociology, anthropology and literary studies. Since Arthur Kleinman's distinction between illness and disease in the 1980s in *The Illness Narratives*, illness stories or narratives have been seen as giving expression to the subjective or lived experience of a particular disease or condition, which is distinct from the clinical definition of disease understood as an organic dysfunction within biomedicine (1988: 3–6). The subtitle of Kleinman's book, *Suffering, Healing and the Human Condition*, emphasises the need for patients to give voice to their suffering and for medicine to find ways to 'record this most thickly human dimension of patients' and families' stories of experiencing illness' (28). Typically illness narratives combine an auto/biographical narrative about living with an illness with reflections upon the wider implications of a particular disease, treatment, recovery and interactions with medical professionals. Kleinman's *The Illness Narratives* does not discuss published accounts of illness by patients and their families, but work by Anne Hunsaker Hawkins, Arthur Frank and Thomas Couser does. In *Reconstructing Illness* Hawkins examines the emergence of what she calls 'pathographies' in the late twentieth century through their relation to the religious conversion narratives that enjoyed a parallel popularity in earlier centuries, and considers the ways underlying myths and metaphors such as rebirth, battle and the journey give form to illness narratives. In addition to writing his own illness narrative (*At the Will of the Body*), Frank has offered a typology in *The Wounded Storyteller* by describing three narrative types: the 'restitution' narrative, the 'chaos' narrative and the 'quest' narrative. While Frank as a medical sociologist is primarily interested in situating clinical ethics and social science 'within a more general ethics of the body' and moving practitioners 'in the direction of thinking with stories' (1995: 23–4), literary critics like Couser (1997) have explored autopathography as a distinctive genre that has both enriched and challenged aspects of the repertoire of life writing.

Illness narrative has grown exponentially in the mid twentieth and twenty-first centuries.[6] Hawkins writes that 'it is surely no accident that the appearance of pathography coincides with the triumph of scientific technological medicine' (1999: xii). In *The Wounded Storyteller* Frank enlists the 'postmodern' (his study is published after Lyotard's 1984 account of the collapse of grand narratives) and the 'postcolonial' to capture rhetorically the 'writing back' to medicine that illness narratives effect (1995: 13).[7] A series of factors and changes after the 1950s seem to have contributed to an increasing interest in representations of illness, pain and suffering by people who experience illness first-hand or those who are close to them. Framing this study as it moves (though not following a strict chronological structure) from the politicised feminist patient of the late seventies through to the increasing use of social media to communicate illness experiences in the present moment, these factors include: medical professionalisation and specialisation affecting doctor-patient relationships; the emergence of the women's, gay rights and disability movements, as well as the powerful influence of AIDS; and of course the popularity of certain life-writing genres (self-help narratives, memoirs) and technologies that facilitated self-publication. These advances remain relevant, and have expanded considerably in the age of the rapid development of digital technology and media convergence.

Illness narratives have garnered positive attention, and their contribution to narrative medicine has linked them with the notion of 'narrative competence' (Charon 2006: 12), turning them into tools that enhance clinical diagnosis and treatment and provide valuable insights to medical practitioners as well as patients. Despite this recognition, in 'The Limits of Narrative' medical humanities critic Angela Woods highlights a series of pressing questions about the use of narrative in an effort to reignite debate about its role in the field. The valorisation of narrative as 'the mode of human self-expression' (2011a: 74) promotes ideas of individual authenticity and a particular kind of self (neo/liberal, Western, middle class). These ideas have been equally questioned by social scientists who seek to locate illness narratives in a wider social context,[8] and by literary/cultural studies scholars who approach them as 'texts' or draw attention to a range of narratives (cross-cultural, queer) that challenge normative assumptions. Woods, however, more fundamentally highlights 'the normativity of narrativity' (76), in other words the suggestion that conceiving one's life as a narrative or story is fundamentally healthy, desirable and necessary. This is an assumption that characterises Frank's typology whereby the quest narrative is presented as an ideal to which everyone should aspire in order to reclaim and reorient the self that has been disrupted by illness:

> Restitution stories attempt to outdistance mortality by rendering illness transitory. Chaos stories are sucked into the undertow of illness and the disasters that attend it. Quest stories meet suffering head on; they accept illness and seek to *use* it. Illness is the occasion of a journey that becomes a quest. (1995: 115)[9]

Woods writes that 'narrative returns us again and again to structure, coherence and unity ... What place is there for formlessness, for meaninglessness, for silence?' (2013: 125). Rather than arguing that we should 'discourage patients and doctors from telling stories or view with suspicion anyone whose sense of self is articulated in narrative terms', she suggests that scholars in the medical humanities can do more 'to foster a critical approach to the normative scripts of particular kinds of narrative', as well as 'more radically' move beyond narrative (2011a: 76).[10] The latter is framed as 'an invitation' that Woods believes 'scholars and practitioners in the medical humanities must be ready to accept' (2013: 126).

Woods' reminder of the limits of narrative is an important intervention in the field, but there is more to say about this term and the ongoing potential of illness narratives to shape wider debates about health, illness and the medical humanities. This is why the title of this book retains the term 'narrative' even as it defamiliarises it by linking it to different media and artistic forms. The proliferation of illness representations in contemporary culture attests to continuing forms of silencing at the hands of biomedicine while also informing a wide range of artistic and cultural practices. (Auto)pathographies and illness memoirs are well represented in illness narrative scholarship, but this is not the case for other media and artistic forms that intersect with narrative. Moreover, stories of particular conditions, and especially of mental distress, are comparatively fewer, and medical humanities is 'culturally limited by a pedagogical and scholarly emphasis on Western cultural artefacts' (Hooker and Noonan 2011: 79). This series of qualifiers, taken up in the following chapters, begs the question whether moving beyond narrative would be necessary or desired if we were to define narrativity more broadly[11] and multiply existing narratives. Even though some critics are adamant that this should be 'only a first step' (Sartwell 2000: 84), I would argue that there is room to challenge *and* expand narrative's conception and role within the medical humanities field, and that the works I consider in this book invite us precisely to do both.

There has been a tendency in the 'first wave of medical humanities', since its establishment as an identifiable field in the early 1970s (first in the US and later in the UK) and the rise of pathography in the 1980s and 1990s, to treat narrative as synonymous with verbal, if not literary, expression and to define it in terms of linearity and coherence. However, as scholars in literary studies and across disciplines have shown, illness stories often challenge chronological causality and unity. Cheryl Mattingly coins the term 'emergent narratives' to describe those stories (in her case within the clinical encounter) that, though still dependent on existing cultural resources, are 'embodied' and 'improvised' rather than told. Emergent narratives are 'clearly allied to performative views of narrative and action' and are not characterised by coherence but rather 'narrative drama'. Mattingly's description of 'how we follow a narrative suspensefully, always reminded of the fragility of events, for things might have turned out differently' (2000: 205) resonates with my discussion of film and performance in Chapters 4 and 5. Illness narratives take many forms and embrace different genres and media, some of which intersect with narrative as it is conventionally understood. In fact, two of Woods' proposed alternatives to narrative discussed in 'The Limits of Narrative' – metaphor and photography – function in this way, rather than as strictly anti-narrative modes. Woods herself acknowledges this when she describes metaphors as 'building blocks of narrative' that drive the story forward even as they lack the larger temporal structure of narrative (2011a: 76). Similarly, the myth of the photograph as a purely visual image has been challenged. Photographs often have captions and titles, if not a longer text attached to them; and as Victor Burgin and others have suggested, even when this is not the case, they are 'traversed by language' when they are interpreted by viewers (1982: 144).[12]

When approached as a communicative act and as essential to the process of meaning-making, narrative is not tied to a single medium. Alongside photography and forms that gesture towards narrative without appealing to elaborate stories (for example, the short animated film that has affinities with metaphor), this book focuses on works which, even though they do not rely exclusively on linguistic expression to give shape to experiences of physical and emotional distress, do not abandon it altogether. In this way, I show how the category of illness narrative can be opened up by addressing some of its limits and conservative assumptions from within, that is, through the works' own generic multiplicity and mixed-media nature that often lead to important aesthetic collisions. Thus word and image in photography; stories and images or distinct visual modalities in documentary film; text and the various other elements of an artist's book; performance art and theatrical conventions in autobiographical theatre; and animated drawing and documentary voice in animated documentary collide, but also enrich each other, in the following case studies. While acknowledging that the term illness narrative can be trivialised through overuse and overinflated, as Woods cautions, I believe that expanding rather than limiting current definitions and approaches to illness narrative can benefit medicine, the arts and cultural studies.[13] As the medical humanities is moving towards a new phase, taking stock of the need to forge alliances with the arts and humanities in order to remain pluralistic and experimental, it is a timely moment to recognise the many narratives of illness in all the senses of this phrase: the multiplicity of illnesses and their treatments; the different arts and media that need to be included in the field; and finally, the range of methods that will foster a more critical engagement with health, medicine and culture.

Many directions have been indicated in the last few years with the goal of enlarging the scope of the medical humanities and sharpening its critical edge. The medical humanities, we might say, suffers from an identity crisis, and nearly every conference or publication in the field includes a discussion of defining or redefining its name, boundaries and approaches. In its response to Howard Brody's three personalities of the medical humanities ('disciplinary list', 'programme of moral development' and 'supportive friend'),[14] the Centre for Medical Humanities at Durham University (2011) in the UK has recently suggested that 'those purposes are very much anchored within the culture and practices of medicine and are engaged in serving it'. The problem with conceptualising the field in an '"instrumental way" is that we prevent it from gaining sufficient distance from medicine to take a radically critical view'.[15] Woods, Anne Whitehead and Alan Bleakley, writing from different disciplines but intersecting in their interest in medical humanities, emphasise the need for a more critical medical humanities. Bleakley favours critique and resistance, a more interdisciplinary approach that avoids 'Western imperialistic tendencies' and a less 'utilitarian and artistically conservative model' (2014a: 23–4). Whitehead also takes issue with the dominant conceptualisation of the medical humanities in 'purely humanising or humanistic terms' (2014: 119). She proposes a shift from practitioner pedagogy and training (or an 'additive' view) towards a more 'integrated' view whereby the nature, goals and knowledge base of clinical medicine might be 'challenged and reshaped' rather than simply 'softened' by its encounter with the humanities (108). While in the following chapters I suggest that the value of the medical humanities is not limited to educational concerns, I am keen not to dismiss the distinct pedagogical potential of the artistic forms I consider – particularly the ways a more critical or radical pedagogy emerging from different sites and media can reshape and challenge existing practices within medical education.[16]

The discussion about the limits of narrative, like the debate about the goals and purposes of the medical humanities, has perhaps been divisive, but it does not have to be approached in purely negative terms. As a terrain where vital issues are being negotiated it has also served as a necessary precondition for renewed transformative articulations in the field, and thus as a form of giving new energy and impetus for conversation. This more positive view, which this book embraces, is evident in Keir Waddington and Martin Willis' journal special issue 'Rethinking Approaches to Illness Narratives'. They argue that 'the limited range of methods presently employed unnecessarily restricts what illness narratives might be allowed to mean, and even what they might look like' (2013: iv). Contributors to this special issue make a plea for 'reclaim[ing]the aesthetic and imaginative qualities from a system that reduces illness narratives (and healthcare more broadly) to nothing more than a further set of utterances that provide specialist medical data' (Willis et al. 2013: 68). Such utilitarian sensibility is something that often characterises approaches coming from the social sciences, where, typically, illness narratives are viewed as data to be solicited through interviews and then transcribed and analysed through certain methodologies. Even when this is not the case, the selection and analysis of illness narratives are normally framed by the doctor-patient encounter rather than other actors, and by the context of biomedicine, instead of situating their contribution in various aesthetic, historical and political traditions. Like these critics, Susan Merrill Squier argues in favour of the introduction of a more diverse set of literary texts and a new set of reading practices that 'can release us from the contract to which we are bound when we accept the implicit frame of both medicine and literature'. She envisages a more inclusive canon that would encompass not only canonical fiction and poetry, but also 'the full range of written cultural expression' (2007: 338). Whitehead similarly endorses the potential of the field 'to engage with an expanded notion of literary genre', including more experimental and 'mixed-media narrative modes' that redress the dominance of realist fiction and autobiography in existing scholarship (2014: 114).

In many ways such calls for more nuanced and sophisticated approaches to illness narratives are beginning to be addressed in the work of scholars trained in literary and cultural studies, including the aforementioned critics. Susanna Egan, for example, has explored the challenges disability and illness pose to autobiography and life writing more broadly, leading to generic experimentation, 'instability in perspective, narration, medium or authority' (1999: 28). Such approaches deconstruct the idea that illness narratives are linear or offer coherence, place narratives in historical and cultural contexts as opposed to following typologies, and intervene in more traditional approaches to literature such as Rita Charon's, which privileges a specific canon and approach to texts (realist fiction and autobiography, and close reading indebted to New Criticism). However, their contribution has not been recognised in mainstream medical humanities criticism, which still revolves around the influential models of Brody, Couser, Frank, Hawkins and Charon.

Neither, though, has scholarship on illness narratives been unequivocally embraced by literary and cultural studies. Many scholars working in these fields have had to actively make room for illness narratives to be considered worthy of literary or theoretical study. Both Lisa Diedrich and Ann Jurecic devote space to counter dismissive views of illness memoirs as 'victim art' and as 'nothing more than a self-indulgent mining of personal experience' (Diedrich 2007: xiv). Diedrich's study conceives illness memoirs as 'affective and effective histories' (xvii) and synthesises theoretical approaches which do justice to both the movements that can be found in such narratives: a movement *in* (the embodied self in relation to itself) and a movement *out* (the embodied self in relation to others; to institutions, including in particular the institution of medicine; and to communities, national and otherwise) (xix). Similarly, Jurecic confronts the suspicion towards emotion and testimony in the academy and argues against the view that *all* illness narratives distract from the structural through their unashamed valorisation of the personal. Responding to Rita Felski's call to consider the ordinary motives for reading and writing, Jurecic embraces illness memoirs for the challenges they present to literary criticism and models what she calls, after Eve Kosofsky Sedgwick, 'reparative' practices (2012: 105).[17] These practices can bridge the divide between mainstream medical humanities criticism, with its interest in the pedagogical or therapeutic/humanistic value of writing about illness, and literary criticism, which is perceived as valuing indeterminacy and complexity.

A central task for the critical medical humanities is to underline the limitations of narrow disciplinary approaches to illness narrative – that is, to show how rigid interpretations in both the arts/humanities and the social sciences fail to address the kind of *work* that these narratives do. *Works of Illness* by social psychologist Alan Radley opens with a series of debates concerning whether illness representations across different forms 'are good art' or constitute 'good science' (2009: 30). The common problem he identifies is that both camps approach such works as transparent windows into a person's experience. This in turn raises the thorny question of truthfulness, or opens the works to critiques of self-indulgence and of aestheticising illness. Focusing on the realm of arts and media with which *Illness as Many Narratives* is concerned, Radley looks at Arlene Croce's 1994 article in the *New Yorker*, 'Discussing the Undiscussable', which has become a common reference point for scholars working with illness narratives. As is well known, Croce refused to attend and dismissed the performance *Still/Here* by HIV-positive choreographer Bill T.

Jones. In her words, she could not review someone who she 'feel[s] sorry for or hopeless about' (1994/5: 17). The performance elicited sympathy and 'a personal, emotional response' from the audience that made 'dispassionate analytical judgement' impossible (17).[18] Radley juxtaposes Croce's non-review with another controversy that also relates to people with AIDS: Jan Zita Grover and Douglas Crimp's commentaries against Nicholas Nixon's *Pictures of People*, a photography exhibition presented at the Museum of Modern Art in New York in 1988. While the exhibition gave faces to statistics by showing pictures of people with AIDS, it emphasised the personal and private rather than the public and contextual. The images, most of which were photographed close-up, exacerbated the victimisation of the subjects, thus eliciting pity as opposed to solidarity. As Radley concludes about the juxtaposition of the two debates:

> On the one hand, Croce strives to preserve art at the expense of hearing the voice of afflicted people. On the other hand, Crimp and Grover seek to empower afflicted people by freeing them from the representations of the photographer/artist, and of the media. At a superficial level there is a sense that art and illness do not mix, that the values of art ... cannot serve the needs of ill people. (2009: 23)

Radley clarifies that the scope of his study is not to determine whether representations of illness should be judged as 'art with a capital A', but to address 'why and how ill people might want to use artistic portrayal as the means to say important things about their experience and their situation. What can one say or show in this way that is not said more directly or more clearly from a medical, scientific or documentary perspective?' (38) Considering how people shape and give form to their experiences of illness for themselves and others shifts attention from the idea of the elevated self in autobiographical writing to 'the fabrication of illness in the modern age' (31). By examining the way works of illness '"do their job" both in the mode of presentation and in the apparent response that they call out in other people' (38), Radley shows how aesthetic practice, which is distinct from aestheticisation, can bear upon ethics as well as the spheres of medicine, science and the arts.

Despite their disciplinary and other differences, what emerges from this recent scholarship is that illness narratives do important work in the contemporary world but that doing justice to its complexity requires a set of tools that need to be actively fashioned. How to create 'critical practices that are grounded in everyday life, practices that are rigorous, compelling and, at the same time, socially engaged and thoughtfully empathic' is the question that motivates Jurecic's hybrid methodology (2012: 17). Diedrich notes of her own practice of 'crossing multiple domains – literary, philosophical, cultural, political, medical' – that it leads to a 'new object' that does not belong to the 'experts' of any of these individual domains (2007: viii). Radley, too, asserts that illness narratives are 'immune from being quite absorbed into the fields of art, medicine or science': 'Made in the interstices between these spheres they are fugitive and yet resilient to the extent that they retain their power to stand up, effectively to be *works*' (2009: 213). It is the active fashioning of tools, this constructive process that draws on different disciplines and perspectives, that I argue should be at the heart of the critical medical humanities.

What all of these urgent and ongoing debates demonstrate is that both in medical humanities scholarship and in literary/cultural studies there have been objections about narrative, and specifically about illness narrative; whereas moving *beyond* narrative is one invitation/provocation that individual disciplines perceive in distinct ways, whether they endorse it or not, another one, taken on in this book, is to continue fashioning tools and approaches that can attend to the polyvalent and important work that illness narratives do personally, culturally and politically. It is precisely this commitment that can generate and sustain the critical dimension of both illness narratives and the medical humanities. While the majority of the scholars mentioned above have shown the importance of expanding our responses to the illness memoir, this book considers a wide range of media and art forms whose aesthetic practices and cultural politics can be productively examined and re-contextualised under the umbrella of illness (as many) narratives and the critical medical humanities. This is not an exhaustive study, given that other illnesses as well as art forms and media, not to mention geographical and cultural contexts, could be addressed in relation to the chapters that follow. However, it is my hope that the critical approaches modelled can be translated across environments beyond what is covered here.

The case studies: towards a critical interloping

There is an assumption that the arts and illness should not 'mix', as already mentioned, but the sheer quantity of projects that treat illness, health and broadly-conceived medical topics demonstrate that they frequently do, whether this leads to controversy or not. Audrey Shafer notes that with the exception of art therapy and art practices within health and care settings, there are many artists, filmmakers and performers who may work with themes and issues of the medical humanities but do not affiliate themselves (or publicly associate) with the field. For Shafer, 'therein lies the next demarcation, dilemma and delight' for the medical humanities. As she explains, 'The delight is the welcome of front-line artists and interlopers from distant disciplines to the cause of medical humanities. The dilemmas include a snubbing of medical humanities as a dilute, noncritical mishmash of applied theory without academic depth, rigor or demarcation' (2009: 3). Shafer's choice of the word 'interloper' is a productive way of describing the work of recontextualisation and cross-fertilisation that takes place in the case studies of this book. The choice of art forms, genres and specific texts as well as juxtapositions/comparisons across and within the following six chapters participate in what I would like to call a *critical interloping* that works in two ways: inserting a variety of artistic and cultural representations that explore illness within the field of the medical humanities to expand its scope and existing approaches, and to create a more inclusive illness narrative canon; and at the same time modelling ways in which the arts and arts/media scholarship can enlarge their practices and critical approaches (for example on aesthetics, ethics, the body, disability and death) through more explicit dialogue with the critical medical humanities.

It could be claimed that the term 'interloping' has negative connotations, since it suggests an unwelcome presence or intrusion. Jo Spence, whose work is examined in Chapter 1, certainly felt like an interloper in the 1980s when she brought her photographic work to the medical community in the UK. As she writes:

> Within the [medical] orthodoxy, I occasionally met with pockets of resistance, glimmers of hope, as people talked about and practised more holistic attitudes towards health. Yet it still seemed difficult for them to understand that, as a photographer, I might have something to contribute to *their* debates. Medicine and photography fragment the same human bodies, if in different ways ... And if I was sick of medical people who viewed me as only an object of study of treatment, I was equally sick of academics within my own discourse who wrote theories of the representation of bodies, without in any way seeming to inhabit their own. (Spence 1995: 130)

Spence saw herself as an outsider from both the medical and academic communities, and her practice of phototherapy – contained neither within institutional frameworks of art therapy, nor documentary or artistic work on the body – can be envisaged in terms of bridge-building, or more polemically, as a form of critical interloping. I write *critical* because interloping does not simply entail adding a range of texts or genres but also, as the passage above shows, engaging with different methods and actively opening up space for them to reshape or challenge existing practices across disciplines.

While the value of the insights many artists bring to the medical humanities is more recognised today, it is difficult to shake dominant assumptions that the more 'relevant' representations, or those that 'belong' under the umbrella of illness narratives and the medical humanities, are those that are directly linked to medicine or focus explicitly on the doctor-patient encounter. This reductive or utilitarian approach prevents the inclusion of alternative genres, contexts and methods within the field, and in turn perpetuates the view of the medical humanities as a narrow area of study that has little to say to writers and artists not working within art therapy or in close collaboration with medical education programmes. Responding to this problematic view, *Illness as Many Narratives* argues for the need of more cross-fertilisation and mutually illuminating conversations between contemporary arts and media practices/scholarship and the fields of illness narratives and the medical humanities, as well as between medicine and broader culture.[19] The latter division is attached more to perceptions of Western 'scientific', rather than non-Western, medicine, and this is why the book's examples are drawn in their majority from a Western context. In showing how illness narratives resist being fully absorbed by either the concerns of the arts or those of medicine, and in the wake of the fascinating debate into 'the turn to memoir as a sign of either the exhaustion of theory or its renewed life' (Cvetkovich 2012: 3) in literary criticism, *Illness as Many Narratives* suggests that engaging with a range of illness narratives and multiple perspectives can help the arts, cultural studies and the medical humanities to overcome divisions and amplify the goals and scope of their respective work.

Though not referring to illness narratives per se, in their epistolary reflections on 'the productive tensions inherent in approaching medicine from multiple perspectives' (2004: 243), Squier and Hawkins testify to the importance of making connections across disciplinary methodologies. Citing Donna Haraway's call to forge 'an earth-wide network of connections, including the ability to translate knowledges among very different – and power-differentiated – communities', Squier and Hawkins conclude:

> Whether we teach in a university or a medical school, whether we write for humanities scholars or physicians, the medical humanities and cultural studies can enable us to make those connections: to see how bodies get made (and remade) in the hospital, the farm, the school and the home, and how in each site we have the choice to cultivate better, less compromised, lives. (2004: 253)

It is the task and challenge of forging, sustaining and expanding such dialogue and conversation, including critique, that should animate the medical humanities as it defines and redefines its future goals. The chapters that follow take on precisely this task by putting in practice the idea of critical interloping.

Illness as Many Narratives opens with two chapters that examine narratives about women's health, specifically breast cancer, and address both the politics of medicine and feminist responses to illness. This is a way of acknowledging the contribution of the women's health movement – which I should stress does not limit itself to breast cancer – to the critique of biomedicine and the development of alternative knowledges/practices about the body. By finding alignments between medical perspectives, feminist theory/activism, artistic practice, pedagogy and the lived experience of illness, the works I focus on in Chapters 1 and 2 open up medical understandings of the body and of breast cancer while also expanding limiting narratives about women's health within mainstream public discourse, such as that of the neoliberal postfeminist subject. Chapter 1 is the only chapter with a specifically historical emphasis, as it compares narratives of scarred bodies from the 1980s to the present. It stages a conversation between the work of two British photographers who have explored breast cancer, Jo Spence and Sam Taylor-Wood, and the responses to mastectomy and prosthesis/breast reconstruction of two American feminist critics/activists, Audre Lorde and Diane Price Herndl, who equally speak from different historical moments. In adding a new interpretative layer to Taylor-Wood's work, considered up to now primarily in the context of contemporary artistic practices and postmodernism, the chapter begins the kind of conversations between artists, theorists and medical humanities scholars that are necessary in order to introduce an alternative range of material and methods to forge a more critical medical humanities.

Despite their national and generic differences or the contexts in which they have been received, when read together, the photographs and texts I juxtapose in Chapter 1 share aesthetic concerns but also mark important stages in the representation of breast cancer and of the post-operative body during the twentieth and twenty-first centuries. As such these works, rather than simply having a private dimension, shape public perceptions and debates about: visibility and concealment in illness representations and the competing discourses of patienthood (politicised or not) associated with them, a topic addressed in the following chapters in relation to various media and illnesses rather than a historical shift; and the conditions under which photography can successfully usurp the power of the medical gaze to re-imagine or re-cover bodies – a subject that prepares the ground for Chapter 2, which focuses on doctor-patient encounters, as well as for subsequent chapters which examine other artistic practices as alternative forms of treatment.

Chapter 1 also introduces a central operation that underlies my notion of illness as many narratives, drawing attention to formal complexity, ambiguity and open-endedness as important tools for challenging instrumental approaches to the medical humanities and pointing to the more radical possibilities of the arts. The collision between narrative and image, or between certain kinds of conventions and the auto/biographical performance of illness – discussed here in relation to the tension between visible self/image and voice/caption, and in the context of feminist politics – is staged in subsequent chapters in relation to other illnesses, media and cultural backgrounds.

If in Chapter 1 Taylor-Wood and Herndl find new ways of inhabiting post-surgical bodies by balancing exposure and concealment or provocation and beauty in their narratives of re-covery, Chapter 2 turns to a form that equally negotiates the private and public and that historically has been associated with both aesthetic and political considerations, as well as with women's artistic practices. In examining the artists' books of Martha Hall, an American woman who unlike the women in Chapter 1 did not inhabit the 'identities' of artist, feminist or activist prior to her illness diagnosis in 1989, this chapter explores a medium that has rarely been discussed in relation to the medical humanities or breast cancer. The artists' books Hall created until her death in 2003 expand customary definitions of narrative, and document her interactions with the medical community as well as her development as an artist. Art historians and book critics typically describe the handling of artists' books in terms of a powerful aesthetic experience that emphasises the visual, tactile and other sensuous pleasures of the book. However, in synthesising approaches to fashion new tools that can mutually enrich the medical humanities and the field of artists' books, this chapter shows how Hall's books also engage and complicate ethical/political discourses of testimony and witnessing through their interactive form and content, thus placing a more radical set of demands upon their readers. As in the first chapter, I analyse the challenges Hall's work poses to mainstream breast cancer culture and the way in which her aesthetic strategies relate to politics. I also assess the provocations of her artists' books for medical communities, to whom Hall attached special importance, and suggest that her work creates spaces for unpredictable and unfinished relational encounters that can reinvigorate models of empathy in medical education. In this way I open up the question of pedagogy, specifically by reflecting on the importance of touch, which Chapter 3 examines further in relation to performance art.

Chapter 3 broadens the intimate context of ethical responsibility and embodied witnessing that artists' books stage for their various readers, as well as their pedagogical potential, by moving beyond the patient-doctor encounter. It shows how performance art can foster important forms of inter-relational and cross-cultural ethics/politics that expand understandings of medicine and treatment for both individual and social pathologies. The focus is on Mexican/Chicano performance artist Guillermo Gómez-Peña, whose work on immigration, politics of language and 'extreme culture', unlike Hall's, does not at first sight appear relevant to debates about illness and the medical humanities. In envisaging him as an interloper into these fields, I return to the key question of what we bring, or fail to bring, into medical education/humanities, raised in this Introduction. I argue that Gómez-Peña's work can enrich the medical humanities not only because it introduces a new 'provocative' medium or a set of 'extreme bodies' that draw on medical imagery, but also because it engages with a range of methods – most notably, radical pedagogical and political strategies – that can challenge instrumental applications of the arts/humanities. His body-based and spoken-word performances over the last thirty years, as well as the pedagogical methodologies that he has developed together with the art collective La Pocha Nostra, have established connections between disparate contexts and discourses. These include the early modern anatomy theatre and the freak show; the technologically augmented/post-human body; global geopolitical events; and, extending key tropes of the previous chapters beyond clinical conceptions of health, 'the *invisible* surgery' to which poor people, racial/ethnic minorities and disabled people are subjected in the popular media (especially since 9/11 and the War on Terror). In this chapter I show how this work speaks to current efforts to expand the province of medical ethics/humanities by addressing a wider context of pain, suffering and cultural healing, and how performance as radical pedagogy can dismantle authoritarian hierarchies and replace specialised knowledge with interdisciplinary dialogue, imagination and opportunities for increased individual and social agency. When La Pocha Nostra describe themselves not simply as artists but 'as radical pedagogues immersed in the great debates of our times', they voice a message that the medical humanities should adhere to so as to avoid shrinking into a narrow field and losing the breadth of vision that will keep it vibrant in the future.

The second part of the chapter turns to Gómez-Peña's solo performances, which explore his personal experience with illness and disability – specifically with liver disease and the risk of neurological damage after a viral infection. This work reframes and extends his earlier collaborative explorations of the body and border identity by creating palimpsestuous narratives that connect illness in the individual and in society and become vehicles for broader philosophical, political and artistic/professional struggles. As in the first two chapters, I examine the political ways of performing illness that Gómez-Peña adopts to counter neoliberal individualised ideas about health and risk management, setting the stage for a more extensive exploration in subsequent chapters of how knowledges and practices among different professionals – in this case, performance artists and medical educators – can be productively translated and used to forge closer critical conversations across disciplines. As I argue, Gómez-Peña's dilemmas about the place of his work in what he calls the era of 'the mainstream bizarre' and his commitment to more radical artistic and pedagogical methods, which do not preclude the possibility of failure, offer instructive provocations to the absolute faith in medicine as the solution to many problems, as well as to existing practices within medical education that recycle superficial forms of empathy and a less critical encounter with cultural difference.

The following three chapters shift attention to collaborative and relational narratives of illness, which are still not as well represented in the field, especially when turning to art forms and media beyond literature. The value of intersubjective and relational approaches to health and well-being has been emphasised recently as an important direction that the medical humanities should take in order to venture beyond a (still dominant in the field) 'neoliberal, humanist notion of the individual body-subject' (Atkinson et al. 2015: 77), and the previous chapters have shown examples of illness narratives where we see this happening. Even though the work already considered does not foreclose collaboration, Chapters 4, 5 and 6 more explicitly address attempts to construct shared narratives, which are often fragile and demanding but also carry their own power. I continue the exploration of how we can challenge instrumentalising approaches to illness narratives by bringing in diverse materials and engaging with different methods, in this case collaborative; but I also raise a series of other questions, such as: what kinds of collaborations/relations do the narratives facilitate or efface? Do they document the many ways in which voices and perspectives can be joined together or instead break apart, and how does this process depend on the medium at one's disposal? In what ways do collaborative narratives complicate the distinction between self-authored illness stories and third-party ones, including how both are customarily received? Ultimately, what is the importance of collaborative methods in attempting to apprehend the experience of illness, and what can the medical humanities and the arts learn from instances of failing to do that?

Attention to third-person illness narratives has been primarily given to family and carer memoirs, and to doctors' narratives of their patients, which may involve a certain degree of co-constructed storytelling. These narratives have been examined as sites for mourning and remembering from psychoanalytic and political perspectives, as well as in the context of supporting individuals who for one reason or another (for example, due to serious communicative disorders) are unable to narrate their stories independently. Whether jointly authored or not, such narratives, while embraced within auto/biography studies for challenging the myth of the autonomous self,[20] often become sites of struggle; they are scrutinised in terms of the ways they negotiate power asymmetries and ethical quandaries relating to giving consent and the appropriation of another's story.[21] Questions of ethical responsibility surrounding artistic practice and spectatorship are important in Chapters 4 and 5, where they are examined in relation to documentary film and auto/biographical theatre. Following threads from previous chapters, these two chapters also reveal the ways illness challenges discourses of mastery, not only in the patient and the doctor but in other professionals too. I argue that a vision that engages with inadequacy and failure can be a productive means of rethinking a number of aspects which are of concern to medical education and the medical humanities, including professional competence, ethics and narrativity.

Chapter 4 discusses Wim Wenders' *Nick's Film/Lightning over Water* (1979–80). Filmed in the last few weeks before American director, and Wenders' friend, Nicholas Ray died of lung cancer, and edited twice, it has been, and continues to be, received with ambivalence by film scholars and viewers more widely, as well as by Wenders himself. The film's perceived failures are due to the difficulty of the subject it treats, which has attracted accusations of exploitation, and its formal self-consciousness, which documents its struggle to come together and successfully settle into one determinate category (for example, fictional film or documentary). While this early work, unlike other more immediately 'relevant' documentaries dealing with questions of death and bioethics, is not well known to medical communities either, I approach it as a collaborative project that becomes a form of 'terminal care' by supplementing medicine's power to largely define how to live one's final days, and presenting us with alternative treatments that can illuminate aspects of both filmmaking and medicine. Through the incorporation of several forms and media including staged documentary, fictional sequences, raw video footage, snippets from Ray's diary and voice-over commentary, the film enacts the process of trying and discarding different conventions and ways of representing illness and dying in film, and constructs distinct forms of witnessing for its collaborators and audiences. As in other case studies, this generic multiplicity allows Wenders to explore the tension between images and stories, loss and consolation, dying and its displacement, ethics and aesthetics, illness in the individual and in the cinema as an art form. These themes further show that illness narratives do not need to be framed by the context of biomedicine, but instead by a wider artistic and human context. Even though the film's ambiguity and the difficult ethical questions it raises are not resolved in the end, *Lightning over Water* affirms the need to continue creating new ways of looking at, and responding to, the experiences and relationships that it portrays. It is precisely the film's open-endedness and 'messiness' that can open a way beyond, on the one hand, the conviction that the values of art cannot serve the needs of ill people expressed by some critics, and on the other, narrow healthcare ethics approaches that equally close down critical conversations with other fields in favour of procedure and a set of moral codes.

Lisa Kron's play *Well* (2004), the focus of Chapter 5, is characterised by a similar 'messiness' and enacts the volatile process of telling a story when things do not go as planned. Not as familiar to medical communities as other plays that have gained popularity in medical education curricula, *Well* brings together autobiographical performance and more traditional theatrical conventions. It constructs a relational narrative of illness that draws on Kron's mother's experience with chronic allergies and on her own story of illness, treatment in an allergy hospital and recovery. While engaging with the uncertainties and debates surrounding contested illnesses such as chronic fatigue and multiple chemical sensitivity, the play intertwines the theme of illness in the individual with a discussion of illness in the community through its exploration of racial segregation/integration, thus opening up the medical to consider a wider context of health and well-being. With humour and ample metafictional gestures, the play gradually dismantles the initially chosen 'professional, theatrical context' in which to explore so-called universal questions of health, and challenges the previously erected oppositions between the healthy and the ill. Drawing attention to the fragility of joint/broken narratives in its content and form, *Well*, like *Lightning over Water*, foregrounds the challenges of the live event as well as of relating to another person. It shows how difficulty, inadequacy and the will to rework existing 'professional' practices can generate *other* ways of performing that can offer insight to the fields of medicine and medical education. Allowing her original agenda and expert knowledge to be affected (and infected) by the mother's and the other actors' interruptions, Kron learns the true meaning of integration – which applies not only to the community but, as I argue, to the play too: 'weaving into the whole even the parts that are uncomfortable or don't seem to fit'. Rather than an indication of failure, the doses of messiness that seep through the play's porous performance structure become signs of 'wellness'.

While Jo Spence met resistance in her efforts to demonstrate the relevance of her photography to public health debates in the 1980s, in recent years a whole range of unconventional media for representing illness are making important contributions and have the capacity to reach increasingly larger and more heterogeneous audiences, especially as they circulate via public broadcasters and the Internet. For example, the animated documentary has become part of the wider ways public health intersects with a vast web of media and forms, rather than consisting of images predominantly drawn from biomedicine. The potential for comics and animation to communicate embodied perception and subjective states of mind that are hard to describe has only begun to be researched in the medical/health humanities. The key focus of Chapter 6 is *Animated Minds* (2003), a series of short documentaries created in the UK to raise public awareness of different forms of mental distress including schizophrenia, agoraphobia, obsessive compulsive disorder and self-harm. These documentaries were created in a collaborative manner, and use real testimony for their soundtrack and various animation techniques by professional animators. Like artists' books and graphic narratives, animated documentaries communicate through an excess of elements – design, movement, shape, colour, texture, voice – despite the absence of conventional visually indexical material such as the body. By bringing together scholarship on the animated documentary as a genre and on witnessing in illness narratives, continuing to synthesise tools and critical approaches, I suggest that the animated documentary's evocative power, which allows it to penetrate subjective experiences, does not merely enlarge the epistemological parameters of live-action documentary. This would make its contribution too narrow, and relevant only to documentary studies specialists. Rather, the dialectic between 'absence and excess' and the distinct kind of self-reflexivity that characterise this form stage an ethical encounter for viewers that escapes either easy identification with the subjects of *Animated Minds*, or misidentification ending in stigma. In this way, and through the 'unfinished' nature of the *Animated Minds* testimonies, the films, like the other case studies, expand narratives about mental health and keep the practices of witnessing and response-ability open.

In addition to developing several of the ideas from previous chapters, such as the ethical responsibilities and challenges of collaboration, Chapter 6 returns to the politics of visibility with which *Illness as Many Narratives* opened. This is not in the (perhaps simplistic) sense that the mentally ill, rather than women with breast cancer, are the invisibly ill people of the twenty-first century, but by reflecting on the ways animated documentary negotiates a similar tension between concealment and visibility as the one addressed in Chapter 1. Animation problematises the idea of embodied presence through the replacement of the real person by an animated character, a kind of mask like the prosthesis that Lorde criticises through her illness performance of breast cancer, even as the soundtrack retains that connection in the documentary. Chapter 6 resituates this discussion of visible self and voice in the context of the complex relation of mental illness to both visibility and invisibility: in other words, in relation to the visual stereotyping of mentally ill people in the history of medical illustration and in mainstream media, as well as in relation to the difficulty of 'finding a language' for mental distress and the relative absence of a range of mental illness stories from public discourse. As the only chapter to explicitly discuss mental health issues, it also returns to common critiques of narrative/narrativity in the field of illness narratives, specifically the problematic assumption that certain forms of mental distress are inherently 'anti-narrative'. By looking closely at the *Animated Minds* audio testimonies, I underline the urgency of paying attention to such narratives and the experiences they document, many of which are surrounded with stigma, beyond an emphasis on pathology.

If the mixing of art and illness often causes heated debates, the mixing of illness and social media in the present moment creates its own controversies. The entrance of intimate embodied experiences, illness and dying into the digital sphere foregrounds questions of boundaries (how far to go with public self-representation online) and genre (are social media trivialising illness experiences?). Following on from the previous chapter, the Afterword offers a snapshot of the new media landscape of illness narratives that has developed in the so-called decade of Health 2.0, or 'participatory healthcare', drawing connections between the ethical, narratological and political questions for both authors and readers raised by these forms and those discussed in the previous chapters. Focusing on their distinctly public nature, immediacy and interactivity, I provide some final reflections on what online and collaborative platforms, and social media like Facebook and Twitter, add to our understandings of visibility, treatment and recovery, as well as to the intimate processes of witnessing and collaboration examined in the preceding chapters.

Throughout the case studies of this book, I argue for the importance of attending to the many narratives of illness, in all the different meanings of this phrase, and of engaging with a wide range of media and methods to forge more explicit and critical links between the arts, cultural studies and medicine so as to ensure that the medical humanities does not degenerate into a narrow discipline. A critical medical humanities can expand current understandings of illness narrative and enlarge the goals and scope of all these fields in ways that can enrich debates about health and illness in contemporary culture as well as cross-disciplinary enquiry more broadly.

Notes

1. See Zagarell 1998.
2. I allude here to the essay 'Imaginary Investments' (Willis et al. 2013: 67).
3. See the epigraph of this book for an example in translation. For a detailed discussion of the register and performative contexts of this tradition, see Sykäri 2009.

4. The term 'health humanities' has emerged as an alternative to the medical humanities to encompass practices that bear upon health outside of medical or scientific understandings, as well as to include a range of health practitioners who are not doctors, such as dentists, nurses, occupational therapists, social workers and others. See for example Jones, Wear and Friedman 2014 and Crawford et al. 2015. I see the critical medical humanities and the health humanities as having certain common goals, and my use of the former term throughout this book is not meant to reproduce the exclusivity that some critics have associated with the medical humanities. Also see Atkinson et al. 2015.
5. Ann Jurecic briefly uses the phrase 'illness as many narratives' in the concluding section of her study to resist narrow interpretations of illness stories, using as her example Anne Fadiman's ethnographic narrative *The Spirit Catches You and You Fall Down* (2012: 128). While the title of this book has been inspired by Jurecic's work, I have adopted the phrase to more widely explore illness narratives across several art forms and media, and to point to their multiple meanings, as outlined in this Introduction.
6. The historical dimension of illness writing prior to the twentieth century has not received the attention it deserves in medical humanities scholarship. See Waddington and Willis 2013 and Whitehead 2014.
7. On postmodern illness, see also Morris 1998.
8. See for example Atkinson 2009, and Woods' overview of these critiques in 'The Limits of Narrative'.
9. Frank further calls chaos stories 'anti-narrative', distinguished by an 'incessant present' tense that precludes temporal development (1995: 98–9). In the Afterword of the second edition of *The Wounded Storyteller* he complements this typology with three new types that acknowledge difficulty: 'life-as-normal narratives, borrowed stories and broken narratives' (2013: 193).
10. Woods engages with philosopher Galen Strawson's distinction between narrative and non-narrative (or episodic) people in 'Against Narrativity' (2004). Elsewhere (2013), she discusses the relevance of Crispin Sartwell and Sara Maitland's work to debates about narrativity and language. Though not examined in this book, such perspectives can offer insights into approaching stories by cognitively impaired people or those diagnosed with Alzheimer's (see for example Freeman 2008).
11. According to Shlomith Rimmon-Kenan, one of the things that illness narratives can teach narratologists is that narrative theory should be rethought 'in terms of contingency, randomness, and chaos rather than order and regularity' (2006: 243).
12. See also McKechnie 2014: 2 about the need to consider the role of the narratee, as opposed to simply the narrator, before assessing the limitations of illness narratives.

13. On multidisciplinary understandings of illness narrative, see Raoul et al. 2007, Mattingly and Garro 2000, and Hydén and Brockmeier 2011. On definitions of narrative across different media, see Herman 2007.
14. See Brody 2011.
15. The personality the Centre has proposed to emphasise resistance is that of 'disruptive teenager'.
16. On how pedagogy fits the 'pervasive calls' in the medical humanities literature for a more resistant model, see Shapiro 2012. On the two streams of the critical medical humanities, situated in medical education and medical humanities respectively, see Bleakley 2015.
17. See Felski 2008 and Sedgwick 2003.
18. For more discussion on this case, see Diedrich 2007, Radley 2009 and Jurecic 2012.
19. On medicine as culture, see Lupton 2012.
20. See Miller 2000, Eakin 1999 and Egan 1999.
21. See Egan 1999, Couser 2004, Tanner 2006, Diedrich 2007, Jurecic 2012, DeShazer 2013, and Frank's 'broken narratives' (2013: 201). In relation to co-constructed storytelling due to communicative disabilities, also see Hydén 2011.

Chapter 1

Re-Covering Scarred Bodies: Reading Photography

Confirming that it is much more than a surgical sign, the site of the amputated breast has generated vibrant conversations taking place through breast cancer autobiography and art photography, in academic and activist circles, as well as in the countless stories of ordinary women.[1] These are conversations that open up and destabilise medical understandings of the body and of breast cancer by articulating connections between lived experience, history and feminist politics, and by engaging with artistic and theoretical discourses on the body, which in turn impact the arts and narratives about women's health. In *The Cancer Journals*, a key point of reference for health feminism and studies on breast cancer narratives since its publication in 1980, African American writer and activist Audre Lorde writes about her refusal to follow the path of prosthesis or, as she calls it, the path of 'silence and invisibility' (1996: 4). Twenty-two years later, American feminist critic Diane Price Herndl, who also underwent a mastectomy, justifies in an article why she did not have 'to wear breast cancer in the same way [as Lorde]' (2002: 150). With this critical dialogue, the chapter juxtaposes visual representations of breast cancer experiences by two British artists who are also speaking from different historical moments: Jo Spence (1934–92), a photographer who has had a huge impact on generations of photographers (especially in Britain), and Sam Taylor-Wood, a photographer and visual artist (born in 1967) who is at the forefront of a new generation of contemporary British artists.[2] In particular, I analyse photographs from Spence's touring exhibition *The Picture of Health?* (1985) and Taylor-Wood's *Self Portrait in a Single Breasted Suit with Hare* (2001).

The debate between Lorde and Herndl, around which my argument unfolds, has a more specific focus, dealing with understandings of prosthetics and breast reconstruction as techniques of 'disciplinary normalization' (Foucault 1995: 296) of the female body. However, it raises broader questions concerning issues of concealment and visibility of the body, more specifically with reference to the site of the post-operative breast, and meditates on various versions of feminist politics that different responses to the disabled body invoke. Spence and Taylor-Wood initially seem to have very few things in common. Unlike Spence's large body of work on illness, Taylor-Wood has produced few images of herself directly referring to her experience with cancer in relation to her other work. Nonetheless, she has been involved in campaigns raising awareness of breast cancer, and her work, especially portraiture, continues to draw on the theme of illness.[3] Although both photographers can be seen as defying the 'male gaze' by casting themselves as the subjects of their own stories in their self-portraits, there are important historical differences that separate their work. Spence's name is firmly placed in the seventies and eighties and is mostly associated with documentary and political photography as well as with phototherapy, a reciprocal peer-to-peer counselling technique that uses photography as a vehicle of self-exploration and social change. Taylor-Wood's work conjures the postmodern and, as her detractors insist, is suspiciously tied to commercial media fields.[4] Her art is populated with characters, including a significant number of celebrities, who are portrayed as captive and alienated in secular, urban and contemporary landscapes, but these settings are often fused with religious imagery informed by Renaissance and Baroque painting. Spence's images are plain or amateur-like snapshots, and her commitment to making the technology of photography accessible to everyone seems to contrast with the glossy technical expertise of contemporary photography, of which Taylor-Wood's work is a prominent example.

By discussing together what may initially appear to be very disparate narratives, this chapter deliberately places images (particularly Taylor-Wood's) in new interpretative contexts. This is not to suggest that the juxtaposition of the textual and photographic narratives in question is arbitrary. I have chosen to read the photographs through the framework of the textual narratives not only because, like the latter, they present distinctive representational traditions (in this case divergent gazes on the female and ill body in particular), but also because the photos can be approached as attempts to shape public perceptions of breast cancer and even change the framework of thinking about the disease. The question of time, namely when these narratives were produced, is crucial as far as both aspects above are concerned. There is a homology between the different pairings in question: although they are by no means identical, texts and photographs produced in the 1980s seem to share similar concerns, and these concerns are not the same as those we find in more recent illness narratives. Both pairings deal with the aesthetic (new aesthetic questions are raised and new representational forms deployed by artists like Spence and Taylor-Wood, who, as noted, use very different photographic practices), but they also speak to the 'development and transformation of the regime of breast cancer during the twentieth century and its implications for the emergence of new subjects, social groups ... and solidarities' (Klawiter 2008: xxvi), as well as narratives about women's health.

Spence's extensive work on illness, belonging as it does to a wider movement for social change, has received much attention and has been discussed before in relation to the politics of patienthood and the integration of disability within feminist studies. She has written about how her work targets people 'within the disability movement as well as within the art world' (1995: 215), 'women who are health workers and women who are cultural workers' (139) and 'forms a bridge between the work done on health struggles, usually dealt through documentary photography, and work done on body as image' (1986: 168). In exploring Taylor-Wood's *Self Portrait in a Single Breasted Suit with Hare* against that background, I intend to extend Spence's bridge – or practice of interloping, as I described it in the Introduction – by examining work that has been considered up to now primarily in the context of contemporary artistic practices and postmodern style, rather than the medical humanities. In particular the chapter poses the following questions: What is the relation of this photograph made in 2001 to a tradition of breast cancer photographs dating from the late seventies that constitute illness as political, rather than merely personal or artistic? Does Taylor-Wood's photographic narrative, which, as I will argue, complicates the relation between visibility and concealment in the ill body's display, gesture towards the creation of 'new forms of embodiment' (Klawiter 2008: 293) and articulate novel 'ways of doing illness' (Diedrich 2007: 35)? It is interesting, in particular, to assess Taylor-Wood's narrative performance in light of the shift from the politicisation to the depoliticisation of patienthood in breast cancer culture, a change that, according to Diedrich, took place at the turn of the twenty-first century, and that Herndl addresses with specific reference to feminist practices towards the scarred body. Staging a dialogue between the photographs along the lines of the conversation between Herndl and

Lorde, therefore, allows for an examination of how word and image mediate illness experiences, and how photographs produced in different historical moments can insert themselves into a heterogeneous tradition of illness narratives inflecting ongoing questions about the politics of medicine and shaping current debates calling for a more critical medical humanities.

The juxtaposition of verbal and visual narratives needs some additional justification, given the contested term 'narrative' and the ongoing debates as to whether it can be applied to photography. As discussed in the Introduction, photographs are not purely visual images.[5] They often have captions and other text, and even when they do not, their narrative potential becomes obvious when they are interpreted by viewers. Moreover, photographic essays and photo-texts blur generic boundaries, thus attesting to the intimate relations between text and image and, in Spence's case, image and performance as well. Spence uses captions and text to accompany her photos and blends photography with drama and therapy in her embodied practice of phototherapy, which records gesture, facial expression and movement. As Spence writes about her photos, it is possible to order and reorder them 'into a variety of mini-narratives, which in themselves can be moved around, providing an infinity of matrices or montages. There is never a fixed story being told, no narrative closure' (1995: 176); and we could add that no single (essential) self emerges from this process, either. Taylor-Wood has stated in an interview with Clare Carolin that many of her works 'are hard to watch precisely because they are not part of a narrative' (Taylor-Wood et al. 2002). Nevertheless, Joost de Bloois (2008) has explored her self-portraits using concepts adapted by Roland Barthes ('narreme' and 'biographeme') that point to a 'jolt of narrative' or 'condensed story'; Taylor-Wood's work moves 'to and fro image and narrative, between impression (with all its connotations of affect) and story'. Even though her work does not offer a linear or unifying narrative, it does not abandon narrative altogether.

Breast cancer photography: from *Property of Jo Spence?* to *Self Portrait in a Single Breasted Suit with Hare*

As in her earlier work on the family album (*Beyond the Family Album*, 1979), which exposes how the struggles of family life or illness are made invisible through the selection of idealised moments, Spence's projects on illness confront herself and her audience with what is missing or has been omitted from representations of breast cancer in both medical and mainstream media images. As she explains in an essay originally given as a keynote paper for the Women's Surgery Conference in Melbourne, Australia, in 1990, what she felt was 'lacking in relation to health education is any notion of how breast cancer could be visually represented better. I mean beyond an image of a woman palpating her breast or "living with one breast"' (1995: 138). Beginning in 1982, at the time she was diagnosed with breast cancer, Spence documented her experiences with illness, medicine and alternative healing practices in *The Picture of Health?*, which brought her work to health conferences, women's groups and medical students. The photographs she made invite reflection about silence and speech. Spence was struggling to be heard by her surgeon so that she could get the treatment she believed she needed, namely a more holistic approach. (Holistic attitudes to cancer were in their infancy in the early 1980s, at least in Britain.)[6] She also wanted to prevent mastectomy, the hegemonic treatment at the time. This struggle is documented in a series of photographs made with Terry Dennett, curator of the Jo Spence Memorial Archive in London, and Rosy Martin, an artist and psychological therapist with whom Spence pioneered phototherapy in Britain. Spence's use of phototherapy was an essential part of her alternative cancer treatment programme. Some of these photographs (most notably *Infantilization* (1984), with Rosy Martin) re-enact and reframe the following episode, which represented a turning point for Spence:

> A young man in a white coat, whom I had never seen before ... stopped at my bedside in a provincial English hospital ... leaned over me and drew a large black cross above my breast, uttering those memorable words: 'That's the one that is coming off.' From that moment on, I was on total alert. (1990: 80)

This performative re-enactment should not be viewed as mere replication of this traumatic event; as Martin explains, phototherapy seeks to re-enact 'memories [and] key scenarios with emotional resonance' (2013: 72) and through role playing (in which roles shift and alternate) not merely represent old pains but 'envisage possibilities for other ways of being' (74).

Spence's snapshots can be approached as a narrative in a broad sense, in that in addition to the text that surrounds many of them (besides captions), they contain temporal order. This is clear in the case of *Narratives of Dis-ease* (*Excised, Exiled, Expected, Expunged, Included*, undated), a series of photographs Spence made with Tim Sheard, a trained psychotherapist who worked with a British cancer charity. In turn, photographs from *The Cancer Project* (Nottingham) and *The Picture of Health?* can be arranged to create a story-line, beginning with *Marked Up for Amputation* (Jo Spence/Terry Dennett, 1982) and ending with depictions of her lumpectomy. Spence describes the process of photographing herself over the years that she was silenced or 'professionally "managed" from asking questions about [her] fate' (1995: 131) as a gradual abandonment of the 'victim position'; the photographs show her becoming 'creatively and productively angry' (1990: 82). By responding to the marking of her body with her own body marking (using a pen and photography), Spence creates what Kristin Langellier and others have called 'the palimpsest of breast cancer' (2001: 145). A broad range of contemporary critical discourses, including psychoanalysis, postcolonial theory, feminism and queer theory, demonstrate the theoretical adaptability and versatility of the notion of the palimpsest.[7] In the field of breast cancer discourse, the palimpsest has been used to refer to layered markings on the breast (mastectomy scar, tattoo and even caption), each inscription overwritten, imperfectly erased, and still visible on the parchment/skin. This is effectively dramatised in *Property of Jo Spence?* (1982), whose eponymous caption is written on the breast itself, like a tattoo, blurring the boundaries between image and text. The photo shows Spence nude from the waist up, filling almost all the frame, her breasts large and slightly drooping. She is wearing glasses that hide her gaze from her viewers, but she faces the camera. On the left breast, a piece of bandage underlines the 'caption' directly above: *Property of Jo Spence?* In the note that accompanies the photo, Spence explains that she chose it (over other *tableaux* with different captions written on the breast) before entering hospital as 'a talisman to remind myself that I still had some rights over my own body' (1986: 157). This photo is therefore not re-enacting a past moment (like *Infantilization*), but projecting into the future, however uncertain that is.

Property of Jo Spence? resembles an earlier photograph by Deena Metzger, who decided to have her mastectomy scar tattooed with a design of a tree branch. This photograph, entitled *The Warrior* and taken by photographer Hella Hammid in 1977, portrays the nude torso of Metzger, her arms reaching out towards the sky in a gesture of openness to life, fully exposing her tattooed breast. Spence's and Metzger's photographs have differences, of course,

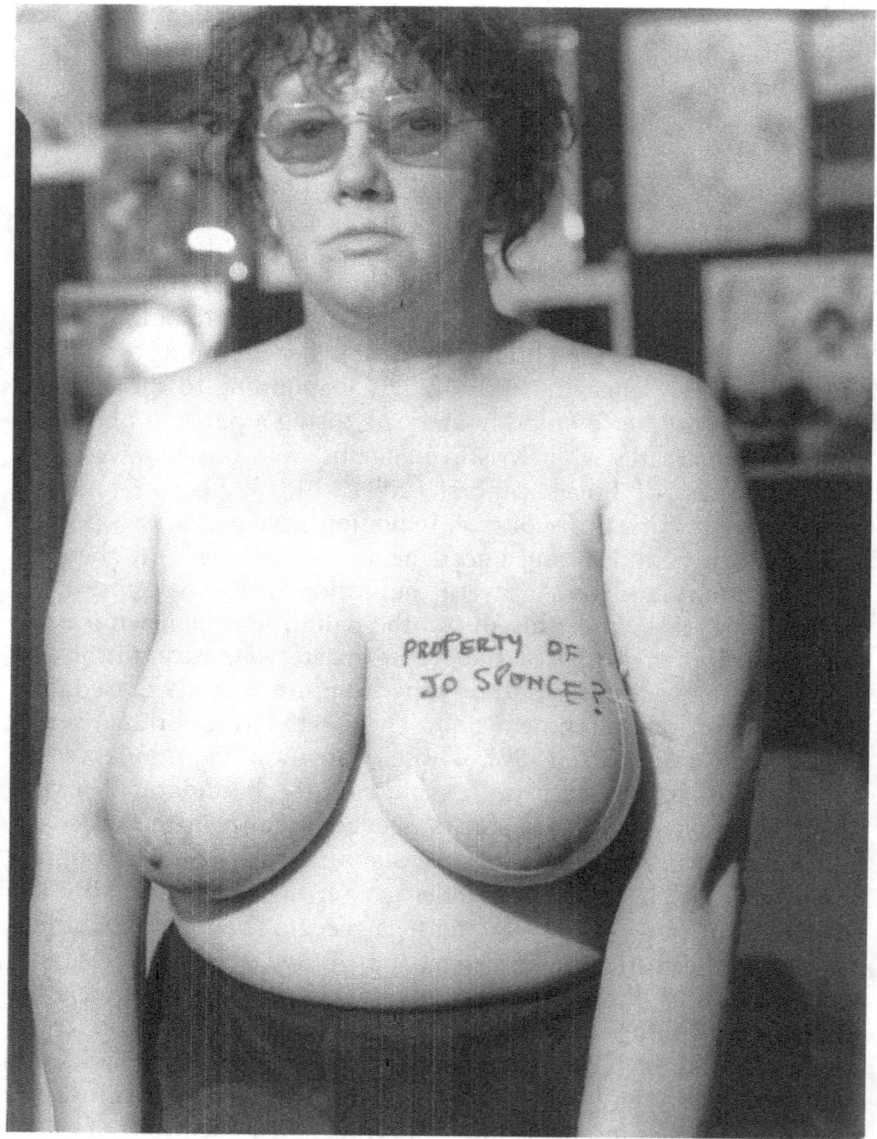

Figure 1.1 Jo Spence, *Property of Jo Spence?* © Terry Dennett.

but in both the body, marked by several socio-symbolic discourses and systems (medicine, photography and also others, since the photos were later embedded in books, re-printed and even circulated online), becomes a site of struggle over the meanings ascribed to female bodies and to breast cancer. Metzger's photograph seems, through its unequivocal optimism, to confirm that she has managed to transform the mastectomy scar from an emblem of shame to one of beauty – Lisa Cartwright has described it as 'the perfect "first" in the non-medical imaging of a mastectomy scar' (2000: 129). Even though Spence reclaims her rights over her body by re-inscribing it through her own rebellious pen, the question mark at the end of the phrase *Property of Jo Spence?* betrays a degree of scepticism. It may suggest that earlier writing – in other words, the doctor's 'black cross' – has been imperfectly erased (to recall the notion of the palimpsest) and is therefore still visible.

Spence's political and photographic autobiography, *Putting Myself in the Picture*, in which some of the aforementioned photographs are included, illustrates, like Lorde's *Cancer Journals*, a practice of writing and photography designed as both personal therapy and social critique. Lorde voices what is hidden, shameful and unspoken and offers a unique insight into the role of the healthcare institution as well as into women's collusion in their infantilisation as patients. Her MLA speech in 1977, subsequently included in *The Cancer Journals*, is appropriately entitled 'The Transformation of Silence into Language and Action', and Lorde uses her own experience of cancer to illustrate how a personal struggle can become politically useful. In this it exemplifies a central tenet of second-wave feminism, namely that 'the personal is political'. In *The Cancer Journals* she affirms, 'If we are to translate the silence surrounding breast cancer into language and action', 'the first step is that women with mastectomies must become visible to each other' (1996: 48). Spence's and Lorde's work challenge what in *The Biopolitics of Breast Cancer* Maren Klawiter calls 'the regime of medicalization' that reigned during the first seventy years of the twentieth century (2008: 84). In her words, this regime:

> isolated women with breast cancer from each other, 'protected' them from knowledge of their diagnoses, prevented them from participating in decision making about their treatment, treated them with a one-step, one-size-fits-all radical surgery, encouraged them to hide the evidence of their treatment and maintain a normal, heterofeminine appearance ... It reinforced the architecture of the closet ... and inhibited the formation of disease-based identities, social networks and solidarities among women with breast cancer. (279)

Although Spence's work cannot address the invisibilities that Lorde, who is black and lesbian, articulates in *The Cancer Journals* and *A Burst of Light* (1988), written after her cancer had metastasised to her liver, it is not surprising that one of the books Spence consulted for *The Picture of Health?* was *The Cancer Journals* (Spence 1995: 141).[8] The following passage is striking for its similarity to what Lorde advocates in *The Cancer Journals* when she refuses to surrender to the construction of the female as 'decoration and externally defined sex object' (1996: 47). Spence writes:

> We question why the patient is pressurized to wear a prosthesis (false breast) after the operation of mastectomy, when it has no function other than a purely cosmetic one. Just as social and political injustices are covered up, so (with perhaps the 'honourable' exception of war veterans) are injuries, deformities and amputations hidden. This not only leaves the individual isolated, unable to recognize and share experiences with other survivors, it also conceals the high incidence of the injury. The tyranny of the acceptable body shape is maintained. (1995: 125)

Like Lorde's vision of 'an army of one-breasted women descending on Congress' (1996: 10), Spence shows her need to be heard by other women, so that her experience can become useful, and affirms her desire to create a community of 'dissident cancer patients' (1995: 214).

Spence's and Lorde's critiques of hegemonic medical practices and women's infantilisation, delivered through discourses (either textual or photographic) that stress speech over silence and visibility over invisibility, are therefore a response to the constitution of breast cancer as a hidden disease and of women with breast cancer as invisible victims. As Langellier argues about such narrative performances, 'they are transgressive in that they break the silence on breast cancer, bring [it] into the realm of discourse and contest [its] dominant, stigmatizing meanings' (2001: 172). Moreover, Lorde's writing and Spence's photography resist the process of immaterialisation, sustained by former sentimental (mostly charity) images of disabled women, and compel us to think about illness in and through the body. Such practices of intervention may come across as angry, raw or aggressive, and as a result they have divided feminist circles, especially when they have found expression through more mainstream media. One recalls here a hugely controversial photo, *Beauty out of Damage* by American ex-fashion model Matuschka, which artfully places the scar at its centre, announcing through a large caption, 'You Can't Look Away Anymore'. Because there is no mistaking that Matuschka's breast has been amputated, this self-portrait caused a range of reactions in the breast cancer community, including empowerment and disgust, when it was chosen as the front cover of the August 1993 *New York Times Magazine*. Like Metzger's photo, the image invites the gaze and qualifies as an aesthetic nude – though, of course, not a conventional one, given its subject matter. While Metzger transforms the surgical scar into something else by covering it with her tattoo, and Spence underlines it through her caption, Matuschka foregrounds it, even as she 'mediates' it visually through the white dress, headscarf, light and overall framing of the photo. However, with Matuschka (who is, like Spence, very provocative), we seem to be far away from documentary photography or phototherapy. Instead, we see a type of photography that explicitly highlights the camera as an instrument that can transform, not unlike prosthesis, the way bodies can look. As Matuschka says, 'If I'm going to bother putting anything on my chest, why not install a camera?' (1992: 33). Despite Matuschka's tenuous position within breast cancer activism (she has described her initiation as happening by chance), the photo is subversive in that it rethinks ideas of beauty and what, in Spence's phrase, 'is fit to be seen' (1995: 125).

If in the images discussed above the body becomes 'a social text open to be read by others and the flesh visibly presents a narrative to be witnessed' (Hall 2000: 417), Taylor-Wood's more covert portraits complicate the nature of witnessing. *Self Portrait in a Single Breasted Suit with Hare*, which appeared on the cover of a supplement in *The Observer* in 2001, is enigmatic and makes a punning allusion to the photographer's difficult recovery from cancer. Functioning on a highly symbolic level, it shows the artist posing in a black suit and flashy trainers against a white background, looking directly into the camera, holding a cable release in one hand and a stiff, stuffed hare in the other. The hare is pointing towards Taylor-Wood's casually-styled thick hair. A journalist comments with reference to this self-portrait: 'How artist Sam Taylor-Wood survived breast and colon cancer and still kept her humour' (Millar, in Taylor-Wood et al. 2002). This is hardly the kind of reaction Matuschka created when her photo appeared in the *New York Times Magazine*.[9]

The first impression Taylor-Wood's photo creates is that it is not about breast cancer or illness at all. Or, to put it better, it is difficult to decode this picture because it does not draw on the kind of imagery (such as the surgical scar or other markings on the body) associated with earlier representations of breast cancer. *Self Portrait in a*

Figure 1.2 Sam Taylor-Johnson, *Self Portrait in a Single Breasted Suit with Hare*, 2001, C-Print, 63³/₈ × 44¹/₂ in. (161 × 113 cm) (framed) © Sam Taylor-Johnson, Photo: Stephen White, Courtesy White Cube.

Single Breasted Suit with Hare does not have the agit-prop quality of Spence's work and does not draw on documentary. Like Matuschka's photo, it is shot in an art studio, exhibits a sophisticated use of the camera and draws on the code of fashion photography. The kind of aesthetic used incorporates whiteness, youth and thinness, though not conventional models of femininity – the black suit and the training shoes have led Jeremy Millar to describe the portrait as an example of 'contemporary dandyism' (Millar, in Taylor-Wood et al. 2002).

More importantly, whereas Spence, Matuschka and Metzger expose private parts for public viewing, Taylor-Wood's self-portrait makes it almost impossible to go beyond the black and white suit to get a glimpse of the 'vulnerable and uncertain flesh' (Perreault 1995: 30), even though the single-breasted suit, with the jacket's one row of buttons, is clearly a metaphor for the scarred female body. Unlike Matuschka's photo, where the white gown she wears is diagonally cut to better display the mastectomy scar while covering the remaining body, here there is nothing other than the caption to suggest that the viewer is looking at a single-breasted woman. And yet, like Matuschka's photo, *Self Portrait in a Single Breasted Suit with Hare* emphasises 'the role of concealment and display in [the ill body's] disclosure' (Cartwright 2000: 129) in its own way.

Taylor-Wood's self-portraits, which constitute a significant aspect of her work, are characterised by a blend of exposure and concealment. An early portrait, *Fuck/Suck/Spank/Wank* (1993), shows the artist standing in a studio with her trousers draped around her ankles, wearing dark sunglasses and a T-shirt spelling the portrait's title. In *Slut* (1993), another self-portrait where the model remains suspended between a desire to be confrontational and a wish to expose her vulnerability, the eyes are covered with layers of make-up while the neck is heavily marked by love bites. This form of displaced self-portraiture culminates in self-portraits hidden within the images of *Self Portrait as a Tree* (2000), *Bound Ram* (2001), and *Poor Cow* (2001), in which it is only the title that reveals the presence of the artist in her work. These images – a solitary tree beneath a stormy sky, bent by the wind; a picture of a ram, its legs tied together with a red ribbon; and an isolated cow in a meadow, staring into the camera – are unconventionally autobiographical: Taylor-Wood has noted in interviews that she took them during chemotherapy, and she has explained how each one of them alludes to a redemptive moment in its own way (Carolin, in Taylor-Wood et al. 2002). De Bloois (2008) suggests that in *Self Portrait as a Tree* 'the use of photography's medium-specificity as the documentation of real presence, that is a "slice of life" taken from the subject's biography, combined with the use of both the formal characteristics and the history of different pictorial genres' (landscape photography, for instance), create 'a singular yet highly complex (auto-)narrative'. De Bloois concludes that through such self-reflexive techniques Taylor-Wood 'resists the immediate exposure of lives and selves' that often appears to be the only mode of (auto)biographical representation left in contemporary photography.

Unlike her previous self-portraits, and unlike the photos by Spence, Metzger and Matuschka, where the eyes are either averted or hidden, *Self Portrait in a Single Breasted Suit with Hare* features a subject staring inquisitively at the camera. With reference to *Fuck/Suck/Spank/Wank*, Taylor-Wood explains that she 'consciously avoided contact with the viewer's gaze' because she 'was not performing for others but rather for myself' (Carolin, in Taylor-Wood et al. 2002). The implication is that in this photo, where she does not avoid the gaze, she is performing for others too, despite the risk of subjecting herself to the scrutiny of the public eye. Yet, even in this portrait disguise remains an important element, especially if we place it next to the images by Spence, Metzger and Matuschka previously discussed. For the purpose of the dialogue on the post-surgical body with which I opened this chapter, I would like to consider the relation of concealment and visibility in *Self Portrait in a Single Breasted Suit with Hare* in the context of Herndl's reply to Lorde's work. If Spence is often accused of 'hanging her dirty washing out in public' (Evans 2000: 114), exposing too much, is the message equally problematic here, but for the opposite reason? More specifically, Taylor-Wood's self-portrait could be seen as conveying the idea that 'you are just as good as you were before because you can look exactly the same' (Lorde 1996: 31) or that the experience of breast cancer can be covered up, as if it never happened. These statements resonate with contemporary anxieties that in consumer-driven and individualist Western societies, breast cancer is increasingly depicted as a private rather than a public issue. Barbara Ehrenreich laments that there is 'nothing very feminist – in an ideological or activist sense – about the mainstream of breast-cancer culture today' and that 'one finds very little anger' (2001: 47–8). The result is a gradual depoliticisation of the disease as it becomes divorced from broader social struggles, of which the fight against cancer is just one part, and reduced to a merely cosmetic issue. Postfeminist narratives about women's health, according to Tasha N. Dubriwny, advance 'neoliberal understandings of health that depict health as both the responsibility and the obligation of individuals', resulting in the affirmation of the power of biomedicine, and in the perpetuation of 'traditional gender roles for women' (2013: 3).[10] Visibility thus becomes divorced from its potential political implications, and empowerment becomes redefined in terms of women's ability and readiness to consume various medical and technological services that promise better bodies and even better selves.

The politics of voice and/or visible self

Herndl addresses the question of changing regimes of disease and feminist politics in the essay already mentioned by measuring her response to breast cancer against Lorde's. She writes that Lorde's refusal to wear a prosthesis twenty years ago 'was an open avowal of something that had remained hidden; the result, I realized, was that I didn't have to wear breast cancer in the same way' (2002: 150). Though Herndl defends her right to define her own desires and make her own choices, especially at a time when breast cancer is no longer shameful and unspoken, she is aware of the implications that her decision to 'look normal' (153) might have, even today: it could reinforce the idea that reconstruction is mandatory and that femininity should be restored at any cost, which is aligned with a postfeminist logic. Her essay therefore partly provides compensation 'for not living up to Audre Lorde's feminism' (144). Herndl's choice not to 'wear breast cancer in the same way' as Lorde does not mean that she wants to cover her experience. 'Wear' is a key word. The other women, Lorde, Spence, Metzger and Matuschka, 'wear breast cancer' as a kind of badge; they display their scars and unveil their bodies to make difference visible. Herndl's definition of wearing breast cancer gestures towards an idea of covering the body. Interestingly, in the essay she describes making her decision to have breast reconstruction 'standing in a dressing room at [her] favorite countercultural clothes shop' (153). However, she describes this moment of looking in the mirror as an alternative 'scene of self-loving' (153) to Lorde's refusal of prosthesis. She clarifies that even though she had cosmetic surgery, breast cancer was never a 'cosmetic' issue for her (151). Thus, even as her visible self hides the scars, she does not wish to mute her difference but to express it differently: 'I thought that I could still follow part of Lorde's lead and make breast cancer visible by talking about it, by claiming the identity of a woman with breast cancer, and that would outweigh my choice to make cancer less manifest to others ... *my voice would outweigh the visible*' (152, emphasis added). Herndl concludes the essay in a similar way: 'I like to think that ... [Lorde] would understand what I did, she would see that I am living my difference and that the *difference between my voice and my visible self is part of that difference*' (154–5, emphasis added).

In both passages above there is a tension between showing or manifesting breast cancer (the visible) and talking about it (the voice) that does not exist for Lorde or Spence. In their work, 'words' and 'image' work together, reinforcing one another, producing a more consistent message; they both unveil and expose the female body, albeit in their own ways. A tension between voice (in the form of an essay or a caption) and visible self (physical body or its photographic representation) can also be found in Taylor-Wood's *Self Portrait in a Single Breasted Suit with Hare*, this time taking place through word–image interaction in the photo. Susan Sontag writes in a different context that 'all photographs wait to be explained or falsified by their captions' (2004: 9). We have seen that in Taylor-Wood's previous self-portrait, *Self Portrait as a Tree*, the caption is essential because there is nothing in the image to indicate that it is a self-portrait. In *Self Portrait in a Single Breasted Suit with Hare*, the eponymous caption underneath, in foregrounding the single-breasted suit, shatters the unity of the body and astonishes its viewer by exposing the misrecognition involved in the contemplation of the photo. I would like to suggest that the caption fulfils the role of compensatory 'voicing' to which Herndl refers; the portrait covers the bodily scars, but does not conceal entirely the experience of breast cancer.

Herndl adds a theoretical layer to her decision to pass as 'normal': she calls her essay 'a theoretical version of self-justification' – it is both 'a confession' and 'a meditation on a fall from one version of feminist politics' (144). She grounds the difference between her voice and her visible self in the developments of contemporary feminist theory, namely in the notion of an 'alienation' or 'an internal difference' from the self that she considers to be 'a condition of postmodernity' (147). Although she claims that Lorde's refusal of prosthesis is not unsophisticated, Herndl seems to align it with a form of nostalgic clinging to 'the pretechnological body' (150). Contrary to this, citing Haraway's 'Cyborg Manifesto' several times in her essay, she emphasises how 'in the full postmodern, posthuman realisation that all bodies are constructed' she 'had no [other] choice' but reconstruction (153). This realisation does not emerge only from her new 'breast' – still her own tissue but 'moved, reshaped, and changed by technology' (151) – but from a long series of interactions with technology that started when (if not before) she was born. Herndl embraces the contradictory meanings of reconstructive surgery and finds that the notion of the posthuman subject serves important goals of disability studies: 'Does reconstructive surgery fall prey to this culture's insistence on feminine beauty at any cost? Of course it does. Does it also help rethink the borders of the natural, sexual, and what counts as feminine beauty? Yes, it does that too' (153). An incident she describes in her essay, when her attempt to convey what it is like to live posthumanly is misunderstood by a woman who only retains the promise of 'bigger boobs' from her story (152), captures perfectly the above contradiction.

Taylor-Wood's choice to represent her experience in the way she does in the portrait seems to derive from certain photographic aesthetic strategies that explore the kind of tension emerging from different media. These strategies often create a simultaneity of narratives within a single image: of her *Five Revolutionary Seconds* series of panoramic images (1997), she writes, 'Whatever narrative you construct from the photograph the soundtrack is deconstructing' (Carolin, in Taylor-Wood et al. 2002). Similarly, in the film installation *Strings* (2003), she takes the basic constituents of film – soundtrack and image sequence – and forces them apart to complicate their relationship. This kind of operation informs the following chapters and is crucial to my understanding of 'illness as many narratives'. Another example is *Mute* (2001), where a professional opera singer is actually singing, but with the sound removed; Taylor-Wood explains that she 'wanted to create a deafening silence that the viewer could feel'. Talking about the relation between image and music more generally, she notes, 'It's the collision of the two that makes something powerful. Music adds that other dimension to really heighten, or change, or highlight something' (Carolin, in Taylor-Wood et al. 2002).

Moreover, if Herndl engages the cyborg or posthuman to add a theoretical layer to her confessional account, Taylor-Wood ties her personal experience with her long interest in the depiction of the spiritual in the history of art and recontextualises imagery used in older pictorial genres and traditions. In relation to what is perhaps the most enigmatic prop in *Self Portrait in a Single Breasted Suit with Hare*, namely the hare, Taylor-Wood explains that it is a homonym for hair: 'It was a portrait in a single breasted suit, as I had breast cancer, with hare, I've still got my hair after chemo' (quoted in Loughrey 2006: 91). It seems therefore that the hare is used as a symbol of regeneration.[11] With roots deep in pre-Christian times, according to Simon Carnell, the figure of the hare has particular affinities with femininity, menstruation and blood (2010: 164) and features extensively in pre-modern medicine (many of its parts were used for the treatment of a range of conditions from baldness to memory loss) (2010: 9). Also, since rabbits and hares reproduce prodigiously, they have become symbols of fertility. Hares appear extensively in the work of twentieth-century German performance artist Joseph Beuys to evoke (re)birth. Beuys uses a dead hare in *How to Explain Pictures to a Dead Hare* (1965) to allude, like Taylor-Wood, to the injuries his body suffered during the Second World War when his fighter plane crashed in the Crimea and he was rescued by tribesmen who wrapped his burned body in animal fat and felt.

The hare, and especially the hare rendered at a point between life and death, is also a familiar component in still-life and *vanitas* painting that is haunted by reminders of mortality. The great French specialist of the genre, Jean-Baptiste-Siméon Chardin, comes to mind. In paintings such as *Still Life with Dead Hare* (c.1760) the dramatic position of the hare (one of its legs pinned to the wall with a nail) conveys the kind of violence that is often concealed in still-life and game painting.[12] At the same time the position is more reminiscent of Christ's crucifixion than a naturalistic game piece. Just as Taylor-Wood has appropriated the outdated genre of landscape photography for *Self Portrait as a Tree*, in other work she turns to still life, which also uses symbolism relating to the objects depicted, but also offers more leeway in the arrangement of design elements within a composition than do paintings of other types of subjects, such as landscape. Her experiments with video create dynamic portraits and concrete still lives that, by going beyond the idea of portraiture as static, reveal connections between existence and time and create new tensions and surprising relationships. For example, in the five-minute film *A Little Death* (2002), a dead hare is pinned to a nail (in the same position as in Chardin's painting) and we watch its gradual decomposition at an accelerated pace. The three-dimensional painting, which seems to be about the finiteness of life, does not stop here. A peach lying next to the decaying animal manages magically to remain intact, raising questions about the meanings of this juxtaposition and the boundaries between nature and artifice. Reflecting on her work more generally, Taylor-Wood has stated that she wants to 'convey the sense of being caught between two worlds, of moments without end' (quoted in Neri 2006). *A Little Death* manages to do this, as the video (in the context of an art gallery exhibition) ends only to start again, repeating a process of decay and regeneration that has no end.

The title of the film further adds to its overall ambiguity. 'A little death' refers to the term French philosopher Georges Bataille used for an orgasm (*la petite mort*),[13] which in turn raises the question of whether the hare is used as a symbol of sexual lust or of decay. The tension remains unresolved. *Self-Portrait in a Single Breasted Suit with Hare* was made after *A Little Death* and, as Carnell notes, the hare held upright by its back legs inverts the traditional position of victimisation in still-life and game painting. Taylor-Wood has noted in an interview that 'in my mind this very erect, stiff hare masculinised me'; Carnell, oblivious to the phallic associations of this image, reads it as an unequivocal example of 'defiant *agency* rather than victimhood' – victimhood is equated here with femininity, the traditional symbolism behind the hare which Taylor-Wood also challenges (2010: 176).[14] While I agree that this self-portrait is in dialogue with dominant representations of the hare in still-life painting, its power lies in the ways it does not erase but rather invokes all the different associations of the hare in earlier work, adding them to the palimpsest of breast cancer representations.

If we explore the cumulative meanings and relationships among Taylor-Wood's various works, both preceding and following *Self Portrait in a Single Breasted Suit with Hare*, we can find a similar unresolved but productive form of tension in this self-portrait. This means that it cannot be celebrated as a straightforward 'triumph of art over nature' (Carnell 2010: 177). Thinking of the arrangement of the picture's elements, it is tempting to propose that Taylor-Wood's body stands for the 'still life', the peach found in *A Little Death* that magically keeps well next to the dead hare of both images. The black suit and white shirt she wears here may allude to illness and death, but next to the hare they also evoke a female magician: 'her gaze directly confronts the viewers' gaze, as if daring them to confront' not only the miracle of the hair, which, like the animal, defies the laws (of death or of chemotherapy) but also 'the miracle of Taylor-Wood's continuing existence' (Power 2006: 12). The limitations of the body, the photo seems to suggest, can be magically transcended by the human spirit and also by the hand of the artist. Taylor-Wood is interested in 'an idea of freedom that carries the implication of restraint'; in the *Self Portrait Suspended* photo series (2004–5), the ropes and knots that were used to suspend her body were later digitally erased from the image to achieve a moment of absolute release and freedom (Carolin, in Taylor-Wood et al. 2002). A closer look, however, reveals the picture to have been manipulated. Similarly, here the cable release cord exposes the trick of Taylor-Wood appearing in her own photograph, just as the caption breaks the illusion of the intact body. Both are reminders of technology that can, either in the form of body reconstruction or photography, perhaps make women anew, but does not allow forgetting. Herndl writes of her reconstructed body that although it makes her mastectomy less visible compared to Lorde's uneven body, there is no way she can pretend that nothing happened: 'Prosthesis is technology and it never lets me forget' (2002: 152). I am not suggesting that Taylor-Wood's photograph embraces or critiques breast reconstruction or prosthetics. Still, for the purpose of the dialogue between text and image that I have been pursuing, she seems to deploy a certain photographic aesthetic that, like Herndl's body narrative, covers but leaves a remainder.

There is always an element of suspension between states in Taylor-Wood's work, as it never ceases to explore oppositions. In *Self Portrait in a Single Breasted Suit with Hare*, the stuffed hare remains suspended between a living and a dead creature; as noted, its earlier signification in still painting is overwritten by Taylor-Wood's comment that hare/hair stands for regeneration. But of course, to recall the palimpsest once more, the earlier meaning is still present. Further oppositions are at work: the hare next to the human model draws attention to oppositions between the animal and the human, nature and culture, disease and illness – the boundaries between them appear fluid and dynamic. While animality or nature are held 'at arm's length' (Carnell 2010: 177) in the self-portrait, art or technology cannot erase the fact that both animals and humans are mortal. The alternating black and white squares of the floor resemble a chessboard that evokes the game's traditional symbolism of the conflict between dualities, including life and death. Moreover, even if the choice of running shoes in the photograph invites an interpretation according to which the patient is once again active, the position of the model's feet on the floor calls to mind tap dancing (there is an effort to balance) and seems to anticipate another later work by Taylor-Wood, *Ascension* (2003). This is a film that shows a man dressed in a black suit and tie lying on the ground while another man, dressed in the same suit (possibly the same man), tap dances on his chest, with a dove perched on his head. *Self Portrait in a Single Breasted Suit with Hare* evokes tap dancing's 'playfulness with gravity, the insane excess of its attempts at lift-off, coupled with the constant necessity of its hammering return to earth' (*Sculpture in the Close* 2005) as, like *Ascension*, it reflects on the boundary between a release from bodily limitations and the transient nature of bodies.

Spence, like Lorde, believed that she could use her camera as a weapon to usurp the power of medicine. Even though her photographs urge us to see how society, medicine, and the media deal with women's bodies, especially at a time of silence and invisibility around breast cancer issues, their success, like Herndl's misunderstood narrative of sharing her experience with another woman, is contingent and precarious. While Spence claims that her process-based practice of phototherapy neutralises the risk of objectification, Darcy

Grimaldo Grigsby has argued that 'in the obstinate persistence of her body, its refusal of transformation, [Spence's] photographs dramatise the violence of the body's subjection to the medium's coercive powers' (1991: 93–4). If both medicine and photography denude, fragment and objectify the body, Taylor-Wood's *Self Portrait in a Single Breasted Suit with Hare* gives us a glimpse of how photography, not unlike prosthesis and reconstruction, can dress, mend and heal the unclothed and wounded body. I echo here Sedgwick's statement about a series of cloth hanging figures – 'stuffed forms dressed in blue leggings and tunics, draped with woven cloth' – that she exhibited as part of an installation for the City University of New York Graduate Center in 1999. Sedgwick had become more and more interested in art and weaving after her own cancer diagnosis, and as she explained (1999), 'the figures' strongest representation ties were to the disorienting and radically denuding bodily sense generated by medical imaging and illness itself on the one hand, and on the other, to material urges to dress, ornament, to mend, to recover, and heal'. But Taylor-Wood's work, as much as it invokes the magical capacity of art, particularly photography, to 're-cover' the scarred body, does not reinforce invisibility. Like Herndl, Taylor-Wood wears breast cancer in a different way, *voicing* her difference on several levels to achieve the oxymoronic effect of the 'deafening silence' that can be found in some of her other work.

Before concluding this chapter it is important to note that breast cancer identities, and representations of illness more broadly, are not fixed. In one of the last self-portraits of Spence, which appeared in *Cultural Sniping* and was taken in 1992 shortly before she died of leukaemia, her body is also covered. We see her lying in a hospital bed, covered with a quilt and about to take a snapshot of visitors to her room; this untitled photo includes the cable release cord we find in Taylor-Wood. The difference from her earlier portraits may be relevant to the fact that the visual language Spence had found for representing breast cancer did not seem 'applicable' to leukaemia, which she claimed was 'almost impossible to represent' (1995: 215). She continued to want to turn her illness into something useful, but simultaneously to feel, as she put it, that

> choosing to go like an Amazon into the lion's den over and over again in order to be politically useful is just too energy-consuming and too conflictual. In the end it didn't seem to me to serve any function at all, so it feels at this point as if I will never do anything except look after myself. (217)

Due to exhaustion and the nature of leukaemia, an aggressive and terminal illness, Spence abandoned direct photography in favour of reframing and reinterpreting her previous works in *The Final Project* (1991–2). In a pre-Photoshop era, without using a computer, she altered earlier work by sandwiching slides together and making camera exposures, thus creating new readings of past images. For example, *Property of Jo Spence?* is presented as a portrait in decay through the effect of a peeling wall that marks her body once more with symbolic ruin. A collaboration with Dennett and Spence's later husband David Roberts, *The Final Project* also explores mortality by looking at cultures that have embraced death as part of life or of a longer journey and by using allegorical props for self-representation – she looked in particular at the Mexican Day of the Dead (*Día de los Muertos*), with its skull motifs and the traditional altars families build for their dead, and at ancient Egyptian rituals of death and burial for inspiration. Like the suspension between states found in many of Taylor-Wood's self-portraits, these photographs, through their theme as well as layering, stage moments of tension between presence and absence, life and death, but with a more persistent finality given Spence's terminal condition.[15]

If Spence's covered body in the untitled self-portrait taken in the hospital challenges static representations of illness, Taylor-Wood's nude photo for well-known fashion and celebrity magazine *Harper's Bazaar* in January 2008 equally puts a spin on the argument I have been making. The body 'as battleground' mentioned in a *Daily Mail* headline announcing Taylor-Wood's portrait ('My Body the Battleground' 2007) is nowhere to be found as there are no cancer scars visible (to the naked eye),[16] and Taylor-Wood's body seems miraculously intact one more time; but it is a different kind of magic presented here. Invisibility is paradoxically stronger in a picture of 'maximum exposure' (Taylor 2008: 100) than it was in *Self Portrait in a Single Breasted Suit with Hare*, where the body was covered. The body in this more recent image passes unnoticed amidst other 'unmarked' or cosmetically enhanced bodies. The photographer, Mary McCartney, explains that she wanted 'intimate, relaxed, and private images' (2008: 20).[17] The expression on Taylor-Wood's face is once more serious, but the image is seductive given the way it is lit and considering the feminine position of the legs, crossed on top of a glistening sofa in her home. Female bodies that have undergone breast cancer and mastectomy can look beautiful and attractive, and it is important for women to challenge stereotypes based on the contrary. Taylor-Wood herself acknowledges in the short interview that accompanies her nude portrait that she loves her body for having fought cancer and given birth to two children (quoted in Taylor 2008: 101), and this photo is perhaps a way of showing her love for her body without feeling ashamed. Normalising breast cancer is not necessarily a conservative gesture, since illness is a normal part of living. While *Self Portrait in a Single Breasted Suit with Hare* invites a more interesting kind of engagement on the part of the viewer, this photograph does not easily counter representations of breast cancer as 'a sexualized illness' (Saywell et al. 2000: 37). However, it is significant that the photograph for *Harper's Bazaar* is not a self-portrait and addresses different audiences from those of Taylor-Wood's own work. If we can extract one message from this analysis of the photograph, it would perhaps be that even though making the personal visible is political for Lorde and Spence, visibility is not necessarily synonymous with the act of politicising, since there are many ways that something can be made visible. Just as invisibility is not necessarily reactionary, visibility is not necessarily radical or transgressive. Both gestures need to be considered in relation to larger contextual factors that make the idea of 'feminist choice', which Herndl's article scrutinises, a shifting, multiple and contingent concept, subject to constant redefinition.

'Feminist cultural criticism is not a blueprint for the conduct of personal life (or political action) for that matter ... it does not tell us what to *do*', reads the epigraph of Herndl's essay from Susan Bordo's *Unbearable Weight* (144). The realisation that the goal of feminism is 'edification and understanding', '*enhanced* consciousness' of the complex operations of culture (144) allows Herndl to work through her initial feeling of failure at her inability to make the 'right' choice after her mastectomy – 'feminist theorist fails, I told myself at first' (149) – and reconfigure the meaning and uses of feminism in relation to the particular context of her decision and moment in her life. We notice here tension between one's narrative performance of illness and certain 'successful' conventions, namely a set of powerful representations revolving around visibility that crystallise as 'the feminist choice' (149) – a tension dramatised in the following chapters in relation to other media and experiences of auto/biographical illness. Many of the critics of illness narrative have suggested that narrative coherence can be a harmful phenomenon, especially when it becomes normative or essential to one's recovery (Woods 2011). In this case it would be harmful to judge Herndl's distinct narrative performance of illness less feminist because it does not rely on the symmetry between voice and visible self that we find in Lorde's or Spence's work. Spence, as we saw, expresses a similar objection, though motivated by another consideration, when she notes that leukaemia does not lend itself to the same kind of (coherent?) narratives as breast cancer representation.

I do not want to downplay the complexity of Spence's narrative performances of breast cancer – simply to understand the opposition she draws between visual representations of breast cancer and leukaemia. Even though the former representations were empowering or useful for her, they cannot be recycled when it comes to apprehending something that is more complicated, and this is why she reorients her photography to different themes and processes – the even more performative rituals of her Final Project.

Alongside the issue of aesthetic collision between word and image or voice and visible self that becomes a productive way of working through instances of perceived failure, there are two more points to take from the previous analysis that are revisited in subsequent chapters. The first is recognition of the limitations of blueprints, however appealing or seductive, a notion that the medical humanities should take on board given the current debates concerning the dominance of instrumental approaches and what the field's future direction should be. Continuous critical engagement with various blueprints and the difficulties surrounding making decisions or adopting certain practices, whether the issue is feminist politics or medical education, is what can revitalise ways of being and acting. The second issue, linked to the first, is that blueprints have a tendency to disregard singularity or difference, a topic Chapters 4 and 5 explore in relation to collaborative treatments of another person's illness experience rather than a split in the individual, which is what Herndl's story presents us with. Carving their own path through Lorde's and Spence's feminist visual politics on the one hand and neoliberal understandings of health where biomedicine and its treatments are all-powerful on the other, Herndl and Taylor-Wood create their own illness performances and treatments. While their narratives of re-covery do not exclude medical and cosmetic (or technological) solutions, their embodied experiences are not silenced by, or subsumed into, these dominant discourses. As I have tried to illustrate by reading the photographs in themselves and through the textual narratives, attending to the formal complexity and ambivalence of such work is important as it reveals the critical and political potential that underlies certain aesthetic strategies.

Whether their choices entail aligning voice with visible self or covering bodily scars but not the scars as 'memorial sites' (Best 2014), the main works discussed in this chapter resist existing and often reductive narratives about women's health (for example, that of the postfeminist neoliberal subject) and create opportunities for the proliferation of feminist subjectivities. In their multiplicity, these narratives are in turn confrontational and contradictory, provocative and beautiful. As Klawiter concludes in her study, 'the flip side of the politics of provocation is often a politics of beauty and bodily reclamation' (2008: 294). If, in their various attempts to make visible what had remained hidden, Spence and the other women artists examined above paved the way for new forms of embodiment in one-breasted bodies, there is more continuity between *Property of Jo Spence?* and *Self Portrait in a Single Breasted Suit with Hare* than may initially appear: adjusting Herndl's final statement in her essay, perhaps Spence would understand what Taylor-Wood did; she would see that she is living her difference, and that the difference between her voice and her visible self is part of that difference.

Notes

1. For developments in breast cancer narratives in the twenty-first century, see DeShazer 2013.
2. In this chapter I am using the name by which she was known before her 2012 marriage (Taylor-Wood) rather than Taylor-Johnson.
3. In 2007, for instance, she did an exhibition of intimate portraits of cancer patients who have visited Maggie's Cancer Caring Centres.
4. She has done music video clips, photography for fashion magazines and more recently directed successful films.
5. For studies that take such an approach to photography and visual representation more broadly, see Hirsch 1997 and Jordanova 2000.
6. Spence opted for traditional Chinese medicine. See *Cultural Sniping* and *Putting Myself in the Picture* for her views on alternative treatments for breast cancer.
7. See Dillon 2007.
8. Lorde must have been aware of Spence's work, as among the Audre Lorde Papers at Spelman College, Atlanta there is an article by Ros Coward reviewing *The Picture of Health?* The article was published in *New Socialist* (October 1985): 28–31. Audre Lorde Papers, Spelman College Archives, Box 51, 3.667. For a discussion of illness and disability in Lorde's work, see Bolaki 2011a and 2013.
9. See Diedrich for an exploration of 'divergent British and American "cultural narratives"' that inform breast cancer narratives (2007: 55). In this chapter I focus on the commonalities that can be observed across the British and American pairs examined, but more could be done with national differences, specifically engaging with Diedrich's schemas of 'an American emphasis on the cultivation of an improved self' and 'a British emphasis on a cultivation of an ironic self' (55). On cultural/national differences and medicine, also see Payer 1996.

10. What differentiates the empowerment of the postfeminist neoliberal woman – what Dubriwny (2013) calls 'the vulnerable empowered woman' – from that of her peers in the era of biomedicalisation (approximately after 1985) is the expectation to manage risk through lifestyle changes that are often dictated by biomedicine and are not available to less privileged women.
11. In *On Generation of Animals*, Aristotle argued that the hare's reproductive power was related to its excessive hair or hairiness (Carnell 2010: 7).
12. The hare was classified early in law as one of the principal 'game' species.
13. See his novel *Madame Edwarda* (1941).
14. On the other hand, this comment can also be interpreted as a way of criticising the obsession with femininity in mainstream breast culture. The connection of the hare with masculinity is also consistent with the widespread opinion that hares were able to shift genders.
15. Other examples in *The Final Project* are the swimsuit portraits in which Spence, wearing only a black swimsuit, lies across the surface of a rocky stream, a field and a cemetery, as well as against an ocean-blue background overlaid with a scene from an operation table. See Spence 2013.
16. The text accompanying the portrait published in *Harper's* also mentions that colon cancer left Taylor-Wood with a curving scar on her stomach (Taylor 2008: 101).
17. Two other women – Beth Ditto, a musician, and Sadie Frost, a designer – are photographed along with Taylor-Wood for the Lavender Trust, a charity for younger women with breast cancer.

Chapter 2

Artists' Books in the Medical Community

In *Tattoo* (November 1998), an artist's book by American artist Martha Hall, there is a description of 'a black and white photo of a nude woman with her arms outstretched ... / a vine with flowers tattooed on the scar across her missing breast' (2003: 30), given to her by her daughter in the form of a postcard.[1] Though unnamed in the book, it is clear Hall is referring to Deena Metzger's *The Warrior* (briefly mentioned in Chapter 1). While Hall admires 'the woman's courage, / her joy / her beauty, / her defiance' and wonders whether she should also get a tattoo, *Tattoo* finishes with two questions: 'Will I dare to prick the surface? Will it help to add another scar?' (32).[2] The book itself highlights these questions through a sewing needle stuck into its cover, connecting the needle that would be used in a tattoo parlour with the activities of sewing and book making.

The book as a form and idea has rich cultural, spiritual and metaphorical associations, including with the body. Words like *skin*, *spine* and *joints* may refer to both the body of the book and the animal/human body. As is well known, vellum or parchment made of calfskin served as the basis of book production into the early years of the invention of printing. If writing is like an inscription on skin, given the etymological meaning of the verb to write (to scratch), we can understand why poet and physician Rafael Campo claims that 'writing good iambic pentameter feels like putting stitches into the anonymous, eternally gaping wound of being human, and [that] rhymes can be intertwined like surgical knots' (1997: 116). Similarly, the binding of a book as the site where its pages stitch together and come apart resonates with the scar.

In 'The Bookbinder' from the sequence *Self-portrait without Breasts*, poet Clare Best, a former bookbinder herself, describes the craft of book making as an alternative, artistic kind of surgery. Both operations rely on what the poem calls 'a vigilant hand':

> Pare the leather, thin the skin
> where it must stretch and crease.
> Then paste: the tanned flesh darkens,
>
> wet and chill, fingers working
> over spine and cords, into joints,
> mitreing corners neat and flat.
>
> Bandage the book in paper, let it
> settle under weights, day after day
> until the leather's dry and tight. (Best 2011: 59)

Elsewhere Best (2013) describes the book-object as 'a cradle', holding through its strength the contents of her work as well as her old and new (post-surgical) bodies through its solidity.[3]

Like Campo and Best, Martha Hall, the key figure of this chapter, performs her own version of surgery and recovery. She does this through the process of writing that one of her artists' books describes as 'making marks' (61), thus restoring the often-forgotten tactility of this act, and by creating her books from scratch using a range of materials and book structures. The cover of *Holding In, Holding On*, a catalogue accompanying a travelling exhibition of Hall's artists' books in several colleges and libraries in the United States published after her death, is adorned with an image taken from her book *Just to Live* (March 1997) that clearly evokes the scar; we see the stitching thread while the colour contrast reveals the pinkish flesh underneath, peeking out of the loose thread against a grey background. The gap that is created invites us to explore the hidden site below the surface and listen to, or rather touch, its story.

This chapter extends the previous discussion of word and image relations by turning to a form that not only compels involvement with the ideas expressed in the text and with visual representation, but also *physical* engagement, as well as a medium that historically has been associated with both aesthetic and political considerations. An artist's book is a book 'created as an original work of art, rather than a reproduction of a pre-existing work' and 'integrates the formal means of its realization and production with its thematic or aesthetic issues' (Drucker 2004: 2). Artists' books are generally understood as a discrete artistic experiment that took place roughly from 1965 to 1980 and then gradually disappeared, but the form continues to be potent today. Even though the specific characteristics of this medium – its complexity, immediacy and intimacy – have received some attention by art historians and book critics, and more recently been debated in relation to the future of the book in the digital era,[4] artists' books have rarely been explored in relation to illness narratives and the medical humanities or, more specifically, breast cancer. Martha Hall created around a hundred artists' books in response to her initial diagnosis of breast cancer in 1989 and the effects of later recurrences until her death in 2003. Unlike some of the women discussed in Chapter 1, Hall did not inhabit the 'identities' of artist, feminist or activist prior to her illness diagnosis. Leaving a career in New York City as a business executive after her first recurrence of cancer in 1993, and returning to art (which she had studied as an undergraduate at Smith College in 1971), she took a series of courses and workshops in book making and familiarised herself with several printing and binding techniques. Acquiring these extra skills was essential to documenting her experience for herself and her family as well as for future use by other women, patients and medical practitioners. Rather than piecing together a conventional illness narrative moving towards a particular closure, Hall's books offer many episodes or moments that are given life through the interplay of the medium's various imaginative elements, only one of which is language. Considered as a whole, her books document cancer as a chronic illness, her development as an artist and her interactions with the medical community.

Part narrative, part object, part performance, artists' books are often defined in relation to other forms and media. In *The Century of Artists' Books* book artist and visual theorist Johanna Drucker sketches out 'a zone of activities' that offers a glimpse of the multiplicity of art forms and cultural production that constitute the field of artists' books:

> fine printing, independent publishing, the craft tradition of book arts, conceptual art, painting and other traditional arts, politically motivated art activity and activist production, performance of both traditional and experimental varieties, concrete poetry, experimental music, computer and electronic arts, and last but not least, the tradition of the illustrated book, *the livre d'artiste*. (Drucker 2004: 2)[5]

Reading artists' books requires not only interacting with words and images but also paying attention to their shape, size, format, colour, texture, typography and even fragrance and sound. In addition to their aesthetic qualities, artists' books are associated with independent publishing, as the artist remains in control of the different dimensions of production and distribution. Their portability, durability and inexpensive nature ensure that they can circulate more freely and outside the gallery system as well as become available to non-specialist audiences, provided that there is a system of distribution.[6]

The above characteristics of the medium are considered to be some of the reasons why the form has been attractive to female artists in a male-dominated art world. Another reason is its intimacy – which differentiates it, for example, from the photographs discussed in Chapter 1, which have a more public presence. As Drucker writes, book making, in addition to being associated with a range of 'feminine' activities (sewing, keeping diaries and decorative tasks), 'matches many women's lived experience' in that it balances 'enclosure and exposure', thus providing a kind of 'intimate authority' to women artists (2011: 14).[7] This is evident in a book like *Tattoo*, which manages to explore scars, breast cancer and Hall's responsibility to other ill people in an equally powerful way to Metzger's defiant photograph without following the same strategies.

Unlike paintings, sculptures and films, artists' books are created for one-to-one interactions but can reach many people. Hall's artists' books encourage us to analyse the special kind of collective space this medium opens and to what extent it is able to transform attitudes to illness, medicine and health as well as art. Her artist's statement included in *Holding In, Holding On* confirms the simultaneous inward and outward-looking character of her books, thus demonstrating the therapeutic, political and pedagogical value of her work. She writes that besides offering her a way 'to have a voice in the world', they allow her to share her experience with other people who are ill and are also 'a means to effect change in the way medical professionals interact with their patients' (15). In addition to using the books to communicate with her doctors Hall helped to found, and served on the board of, The Cancer Community Centre in South Portland, Maine, and received invitations to speak to medical professionals in US hospitals and colleges. Although she does not allude to the political origins of the artist's book, she wanted her work to be in public, rather than private, collections and museums – particularly college libraries, where the books could be held and read by individual students, including medical students.[8] Her books are currently used in Medical Humanities units, and the Maine Women Writers Collection (University of New England), which owns twelve of her books, regularly receives requests to have the books used in medical schools across the United States.[9]

Artists' books and the medical humanities

Hall's work does not feature in any of the key volumes surveying the field of artists' books. There are, however, a number of better-known books that deal with experiences of illness or have a broader medical theme, although many of them are not well known to a wider public beyond the community of book artists, collectors, librarians and curators. Moreover, in these specialised circles they are often discussed with different aims in mind. In both Drucker's *The Century of Artists' Books* and Renée Riese Hubert and Judd D. Hubert's *The Cutting Edge of Reading Artists' Books*, artists' books that explore illness are grouped with others on the basis of their shared formal characteristics (interesting deviations in terms of binding, typography and visual form) or their functions as 'documents' and as 'agents of social change', to use some of the headings of Drucker's study. This misses what exactly the books can communicate about experiences of illness, mourning and death, or about the relationship of the individual to institutions like medicine. Even though attention is paid to the ways they integrate their formal and thematic aspects,[10] or how a specific book can raise public awareness of certain topics, often the aim of such scholarship is to adjudicate the books' generic status – that is, to show whether it meets the criteria of an artist's book.

Consider, for example, Joan Lyons' *The Gynecologist* (1989). This book includes an interview between a patient and a gynaecologist who insists on surgery to remove her uterus, ovaries and cervix as a solution to her problems. The opening line, 'He has wanted her womb for years' emphasises the victimisation and power struggle exposed in the book. In addition to the text, also consisting of an 'Afterword', a feminist assessment of the American Medical Association and its attitudes towards women, there are reproductions of woodcuts and engravings from medical books, such as drawings by Leonardo and Vesalius, which focus on the uterus and show the body of a woman wide open. As Hubert and Hubert conclude their reading of this book: 'Although readers will learn that patriarchy prevails within and far beyond the medical field, they should by no means consider this strong feminist book a treatise, let alone a pamphlet, but view it as highly sophisticated bookwork' (1999: 145).[11] This cautionary remark is important in that it shifts attention from content to form, or rather to their dynamic connection, thus emphasising the importance of close reading and of a particular kind of attention to the work, often overlooked in instrumental medical humanities approaches. However, it also creates a rigid opposition between politics and aesthetics in order to demarcate the proper terrain of artists' books. In the process, as the political becomes narrowly interpreted in terms of content, or worse, propaganda, what gets missed is that aesthetic strategies are always already political; an aspect that Hall's books powerfully demonstrate, as we will see.

A similar problem can be observed in relation to artists' books that draw on personal experience. What many book critics attempt to establish is whether 'the concept of the personal degenerates' into 'the sappily confessional which ends up being so generic as to negate the very idea of the individual voice', or whether we are dealing instead with 'original' works of art (Drucker 1994: 24–5). Books such as Matthew Geller's *Difficulty Swallowing* (1981) and Linn Underhill's *Thirty Five Years/One Week* (1981), both documenting the death of people close to the artists, have been measured against this ideal of artistic 'originality'. The former, a medical chronicle of the death of Geller's girlfriend from leukaemia, is composed of medical reports, diary entries by Geller, photographs and handwritten letters or notes by the patient. The medical report pages are filled with symbols and abbreviations and, in their documentary neutrality, could be seen as countering sentimentality. Their effect is either to slow down the progress of reading the book or, paradoxically, speed it up, as we can imagine readers feeling compelled to simply turn these pages to reach the larger and more intelligible story at the heart of the book. But the medical notes by different doctors and nurses can be also appreciated as medicine's intrinsic aesthetic component (a version perhaps of Bakhtin's heteroglossia) or for the mystery and possibly dread that they evoke to the lay reader who, like the patient, is excluded by the strange language and is withheld full knowledge. Linn Underhill's book tells the story of her younger sister's battle with melanoma through diary entries (both handwritten and typed) and photographs, some of which have a medical theme. As in the case of Wenders' film *Lightning over Water* (discussed in Chapter 4), where the use of video shots is paralleled to Nick Ray's cancer (it is a tumour in the film), we can read the progressively faded or blurry images in this book as a comment – albeit aestheticised – on the progress of metastasised cancer that in one week took the sister's life.

The questions and debates in which artists' books often become implicated resonate with the complex and contested space that illness narratives occupy in contemporary culture and the medical humanities. For example, Drucker's point about the danger of self-indulgence and the 'degeneration' of the personal into the confessional recalls the accusations against the memoir, and the illness memoir specifically, that were outlined in the Introduction. Like memoirs eroding literary value, the confessional nature of many artists' books today risks detracting from a 'true' work of art. Illness narratives are not, however, reducible either to their aesthetics or to their political dimensions (we can recall Diedrich's attribution 'affective' and 'effective' to capture the ways they are about the poetics of suffering *and* politics): they are not just personal expressions of grief or merely therapeutic instruments; neither are they reflections of ideology, or designed to just influence healthcare. What critical medical humanities scholars can offer to these debates – and what I am offering in this study, through what I have described as a critical interloping – is an alternative way of approaching the work involved in the making of some of these books that focus on illness experiences. This is not to deprive them of the label 'art' or 'artist's book' (the books mentioned above were made by people who see themselves as artists) but to also understand them 'in terms of aesthetic practice – of an ethic that problematises the person's situation as a work of freedom' (Radley 2009: 37). In paying attention to this kind of work, we can, following Radley and others, illuminate how works of illness are fabricated to 'allow something important to be made again, to be seen anew by others, to be grasped afresh' (2009: 184) – in other words, to be shared. Approaching illness stories and artworks in this light has a twofold dimension: it encourages a perspective that addresses aesthetic practice in itself (how the works are made or put together) and how such practice bears upon ethics and the social world, including the spheres of art, medicine, science and politics.

While most book critics describe the handling of artists' books in terms of an experience that emphasises the visual, tactile and other sensuous pleasures of the book, in the following reading of Hall's books I show how books that deal with illness also engage and complicate discourses of testimony and witnessing, which have been foregrounded in trauma and, more recently, disability and illness narrative studies scholarship.[12] In this way, I synthesise approaches to fashion new tools that can mutually enrich the medical humanities and the field of artists' books. In raising questions of ethical responsibility, artists' books place a new set of complex demands on their readers that have interesting affinities with the modes of address within illness narratives more broadly, even as they find unique expression through this medium's characteristics. Subsequent sections of the chapter turn to the kinds of political and pedagogical provocations Hall's books present to mainstream breast cancer culture, medicine and medical education, including a consideration of their place within the dominant field of narrative medicine. Like the works discussed in the following chapters, her books create spaces for unpredictable and unfinished relational encounters that demand a more radical form of witnessing which does not entail reducing difference to the same; and they do so through the powerful aesthetic as well as the ethical force of touch.

The secret life of the book: touch as witnessing

Artists' books engage their readers intellectually and emotionally, but also physically, and require greater effort than most ordinary books.[13] Breon Mitchell characterises the reading of an artist's book as 'a performance'; the 'ideal' reader is someone who 'plays' the book, 'actualising' the various elements the artist has built into it, as if it were a 'musical score' (1996: 162). Touch constitutes a central element in the reading process of Hall's artists' books. As the formal means of realisation and production are integrated with the thematic or aesthetic issues in many artists' books, the choice of paper conditions and enhances the viewer's tactile experience of a book's contents. In the book *Shell Bones* (July 2002), for instance, where Hall tells a story about finding thick and strong shells on the beach and taking them home, heavyweight wrapper is used with worn and torn edges. Rather than being reduced to the pages that communicate (through the words inscribed on them) this story, the heavyweight wrapper becomes a skin that reveals the scars of the experience that is narrativised:

> I loved them because they were so
> heavy in my hand.
> ...
> I wanted my bones to be thick and
> strong like the shells
> ...

> I didn't notice until today
> that some of the shells have deep holes.
> I didn't want them to be like my bones. (80)

The box in which the book is found also contains a shell with holes. In this way, the reader engages with the piece on a number of levels, experiencing the text rather than simply analysing it.

Touch and vision are not separate, as many of Hall's books demonstrate through the use of colour. Colour works expressively to enhance the affect of some books – for example in *Dark Room Days* (April 1999), a book about Hall's depression and thoughts of imminent death, the fragments of black and white photos used on black board paper conjure the darkroom where photographic prints are processed, but also the radiation room with its frightening X-ray procedures. The book closes with the line, 'where are life's colors?' (42). *Playing with Fire* (May 2002) makes further use of colour, resulting in an almost synaesthetic effect. The text is about being 'burned' and scarred by the red eye of the laser beams, and the experience of being burned is conveyed through the intense colour of the cover and the technique used: pochoir and hot foil stamping with laser print. Pochoir, the French word for stencilling, is used to create prints of intense colour. Foil stamping uses heat and metallic film in a specialty printing process that produces a shiny design on any material. The effect is arresting, as colours come alive, and creates the illusion that if readers touch the book they may be burned.

Hall's books also bear the body's marks and hold its traces through the inclusion of hairs as well as autobiographical objects, such as used medical appointment cards and original prescription bottles. These objects do not merely function as signs, but have a material presence. Writing about the AIDS memorial quilt in her chapter 'Objects of Grief', Laura Tanner urges us 'to resist the pressure of immaterialization that would exclude palpable, multisensory experience ... from the realm of knowledge' (2006: 209). As she elaborates, objects on the quilt do not only function in a symbolic way. The quilt's material presence and the tactile specificity of each panel, some of which have objects sewn onto them, return us to their embodied use by the people they belonged to as well as to our own bodies. Tanner mentions her children's normal desire to touch the quilt and its objects during an exhibition against the constant reminders not to touch, and observes how most cultural critics who have written about the quilt 'invoke embodiment only to metaphorize it' (202). For example, Judy Elsey (1992) has compared the quilt to the novel, thus obscuring the kind of physical intimacy and engagement that it invites.

Physical intimacy can be threatening when the object one comes into contact with deals with trauma or serious illness. Hall seems to perceive the threat posed by the viewers' literal contact with her books: 'People may not want to "touch" the topics I explore in my books; yet the books invite handling, touching, interaction' (14). She places in quotation marks the word *touch*, enacting a similar process of metaphorisation to the one discussed by Tanner – touch, as Jacques Derrida tells us in *On Touching*, is often used in a figurative sense as an alternative for 'to speak of' or 'to refer to' – only to then disrupt it by returning to the ways her books hold the traces of her body and of illness; in other words, the literal and the figurative meanings of touch 'invade' one another (Miller 2008: 151). But touch, especially the caress and other forms of affective contact, to which we could add the 'spatial embrace' of the book (Drucker 2004: 360), also becomes associated with an exposure to the other's alterity in Emmanuel Levinas' ethics-centred philosophy. Levinas distinguishes the 'caress' from 'palpation', a word often associated with a medical examination; as he writes in *Totality and Infinity*, 'The caress consists in seizing upon nothing, in soliciting what ceaselessly escapes its form towards a future never future enough, in soliciting what slips away as though it *were not yet*. It *searches*, it forages. It is not an intentionality of disclosure but of search: a movement unto the invisible' (2007: 257–8).[14] This description resonates with the tension between the fixed sequence of the codex (or traditional book form) and the expansive effect of reading and viewing. At the same time, 'the movement unto the invisible' that Levinas writes about brings a form of affective contact that goes beyond vision to bear upon a certain kind of ethics and responsibility towards another.

Hall's book *Jane, with Wings* (January 2001) provides a reflection on the complex nature of touching and the ethics of responsibility that it generates. It consists of hand-made paper that incorporates hair, thread and linen. A polished stone serves as a knob for lifting the red cover of the black box that houses this book; it is an invitation as much as it attests to the need for secrecy. The book uses a multi-layered folding structure[15] which, in allowing readers to 'enter' it or be enclosed by it, encourages a different kind of engagement to the one prompted by turning pages. As Radley and Bell note, 'to read this book is perhaps above all to learn to handle it': 'To read

Figure 2.1 Martha Hall, *Jane, with Wings*, image courtesy Bowdoin College Library, Brunswick, ME.

the words one has to handle the book very carefully, going deeper into the "origami" folds so as not to tear the paper' (2007: 381–2). At the same time, because this book lacks the sense of limit usually provided by an edge, binding and spine, it further foregrounds 'the infinite space of the page', capable of drawing the reader not only 'in an endlessly expanding experience of sensation and association' (Drucker 2004: 359) but also, as I show below, of infinite ethical responsibility.

Jane, with Wings opens with a series of phrases that attempt to locate and illuminate 'a pattern in the darkness':

> a crack
> in the middle,
> or on the edge,
> on the out
> or on the in –
> stitched together
> and coming apart.

This is the liminal space of the scar, existing at the interstices of visibility and interiority, both inside and outside, and as a result it is difficult to testify and bear witness to. While the construction of the book invites opening, going deeper into its origami folds, the text advises the reader to 'close it away', creating a productive tension:

> Close it away.
> the fear ...
> Close this page.
>
> You are not
> the one
> who is dying.
>
> You do not
> need to see
> beneath the surface
> the skin,
> the scars. (56)

The delicate boundary between concealing and revealing that *Jane, with Wings* negotiates seems apt considering it explores traumatic experiences that are hard to articulate but at the same time, as we have seen in Chapter 1, impossible to forget. An appeal for recognition or empathy is made more difficult when an illness narrative addresses people who do not suffer from the same condition; through the pronoun *you*, the book not only relates the reader to the author but also the healthy to the sick ('you are not the one who is dying'). Hall's books present a challenge to reading conventions as well as to dominant attitudes towards illness, and utilise strategies specific to the genre of the artist's book: at first glance, the reader/viewer is faced with the creativity and uniqueness of the books as works of art and is therefore lured into opening them (or the boxes in which they are housed) without always knowing what to expect. Given that the books are handmade, and, in many cases, handwritten, there is a much more immediate sense of exploring privacy; the reader, inevitably, takes the role of *voyeur* (the injunction to 'close the page' or the invocation of 'fear' in *Jane, with Wings* may have the opposite effect as they fuel readers' curiosity), but soon realises that the book makes different demands on him or her. By that time, however, it is difficult to withdraw, not only because this goes against reading conventions (namely, against the desire to reach the end), but also because, as Shlomith Rimmon-Kenan writes in a different context, it is as if the text says: 'You can't leave me now that you know my condition' (2006: 248).

It is clear, then, that reading this book demands taking up the interactive/ethical challenges it presents. Returning to Mitchell's idea of performance, *Jane, with Wings* can be thought of as a kind of *interactive* art. The experience it offers is indeed 'actualized' by its reading, but we are not dealing with merely a 'unique aesthetic experience' (Mitchell 1996: 162). The book not only engages the senses but also constructs the reader as responsible, in Kelly Oliver's sense of 'response-able' (2001: 7), and therefore engages him or her as witness to its testimony. Whether one chooses to advance in the reading of the book or not, there is no way not to interact; the piece already, through its form and text, establishes an intersubjective relation between writer and reader/viewer. Mitchell suggests that learning to read or 'perform' the different elements of an artist's book rewards patient readers by giving them access to what he calls 'the secret life of the book', the unexploited 'living potential' of books that 'slumber in book libraries and museums' without having been read properly before (1996: 165). While *Jane, with Wings* seems to compel a specifically *ethical* form of engagement, the reader (even the 'ideal' one who reaches the book's centre) is paradoxically told that he or she is to close the book without knowing, without seeing 'beneath the surface / the skin / the scars'. In other words, *Jane, with Wings* demands *and* exceeds a response at the same time. What may initially seem like a performance of failed interaction can in fact transform us as readers in that it compels us to bear witness to what, in Oliver's phrase, is 'beyond recognition', though no less real. What matters is not to 'comprehend' it (a finite task) but 'encounter' it (an infinite task), and respond to it in a way that affirms response-ability (2001: 90). This is where the 'secret life' of this book lies every time it is handled; the other secret (gestured in the text) remains untold.

Transforming medical and breast cancer cultures

Hall's books not only stage intimate moments of witnessing but also critique how bodies of cancer patients are handled during surgery, radiation and chemotherapy, intervening both in breast cancer and medical cultures, particularly in the latter's increasing reliance on science and technology. They do that through the words on the pages but also through the formal aspects of the books. Hall's medical history reveals a series of interactions with the medical community over a long period of time. After having a mastectomy, followed by months of chemotherapy in 1989, she had a recurrence of breast cancer in 1993 after months of having been un/misdiagnosed. She was treated with high dose chemotherapy and had a bone marrow transplant and radiation. In 1998, a recurrence of cancer in her neck was treated with radiation, but in 1999 she was diagnosed with metastatic breast cancer in her ribs, spine, skull and liver, for which she was treated with chemotherapies until her death (100–1). In light of this medical history, her books move beyond the cultural narrative of triumph, making room for feelings of pain, loss, anger and suffering.

Two books that express a range of emotions concerning her prolonged illness and treatment through their layout and formal aspects are *What You Don't Want to Know* and *Black Box*. The former, created in December 1998, is an altered book that Hall made by pulling apart and reassembling a publication of the National Cancer Institute entitled *What You Need to Know about Breast Cancer*. The pages of Hall's altered book are stitched, stapled, torn, glued, cut, crumpled, marked and resequenced. In addition many of the words in the original text, including the title of the book, are erased or highlighted with black ink. Drucker calls transformed books more broadly 'interventions into the social order' and adds that there is 'an aggressiveness' to such transformative practices that 'is related to the gentler act of making a layered palimpsest' (2004: 109). In her artist's statement, Hall notes that 'the process of stitching, crumpling, tearing, cutting, and stapling the pages helped [her] express and release anger' (13). But this book does not only have therapeutic value. Erasing parts of the original text, altering the title and substituting new words and images, Hall – like Spence, who repeats her doctor's marking of the 'bad breast' with a difference – intervenes into the official medical narrative and attempts to reclaim part of her agency. The publication of the National Cancer Institute with the title *What You Need to Know about Breast Cancer* provides information about diagnosis, treatment choices, breast reconstruction and follow-up care, and even includes a list of questions that women might want to ask their doctors. Hall's interventions suggest that this book, however significant in providing information, cannot address fundamental aspects of the lived experience of illness (which would differ from woman to woman). Indeed the existence of other books with the same title, or books that echo or revisit this title,[16] show that the question of what a woman 'needs to know about breast cancer' is one that will always cause debate and invite rewriting. Given that

Hall's new book is composite as it is held together by different voices, it becomes a site of struggle over the meanings ascribed to breast cancer and the people (or the experts) who can advise about it in the most comprehensive and satisfactory way.

Black Box, also created in December 1998, serves a similar function. This is literally a box that contains ten black and white books (one of them is the altered book *What You Don't Want to Know*). The term 'black box' in science and engineering refers to a device, system or object whose internal workings are opaque or unknown. In aviation, it is what records conversations and information that can be retrieved in the case of an accident. These meanings of the term resonate with various aspects of illness (for example, the unknowability of the body's interior by the patient, or illness as an accident) but also posit the books as what will survive – what Hall more positively calls her 'legacy' in one of her later books of the same name. 'Black box' in pharmacology also refers to the type of warning (a 'black box' warning) that appears on the label of a prescription medication to alert patients and healthcare providers about any important safety concerns, such as serious side-effects or life-threatening risks. This warning is referenced in some of the excerpts from the books inside the box. One of them is in the shape of a fan – an appropriate book format for deciding how much to reveal or conceal – and when spread out fully, presents a list of words/phrases the artist does not want to hear about. These range from 'hair loss' and 'palliative treatment' to 'survival rate', 'life insurance refused' and 'no cure' (35–6). At the end of a long list of items resembling a kind of exorcism, Hall notes the irony of this ritual, the fact that the words and phrases need to be recalled and put down first: as she corrects herself, 'I should write, "What I don't want / to hear about *again*."' (37) But like Spence's practice of phototherapy, whose aim is not simply to repeat traumas but to envisage new possibilities of acting and being, this process cannot be simply reduced to an instance of replication, if only because it engenders something new in the very material form of the book.

The text in many of Hall's books draws on specific interactions with the medical community. Such is the case of *Just to Know* (March 1997), a book in which Hall is not only examined but also herself 'examines' the female technician who administers radiation therapy:

> 'Take in a deep breath. Hold it.' The test. The technician's voice sounds eerie, comes from a speaker in the machine. She is in the other room, eyes on the computer, not me. The machine whirls softly

> as if something is spinning around and around at high speed inside. 'Breathe.' The machine moves forward a fraction of an inch. 'Take in a deep breath. Hold it.' Then the muted whirling sound. 'Breathe.' Again and again. Perhaps a hundred times. She must be tired of repeating the same phrase. (20)

The invasiveness of medical technology is emphasised here not only in relation to the patient (there is nothing in Hall's books that recalls Herndl's response to the blurring of body and machine through her invocation of the cyborg), but also the technician – her 'eerie' disembodied voice and her repeated words suggest that she has become machine-like in her interactions with her patients. In his memoir *The Desire to Heal*, Campo draws a compelling comparison between 'withholding words' through the conscious process of 'forbidding [him] self the application of heartfelt, meaningful language' and that of commanding his patients 'to hold their breath' (1997: 114). *Just to Know* similarly shows that the increasing presence of technology in the medical encounter hinders important emotional intimacies and leads to detachment and distance.

Test Day (February 1999) expands this critique through the distinction between scanning the body and scanning the self or soul:

> I will light up their screens,
> My insides black and white.
> Circles, shadows, lines.
> But the watchers will not see me;
> Will not see my self, my soul; (38)

The focus on shapes – 'circles, shadows, lines' we see on the pages of the book containing the bone marrow scans – confirms that 'knowledge, authority and domination are exerted through a visual ordering of bodies' (Cartwright 1995: 170).[17] *Test Day* also pursues a contrast between light and darkness both through its composition (shadow painting) and the words; the patient will 'light up their screens', but what the watchers' technology cannot penetrate is her 'black' anger, which nevertheless does not 'cloud their machine vision', and her fear (38). The reference to 'soul', rather than having religious connotations, suggests something more amorphous that cannot be ordered or seen through the technicians' optical tools (we can recall here the 'pattern in the darkness' in *Jane, with Wings* that will not be exposed to vision in the end). Anatole Broyard also alludes to the soul in his autobiographical essay 'The Patient Examines the Doctor'; he notes that 'soul is the part of you that you summon up in emergencies' (1992: 41), and comments on medicine's unwillingness to see him as anything more than his illness. Even though Hall's tone is less playful than Broyard's, in providing alternative 'examinations' of those who examine bodies *Just to Know* and *Test Day* offer the kind of 'countersurveillance' (Cartwright 1995: 170) that can reconfigure medical imaging technologies and the ways they shape the doctor-patient relationship.

Illness narratives return again and again to the incommensurability that characterises the perception of illness by patients and the medical community. Broyard captures this perfectly when he writes: 'To the typical physician, my illness is a routine incident in his rounds, while for me it's the crisis of my life' (1992: 43). *Small Rooms* (March 2002) dramatises this incongruity:

> The nurse asks, 'And how are you today?'
> I answer, 'I'm in terrible pain.'
> and she responds, 'Oh.
> I like the color of your sweater.'
> She doesn't look at me. (70)

The text evokes a never-ending cycle of superficial interaction rather than meaningful communication between patients and doctors:

> I leave the long corridors,
> the waiting women,
> the nurses and doctors asking
> someone else,
> 'And how are you today?' (72)

This is one of the books that attacks the mandatory 'cheerfulness' in mainstream breast cancer culture to which critics such as Ehrenreich have drawn attention, and expresses the artist's anger. The reference to Ehrenreich is not arbitrary, as in the Martha Hall Collection in the Maine Women Writers Collection there is a small amount of foldered material owned by the artist, including a copy of Ehrenreich's 2001 article 'Welcome to Cancerland'. Although *Small Rooms* does not express Ehrenreich's strong feelings against 'the prevailing pinkness' in breast cancer culture (2001: 52), it subtly alludes to it through the note that one of her nurses is 'wearing a pink ribbon pin' (70). Hall could have been aware of the *Think Before You Pink* campaign, launched in 2002, that encourages consumers to ask critical questions before buying pink ribbon products. *Small Rooms* ends with Hall parodying her doctor's words: 'I'm "fit as a fiddle". / I have stage IV breast cancer' (72).

Small Rooms is made to look like a series of examination rooms with acrylic windows and X-ray transparencies projecting onto them, thus turning the book into a physical space and enabling us to experience the kind of claustrophobia, entrapment and exposure thematised through the words:

There is no changing room.

There is no place to put my clothes.
I fold them, bra inside
and put them on the basket
where the used gowns go.

You can see the parking lot
and Route One
from the examining room.

Why do I have to take off my socks? (70)

The last question is a desperate attempt by the patient to counteract what in Chapter 1 was described as the 'radically denuding bodily sense generated by medical imaging and illness itself' (in Sedgwick's words) by clinging to the socks; an item of clothing that is here invested with a surprising potential to 're-cover', given that more private parts of the body are exposed during the tests. A similar urge to 'dress' and 'ornament' the body is expressed in *Playing with Fire*, in which Hall talks about the black stones she holds in her 'clenched hand' while she is having radiation treatment. Book artist Susan King in *Treading the Maze* also chooses a necklace of beads (this time blue glass ones) as her 'amulet', 'something to wear on my body, close to my breast' in the hope that they will 'absorb and neutralise excess radiation' and that their 'coolness' will 'soothe [her] skin' (1993).[18]

Time is medicine's central axis not only in terms of the process of diagnosis, treatment and cure but also the relationship that develops between doctor and patient. The medical waiting room, tests and even the word *patient* conjure waiting and the uncertainties and fears that go with it. Several of Hall's books address this theme. *The Rest of My Life* (November 2000) opens with the words that it has been more than a year since she was diagnosed with a recurrence of breast cancer:

Friends ask, 'How much longer?'
They mean, 'when will chemo be done?'

...

Now,
what is the answer?
'Never'
'Until I die.'
or
'As long as I live.'

...

'I am living with cancer.'
'I am buying time.'
'I have a chronic disease.'
'I'll be back for more treatment
on Monday.' (54)

The Rest of My Life emphasises how a chronic patient experiences time as directly linked to medical treatment through its construction too. The book consists of a handmade box covered in colour Xerox copies of Hall's planning calendar, and is bound with medical bandage taping. The accordion segments of the book are the actual appointment cards for one year of cancer treatments: October 30, 2000–October 2001. There are two simultaneous texts (in addition to the appointment dates and calendar pages) and these are inscribed on the appointment cards themselves: notes on everyday events made during treatment, and a history of the past ten years of Hall's life with cancer in red pen. The book can be opened from either end, and also includes brown envelopes that contained medication given to the artist before chemotherapy treatments. The expressive (here visceral) power of this book is glimpsed by the fact that within its small scale (its dimensions are 2¼″ × 4½″ × 3″) an attempt is made to contain the experience of a whole life or, more precisely, the rest of one's life. A second book with the same name, *The Rest of My Life II*, made in 2003, adopts a similar structure and themes even though it contains appointment cards from later dates.

Prescriptions (April 2002) further zooms in on treatment and expresses Hall's agony over the number of pills she needs to take and over her doctors' quickness to prescribe them. The book relies on repetition, especially the refrain 'I have too many prescriptions', which foregrounds frustration and the inevitability of the situation. Hall fears that she might get addicted to her pills and is self-conscious about how she acts at work when she is under their (side) effects: 'was I still me?' (75). She even worries that some of her pills, having become street drugs, will be stolen from her

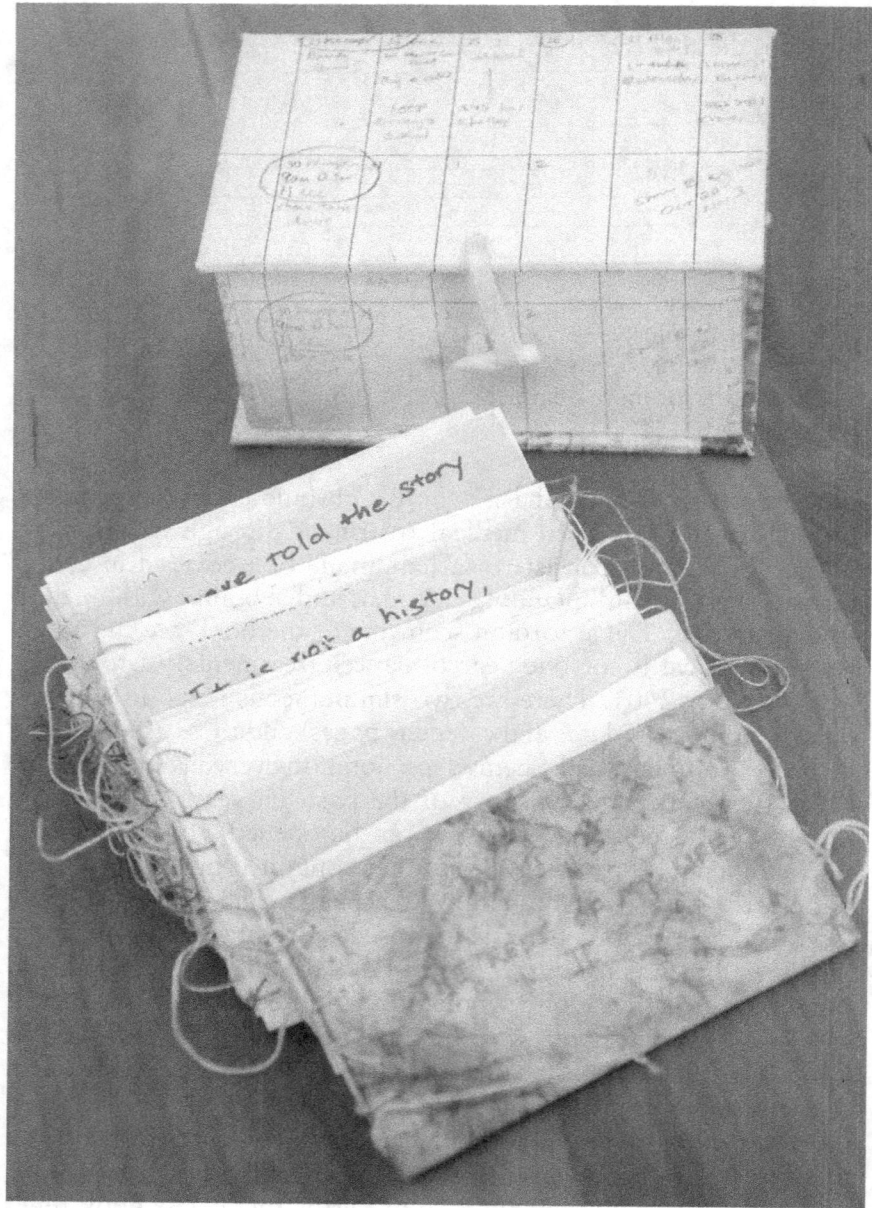

Figure 2.2 Martha Hall, *The Rest of My Life II* (2003), Maine Women Writers Collection, University of New England, Portland, ME. Photo by Laura Taylor.

(77). Her question, 'why is my oncologist so quick to prescribe a drug ... I wish my doctor would address the cause, / and not the symptom' (77) can be read as an indictment of American medicine in particular. In her study *Medicine and Culture*, Lynn Payer describes American medicine as 'aggressive' and notes that American doctors often choose surgery over drug treatment, but when they use drugs they are more likely to use 'higher doses and more aggressive drugs' (1996: 124–5). The 'can-do attitude' of American medicine towards illness, which Payer traces back to the influence of the frontier on the American character, is glimpsed in Hall's artist's statement where she mentions the phone call she received in 1989 by the (unknown to her) surgeon who announced that she had breast cancer: 'You have breast cancer and you better decide quickly whether you're going to do something about it here or in Portland ... With that threat, he hung up' (10). Lorde reports a similar incident in *The Cancer Journals* and *A Burst of Light*, but even though she initially opts for surgery, she decides to pursue alternative treatment in Europe (Germany and Switzerland) after the recurrence of her cancer.

The pages of *Prescriptions* consist of transparent leaves with photocopies of original prescriptions and pill containers. Transparencies are often used in artists' books for their ghostly effect, generated by their similarity to X-rays, but in many of Hall's books the X-rays are clearly referenced rather than simply evoked.[19] However, the invasion of medicine is also conveyed through the names of the pills themselves, words that enhance its 'mysterious' clinical language as they interrupt her verses:

> The days I don't take any drugs,
> other than my daily dose of
> Xeloda, Ambien, Arimidex, Zoloft,
> Synthroid and Coumadin
> I feel happy.
> I tell my husband
> I had a good day. (77)

This text highlights the irony of having 'a good day' when there are at least six different names of pills listed, but no need to take 'any [other] drugs'. But 'a good day' is not paradoxical if we consider Havi Carel's concept of 'health within illness', which unsettles the rigid opposition between health and illness and fits better the experience of chronic illness (2008: 77). Chronic patients have good and bad days, like Hall, and experience periods of stability and well-being. Though overlooked, health within illness affirms the diversity of illness experiences and the different degree of adaptability by individual patients to their new or more limited capacities.

In *Anxiety (to Martin Antonetti)* (May 2001), Hall explores waiting by alluding to her double identity as artist and cancer patient:

> I have been waiting
> nearly three weeks
> for you to call –
> or is it three days … (58)

The book starts with Hall waiting for Martin Antonetti (curator of rare books in Smith's Mortimer Rare Book Room) to call in order to let her know whether he will buy her book entitled 'The Rest of My Life', but her anxiety quickly shifts; the book closes with Hall waiting for her doctor, this time, who will call her 'about *The Rest of My Life*' (59), not a book with this title, but literally the rest of her life. *Anxiety* emphasises feelings of dependency by evoking Hall's insecurity about the future of her art *and* of her life, which remain inextricably connected. If the curator buys the book, its life will be extended in the same way that her biological life can be extended if the doctor brings good news that her treatment has worked. *Anxiety* is an atlas foldout, and symmetry is created as the top part concerns the curator, and the bottom the doctor. As the book can be read either horizontally or vertically, the conflation of identities and positions intended by Hall is foregrounded.

The simultaneous invocation of the curator and the doctor, and the feeling of anxiety towards both figures in this book, could also be read as a way of drawing attention to common discriminatory forces within the realms of medicine *and* art. As already mentioned, even though there is no single easily identifiable reason why women artists are drawn to artists' books, art historians have suggested that they offer an alternative to embrace an art practice that has not been historically male-dominated (painting, for example). In *I Make Books*, a documentary created by the University of New England Media Services Department in 2004, Hall mentions her lack of confidence as an artist, especially when she started making books, and notes that when she showed her books to one of her doctors, he responded with surprise, 'Oh, you could be an artist!' While Hall's critique of patriarchal artistic traditions is subtle, this changes when she moves to the realm of medicine.

Her book *Test Day* compares the female patient with an obedient pupil who needs to do as told in order to earn a passing mark:

> I hate it when the postcard comes.
> I want to RSVP no,
> As if it were an invitation
> Not a command.
>
> I will be obedient,
> As if my desire to please
> Will earn me good grades,
> A passing mark.
> Small child thoughts
> In my woman head.
>
> ...
>
> I will do as I am told. (38)

The 'watchers' (38), referring to the imaging technologists that examine her in this book, conjure a surveillant gaze. But this is not the traditional male voyeuristic one; the 'watchers' are many, and, as another book, *Just to Know*, specifies, the technician is female. However, the reference to 'small child thoughts / in my woman head' above implies that there is more continuity between a patriarchal era of medicine and contemporary reality. *Test Day* brings together women's infantilisation (on different levels) with the kind of infantilisation inflicted upon patients by the medical community to emphasise the extensive history of vulnerability to male objectification that distinguishes female from male patients and their relationships to their doctors. The words of this book resonate with Ehrenreich's argument that women with breast cancer 'are encouraged to regress to a little-girl state, to suspend critical judgment, and to accept whatever measures the doctors, as parent surrogates, choose to impose' (2001: 52). Spence has also treated this theme in one of her phototherapy sessions with Rosy Martin entitled *Infantilization* (1984) from *The Picture of Health?* While the first photo re-enacts the incident when her breast was marked by her doctor (as discussed in Chapter 1), in the following image she poses as a baby with a pacifier in her mouth, acting out the loss of autonomy and disempowerment at the hands of the medical system. Like Hall's 'obedient pupil', Spence wilfully takes the role of the docile patient, but her anger in front of the camera is obvious.

Such comparisons invite the question whether the various aesthetic and ethical strategies for 'doing illness' (Diedrich 2007: 25) that the artist's book as a medium can bring into being can also be described in feminist or broadly political terms, a matter with which Chapter 1 was concerned. Hall's books do not establish links to radical activist agendas such as environmental or gay/lesbian movements, and do not explicitly grapple with questions of difference, such as class and racial disparities, that often determine who is more likely to have access to healthcare and, possibly, better survival chances.[20] However, as we have seen, they address discourses of victimhood/survival and infantilisation, and express anger and frustration, thus questioning the prevalence of restitution or triumph narratives within breast cancer culture and patriarchal attitudes perpetuated within medical communities.

These are also some of the threads of Ehrenreich's argument that seem to have inspired Hall's response in some of her books. To conclude this section, I want to draw attention to a detail in Ehrenreich's article that may also have 'spoken' to Hall in a certain way. While commenting on the ultra-feminine and infantilising theme in breast-cancer discourse, represented by the teddy bears and the prevailing 'pinkness', Ehrenreich specifically refers to the contents of a bag distributed to breast cancer patients that besides cosmetics includes, to her amazement, 'a small box of crayons' (2001: 46). The founder of the Foundation who distributes these bags explains what the crayons are for – they go with a journal and sketch book also contained in the bag, 'for people to express different moods, different thoughts' – but admits to Ehrenreich that she has never tried to write with crayons herself (46). Rather than negating the power of writing, crayons, as Hall's artists' books demonstrate, can 'extend its communicative potential' (Drucker 1998: 18). 'Painting in fierce colors' and 'making marks', as Hall describes the process of making books in *I Make Books*, is not a solipsistic or merely cosmetic activity that promotes infantilisation. Nor is it dictated by the parameters of American consumer culture that Ehrenreich finds troubling in the context of mainstream breast cancer culture. While surveying the pink-ribbon-themed breast cancer products, Ehrenreich notes, 'I can't help noticing that the existential space in which a friend has earnestly advised me to "confront my mortality" bears a striking resemblance to the mall' (2001: 46).

I am not suggesting, of course, that all women with breast cancer should become book artists so that the mall can give its place to what is often perceived as a more elitist space, namely the art gallery – even though artists' books often operate outside the constraints of the art market and gallery system. Even so, creating a book and sending it out into the world is not the same as putting down thoughts in a diary that will not be read by others. As Drucker writes about printing, an important component of book making:

> It provides a fundamental means of transforming personal expression into an authoritative form within the social order and the public sphere. The physicality of printing makes that transformation a somatic experience, an act of the body, which moves the interior voice, the personal word, into the cultural domain. (1998: 4)

The implication is that not all women who write about their illness or create artefacts can reclaim discursive authority, but my point is that writing and drawing do not only serve to communicate personal experiences. Artists' books may offer some women a voice, they are therapeutic – but they are also political, insofar as the books are shareable and can thus lead to collective empowerment. Moreover, as I suggest below, they can be used to effect change in the ways medical professionals interact with their patients: both in terms of challenging the authority and language of medicine; and pedagogically, by demonstrating a more radical form of ethical responsibility with the potential to reinvigorate understandings of empathy within medical education that either revolve around notions of measurement and efficacy, or are predicated on knowing the other.[21]

Doctor book patient relationships

In the documentary *I Make Books*, Hall explains that she used many of her books to communicate with her physicians, nurses and the medical community in general, and stresses how much importance she places on this audience. A physician often interacts with the patient's chart as a textual object (for example, before the initial encounter with the patient), but this is to gain clinical knowledge. The demands made by Hall's books on her doctors are of a fundamentally different nature. As she adds in her artist's statement, the books 'elicited various responses including denial, disbelief, and discomfort' (13), which seem to qualify the still dominant view of the humanities as medicine's 'supportive friend' (Brody 2011:1). One of those books discussed in some detail in the documentary is *Voices: Five Doctors Speak* (August 1998). The book, subsequently made into an edition of twelve, emphasises the interpersonal dimension of medicine in an intriguing way. It reads like a theatrical play or script; if one is accessing this book through the exhibition catalogue *Holding In, Holding On*, there is a section at the end that provides information on the 'cast' by giving the full names corresponding to the five voices, distinguished in the text through the use of their surname initials. However, this is not how the original book sorts out the doctors' voices. There, Hall uses a different font and paper to distinguish each doctor and the concertina spine with tipped-in single pages draws further attention to their autonomy. *Voices* also consists of skull, eye and skeleton stamped images, and of a miniature book entitled *Legacy* attached to one page inside an envelope. This idiosyncratic script can be better described as a series of monologues, since the voice of the patient is not audible. The choice not to turn the sections of which this 'performance' consists into dialogues is perhaps a statement in itself: medicine takes away the voice of the patient, confirming instead the doctors' 'monological authority' (Frank 2004: 103).

Voices documents what five doctors each said to Hall when telling her about her second recurrence of breast cancer over a nine-day period (July 7–16 1998), and they can be read comparatively to emphasise different approaches and patterns of interaction between doctors and patients. Some of the voices are more generous and, though they communicate the same bad news, do so with more empathy and caring, while others consist of thoughtless comments ('Four and a half years is not bad'; 'We are buying time') or superficial interactions and uncaring comments ('Do you want to speak to me on the phone or in person?'). A few of the voices contain condescending or patronising comments ('You are my poster child. You've done so well') or, on the contrary, blame the patient for failing to do well ('You failed'), sustaining the ideals of female infantilisation and dutiful compliance (26–9). In the documentary, Hall explains that the doctor who said that she had 'failed' used the term merely 'in a medical-terminology sense', but it was only after she confronted that doctor by showing him the book that the burden she had to carry for a long time softened, and the clash of contexts was revealed. This is an example of the kind of 'divides' between doctor and patient that Charon outlines in *Narrative Medicine*; they arise from the conflicting understandings of mortality, the contexts of illness, causality and emotional suffering that separate clinicians from patients (2006: 22). If these deep-routed divides can be encapsulated through the hyphen separating the two subject positions in the phrase 'doctor-patient relationship',[22] I want to explore what happens when the book, inserted in the place of the hyphen (as captured by the subheading of this section), is given the task of bridging the gap and distance between these two positions.

Hall showed *Voices* to all of her physicians, including the one she was most angry at, who delayed seeing it, providing various excuses. When he finally found the time to read it after Hall directly challenged him, Hall notes in the documentary how at first the two of them were sitting far apart on each side of the room. It was the book that allowed them to bridge the distance between them, starting with drawing their chairs closer, and then beginning to consider each other's perspectives. Hall shows him the page with the question 'Do you want to speak to me on the phone or in person?' (25), which she identifies as his words. She explains that it was very important for her to see him in person to discuss her test results, but he counters that his question was necessary given that most of his patients are reluctant to do so and prefer the distance of the phone. Alluding to another moment of sharing her books, Hall explains that *Tattoo* led one doctor to ask 'what do you mean when you say radiation's burn?' Here the doctor misunderstands Hall's exploration in the book of the blue dots tattooed on her chest 'to mark radiation's burn' (32); she is not referring to a literal burning, but her doctor lacks the kind of 'imaginative flexibility' (Charon 2006: 174) required to do justice to these words and to the experience they communicate.

Overall, the documentary reveals Hall's openness to dialogue and conversation, and how linked the legacy of her books and the value of her work are to the prospect of being read by the medical community; she emphasises how keen she is to get medical students' reactions to her books, even if they end up calling into question her feelings. In her words (2004), 'The dialogue is something I am going to miss in letting my books go to an institution [University of New England] and I would hope that – I am carrying out half of the conversation – from time to time somebody would carry on another piece of the conversation. That would be a real gift.'

In his chapter 'Physicians' Generosity', which draws on Bakhtin's idea of dialogism, Frank argues that 'identification with others requires giving up monologue'; dialogue is achieved when a 'physician reconstitutes him- or herself *in the voices of his or her patients*' (2004: 101). In *Voices*, we also notice a reverse process taking place that confirms the mutual positive impact meaningful communication between doctors and patients can have. One of the voices, belonging to her oncologist Letha Mills, tells Hall the following:

> In order to live you must live
> with the fear of dying.
> Your books will be your legacy
> for family and for friends.
> And if you live to be an old lady
> You'll reminisce. (26)

This is the only voice in the book which does not fall back on routinised responses, and embraces uncertainty rather than the mythology of progress. This is clear through the reference to the 'fear of dying', the use of the conditional 'if', as well as an emphasis on quality of living as opposed to survival rates. Broyard describes the doctor in terms of 'a storyteller' who can turn patients' lives 'into good or bad stories, regardless of the diagnosis' (1992: 53). In the same vein, Hall notes in the documentary that even when Mills communicated the same news to her, she had a different style that distinguished her from the others' 'black and white' or distant 'professional' discourse. She is the only doctor, Hall reports with delight in the documentary, who has been at her house and had dinner with her family.

Mills' statement encouraged Hall to continue to make books and also inspired the miniature book *Legacy* (March 2001), in which Hall uses the image of a dancing skeleton to dramatise her doctor's 'story'.[23] Usually books within books, like the small separate book *Legacy* within *Voices*, are used to expand upon the themes of the main text. Such books, like the collision between photograph and caption discussed in Chapter 1, also open spaces within the fixed structure of the book – 'embedding', as Drucker notes in a different context, 'the exploded narratives ... in the frame of the original, deceptively contained work'. She further compares them to 'tunnels out of the work or into its interior' (2004: 151). *Legacy* serves as an example of the patient piercing the monological structure of *Voices*, but also, more strikingly, doing so by reconstituting herself in the voice of her practitioner. As Hall admits in the documentary, Mills' words were the most important thing anyone ever said to her. Hall of course shows the finished book to all her physicians, and this means that now that Mills' words have been transmuted into her patient's book, the doctor, following Frank, can also reconstitute herself in the voice of her patient in future – the circle is complete, but can open again. In her foreword to *Holding In, Holding On*, Mills constantly returns to Hall's work, speaking in her voice, in order to illustrate the impact her art has had on her medical practice and life: 'Martha's stories will speak to each of us differently and their meaning will change as we change and grow' (2003: 7). Despite its small size, *Legacy* communicates the intrinsic value of Hall's books, as well as their role as 'redemptive' in Radley's understanding of this term: even if they cannot provide a remedy or cure, they are life-sustaining (2009: 113), and the kind of freedom they offer is realised precisely through the act of making something. Hall's *I Make Books* (May 2001), a much bigger book with painted pages and the following words inscribed on the spine of each page, captures this idea perfectly:

I make books.
I write what I cannot say.
I make marks with meaning only in
their making.
I paint in colors fearsome and strange.
I make books so I won't die. (61)

The last page of *Voices* is a haunting piece of text filled with a single phrase repeated on every line in all the different fonts of the doctors: 'I'm sorry.' The use of distinct fonts suggests that all of the five doctors have said these words to Hall at some point. The litany of 'I'm sorry' leaves barely any white space on the page, creating the effect of concrete poetry or of a painting made of words rather than images. Besides causing a visceral response, this page raises questions concerning the frequency with which 'I'm sorry' is/is not being uttered by physicians,[24] and its implications. Is 'I'm sorry' meaningful in any way, or simply a distancing technique from an emotionally difficult situation, as in the example of the voice by a doctor already discussed – 'Let's take this one step at a time. *I'm sorry*. Do you want to speak to me on the phone or in person?' (26, emphasis added)? Does it evoke, instead, the difficult issue of failure?

Medicine and science are resistant to the idea of failure; the modern medical narrative can only be sustained if progress and efficacy are confirmed through good survival rates for patients (the restitution narrative) and expensive treatments that work, rather than through the acknowledgement of victims that belie the triumphant discourse of science.[25] If through 'I'm sorry' a doctor relinquishes his or her authority, does this signal a shift from an emphasis on cure to care, which has been foregrounded in some recent memoirs (especially by doctors treating AIDS patients)?[26] Diedrich, who concludes *Treatments* with a chapter entitled 'Toward an Ethics of Failure', stresses that an

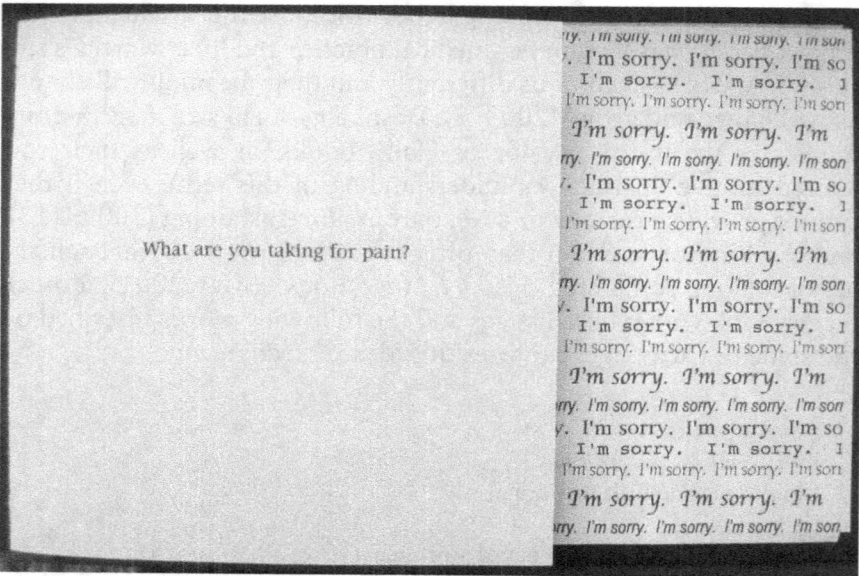

Figure 2.3 Martha Hall, *Voices: Five Doctors Speak, July 7–16, 1998 / [Martha A. Hall; voices: Tom Ervin, William Herbert, Hector Tarraza, Letha Mills, Rodger Pryzant]* (2001), Maine Women Writers Collection, University of New England, Portland, ME. Photo by Laura Taylor.

ethics of failure 'takes failure not as an ending' (as, for instance, in Hall's doctor's statement, 'We failed. You failed' in *Voices*) but 'as a beginning' (2007: 166). This possibility, however, is not acknowledged in the book *It's Nothing* (December 1999); an ironic title for a story of misdiagnosis. Hall insists that she is in pain, but since the tests do not show anything her judgement is disregarded. The new tests, nevertheless, reveal multiple lesions 'there where I had shown you / I had pain. There' (45). The medical notes mute this incident: alluding to the typical idea of the patient as a poor or unreliable historian, they refer to 'aches which [the patient] has minimized and really brought out fully today' and describe Hall as 'slightly more depressed than she has / been in the past' (45).

Like other books in which Hall shifts between the positions of breast cancer patient and artist, *It's Nothing* compares and contrasts the consulting room and the art classroom as spaces of body examination. The suggestion is that the latter can become a model for a more holistic approach to health and healing. The book starts with Hall preparing to draw her body in art class; the first step is to trace it through touch. She starts with her bald skull, exposed to the class, holding it cupped in her hands before gently moving her fingers down to the rest of her body. While this exercise is painful (Hall hates knowing where 'the jabs of pain would be – long / ago memorized'), it is also a healing experience:

> So in art class I draw my ribs, my
> vertebrae, my skull. I draw my pain.
> I draw delicacy that hides anger,
> fragility that holds strength. These
> are my bones. I need to draw them to heal. (45)[27]

The book challenges the knowledge monopoly of doctors by indirectly referencing women's health groups and self-examination procedures, but it also posits an alternative 'imaging' of the body through the art of drawing which is guided by touch rather than vision, in this way taking Herndl's and Taylor-Wood's narratives of re-covery one step further. The emphasis on touching the body (a range of verbs are used in the text, such as 'feel for', 'trace', 'gently move' and 'knead', and the book is handwritten in pencil), which takes place in art class, complements the medical gaze, or 'the machine vision' of 'the watchers', as Hall calls it in *Test Day*. Imaging technologies boast of almost military accuracy, but many would agree that despite the battle for the succession of technologies in medicine (the stethoscope and the doctor's senses replaced by the X-ray, for example), effort should be placed in linking older with newer technologies. Hall's ritual in this book – especially the reliance on senses such as touch and sound, as opposed to just vision – resonates with the kind of examination Abraham Verghese offers to one of his dying AIDS patients in his memoir *My Own Country*:

> I percuss his chest, and the sound of his right lung is disturbing. Only at the very top, near his collarbone, do I hear the *thoom* of resonance ... The sounds of my percussion on his body fill the room. Thoom, thunk, thunk, thunk, tup, tup, tup – even Luther seems to pause in his delirious muttering, his floccillation, to listen to the music of his body, to relax, to smile. (1994: 343)

Hall's concluding determination in *It's Nothing* to 'keep listening – to hear / what [her] bones are saying' (45) can be read then as an affirmation of the art of physical examination (whether this is by a doctor or a patient), which is disappearing fast in an era of sophisticated imaging techniques and impersonal technologies.

While the development of narrative medicine has responded to many of the concerns about how medical practitioners interact with their patients, the attention given to acquiring narrative skills in medical humanities programmes is slowly being supplemented through the insights of other arts outside literature. Bleakley, a long-time advocate of what he calls 'an aesthetic medicine' that is 'taught and learned imaginatively' (2006: 197), has emphasised the importance of working closely with a range of artists:

> While doctors use the senses in the art of diagnosis, let us also involve experts with developed sensory awareness – visual artists for the eye, musicians for the ear, perfumiers and oenophiles for the nose and taste buds, tabla players for the fingertips and designers for the synesthetic experience of multiple senses acting in harmony, just as we draw on the inspiration of writers to help to educate narrative intelligence for close listening, appreciation and interpretation of patients' stories. (Bleakley 2013: 12)

The intermedial nature of artists' books and the ways in which they implicate different senses in their creation and reading mean that this form is in a unique position to redress the emphasis on *narrative* medicine.

Charon has suggested that literary studies can help reinforce the 'realization that our intimate medical relationships occur in words. Our intimacy with patients is based predominantly on *listening to what they tell us*.' She qualifies this statement, 'Yes, doctors touch patients and do rather extraordinary physical things to them, but the textuality and not the physicality defines the relation' (2006: 53). Such an emphasis on textuality risks overshadowing other dimensions of narrative medicine. In the same way that I have traced the links of photography in Chapter 1, and artists' books in this chapter, to performance, in 'Performing Narrative Medicine' Langellier binds narrative medicine to performance. She recasts the type of close reading advocated by Charon as 'a bodily performance'; 'stereophonic listening' as 'listening out loud'; and the writing of 'the parallel chart' by doctors as 'critical performance' (2009: 153–5).[28] Charon herself acknowledges the tension between textuality and materiality in her outline of narrative medicine. Through her examination of 'desire', the fifth aspect of her training drill for reading texts, she notes, for instance, that 'readers can come back to earth, back to materiality, grounded again after the abstractions of temporality and metaphor, home once again in lives of bodies and health' (2006: 126). The advantage of artists' books over literary texts, if used within medical education, is that materiality is foregrounded so that moving from the text to the body is made easier.[29] Like patients, artists' books can be seen from either a clinical distance, when for example they are exhibited behind a glass case or cannot be opened/performed, or close at hand. Appreciating their full potential requires 'close reading' and 'stereophonic listening' – the patient's 'many voices in their contradictions, their secrecy and their exposure of the self' (Charon 2006: 97) can be recast as the folds, layers, marks, secret passages and routes opened by the books as they are touched and handled. Similarly, the 'contradictory impulse' in the diagnostic act to capture the 'singular' and at the same time categorise or make something 'readable' – what Charon associates with narrative and scientific knowledge respectively (45–6) – can be linked to characteristics of the artist's book medium; it is an object that is readable through its connection to the book, but by extending its conventional elements in several directions it becomes singular and unique. In a lot of artists' books, as we have seen, even individual pages are made of diverse material or have a different size, emphasising their uniqueness even as they are perceived as pages.

While narrative has become synonymous with reflection in 'reflective writing', as practised within narrative medicine, artists' books can open medical practitioners to practices of reading and touching that focus on the intimate and the immediate and produce an alternative kind of reflection that engages both body and mind. This extends Catherine Belling's call for greater attention to 'the lyric' as opposed to the narrative mode of literary discourse in fictions of medicine, as it encourages a kind of 'mindfulness' or complete engagement in the present moment (2012: 2–6).[30] Artists' books cultivate such an absorbed form of engagement, as students from the University of New England who had the opportunity to write to Hall while she was alive and respond to her work have confirmed. Answering their letters, Martha Hall wrote to Jennifer Tuttle in 2003: 'Please thank [your] students most of all for writing about the silence in the room as they looked at the books. I think it is remarkable, and certainly feels especially gratifying, that they took such an intense interest.'

In staging moments of silence, witnessing and presence, artists' books are able to reconfigure the patterns of relationality between patient and doctor:

> I am afraid
> to speak my fears aloud,
> to ask questions,
> to hear your answers,
> to know what you know,
> so do not tell me.
>
> Just turn the page
> And close the book.
>
> Do not tell me
> now. (86)

This excerpt is taken from *Tell Me* (January 2003). The book facilitates a silent but meaningful encounter between Hall and her addressee that involves a form of communication beyond spoken words, mediated by the book that connects the two as if it were a skin. If we were to read the text as referring to a doctor-patient encounter, the doctor is asked to simply turn the pages of the book and delay telling the patient what she fears to hear. Writing about the importance of 'an ethics of touch', Sara Ahmed suggests that 'thinking of speaking and hearing in terms of touch might allow us to challenge the very assumption that communication is about expression, or about the transparency of meaning' (2000: 155). Transparency is what is aimed for in most patient-doctor exchanges, even though the emotional difficulty entailed makes communication difficult. This is why neutrality and silence, in the form of withholding words that can touch another person's heart, are opted for by the doctor, and sometimes by the patient too. In this case, however, silence attests to making oneself available and fully present.

Considering the 'doctor book patient relationships' that Hall stages for her readers, the book as an object placed between the subject positions of doctor and patient is assigned a difficult but not impossible task: transforming the empty space or distance between the two into a space of proximity, and the silence (or the words on the page) into a form of contact through touch. Hall describes actual moments when this happens in the documentary *I Make Books*. Such moments call the doctor to be uprooted from his or her usual routine – be it physical examination that searches for something specific, or talking/listening to the patient, which like vision also works across distance[31] – and face the patient anew by responding to the book between them. This response can be better described in terms of Levinas' caress; as mentioned before, it is different from palpation in that even though it is a kind of search, it does not seek to disclose something. As Oliver further explains, the caress 'seeks the continuation of relationship, the future of relationship, even while it constitutes it' (2001: 205). While Hall's artists' books empower patients to demand better healthcare and to remain critical of certain discourses within mainstream breast cancer culture, they also instruct her doctors and readers more generally to touch them in this non-instrumental way, to seek the continuation of the affective and ethical relationship that they open up in the present.

Notes

1. Dates (month and year) when Hall created individual books are given when a book is first mentioned, but all quoted excerpts from the books, Hall's artist's statement and biographical information refer to the exhibition catalogue *Holding In, Holding On* (2003). Only page numbers will be provided in brackets for these references.
2. *Tattoo* was a very important book for Hall, as it encouraged her to share her work with others. This is thematised in the text itself; for a detailed analysis of this book, see Radley 2009: 74–5.
3. Clare Best underwent double prophylactic mastectomy to reduce the risk of developing breast cancer in light of her family history.
4. See the work of the network Transforming Artist Books (February–August 2012), <http://www.tate.org.uk/about/projects/transforming-artist-books> (last accessed 27 July 2015).
5. On definitions and the history of artists' books see Bury 1995, Klima 1998 and Lauf and Phillpot 1998.
6. For many art historians, however, this vision has not been fully fulfilled: the majority of artists' books today are in limited editions, hosted in special collections and generally difficult to access.
7. For women and artists' books, also see Drucker 1998, Prince 2008, and Wasserman 2011.
8. Permanent collections in which Hall's books are held include the National Museum of Women in the Arts, Washington, DC; Bowdoin College, Brunswick, ME; Dartmouth College, Hanover, NH; Smith College, Northampton, MA; University of California at Santa Barbara; Harvard University, Cambridge, MA; University of New England, Portland, ME; Yale University, New Haven, CT; The Cancer Community Center, South Portland, ME.

9. See 'Martha A. Hall Collection, 1998–2003', University of New England, <http://www.une.edu/mwwc/research/featured-writers/martha-.-hall-collection-1998-2003> (last accessed 27 July 2015).
10. Two books that are particularly interesting for a medical humanities audience are Scott L. McCarney's *Memory Loss* (1988) and Susan King's *Treading the Maze: An Artist's Journey through Breast Cancer* (1993). Both books place their viewers into the experiences they represent using a venetian blind and a maze structure respectively, as tangible metaphors of disorientation and struggle.
11. Conversely, Hubert and Hubert suggest that Margot Lovejoy's *The Book of Plagues* (1994) 'originates rather ironically in magazine displays and commercial brochures' (1999: 145).
12. See Felman and Laub 1992, LaCapra 1994, Blanchot 1995, Caruth 1995, Diedrich 2007, Tanner 2006, Oliver 2001, Hallas 2009, Charon 2006, and Kaplan 2005.
13. One example is Heather Weston's *Binding Analysis: Double Bind* (2000), about schizophrenia, which contains a riddle in its structure. See <http://www.vampandtramp.com/finepress/w/weston.html> (last accessed 27 July 2015).
14. The significance of touching is elaborated in *Totality and Infinity* almost exclusively in the context of erotic love (and the feminine), but Levinas returns to this concept to describe the ethical structure of sensibility (see 1996: 80). For the role of the feminine in his ethics, see Chanter 2001.
15. A clue to the title of the book can be found in Hall's statement that she enjoys 'the challenge of finding or devising book structures that give wings' to the words and images she has created (15).
16. One example is Robert Buckman and Tereza Whittaker's *What You Really Need to Know about Breast Cancer* (2000).
17. See also Hall's book *Playing with Fire*, which refers to various body parts which are 'counted, named, numbered' (78).
18. In *Playing with Fire* the beads are also associated with the ocean, even though there is no way of knowing whether Hall was aware of King's book.
19. See Francine Zubeil's artist's book *Panique Générale* (1993) for the ghostly effect of transparencies.
20. In her artist's statement, Hall calls the themes she explores through her books 'universal' (15).
21. For critiques of empathy in medical education, see Rossiter 2012.
22. Diedrich has described the hyphen between the two positions as a *différend*, drawing on Jean-François Lyotard's term (2007: 150).
23. *Legacy* seems to have been included later in *Voices,* possibly when Hall decided to turn *Voices* into an edition of twelve books in 2001.
24. See also Friedman 2005.

25. This discourse is also scrutinised in *Ghost Friends* (August 2001), consisting of lyrical elegies and remembrances of Hall's acquaintances who are also cancer patients but do not survive. The bookcloth-covered clamshell box housing the sixteen books of *Ghost Friends* – each one of them sitting in an expandable file format – creates a realistic filing cabinet, as expected to be found in a hospital or clinic.
26. See Campo 1996 and Scannell 1999.
27. Hall's books themselves can be described as delicate objects that hide anger or as fragile objects that hold strength.
28. Also see Frank 2007.
29. See the artists' books 'Core Sample' and 'Spine', created by Allison Cooke Brown in 2003, <http://www.vampandtramp.com/finepress/b/allison-cooke-brown.html#wearable> (last accessed 27 July 2015). Hall collaborated with Brown for *Paper Passages*, a seven-month correspondence (starting in 2001) in various book formats surrounding both artists' experiences with breast cancer. Judith May Walton explores the analogy between the 'lived body' and the 'lived book', drawing on Claudia Kolgen's artist's book *Ein Hauch von Erinnerungen* (*A Hint of Remembrance*) (1987), which 'breathes through a small aperture in the dark grey cover as you open and close it, forcing air in and out of the white rubber bellows, lungs' (2010: 27).
30. See also Epstein 1999.
31. On distance in relation to the different senses, see Oliver 2001: 191–216.

Chapter 3

Performance Medicine and Radical Pedagogy

In his essay 'In Defense of Performance', Guillermo Gómez-Peña answers a question he is often asked by journalists about the function of performance art: 'Performance artists are a constant reminder to society of the possibilities of other artistic, political, sexual or spiritual behaviors and this I must say is an extremely important function.' He adds, 'It helps others to reconnect with the forbidden zones of their psyches and bodies, and to acknowledge the possibilities of their own freedoms. In this sense performance art may be as useful as medicine, engineering, or law and performance artists as necessary as nurses, teachers, priests, or taxi-drivers' (2005: 43).[1] Unlike Martha Hall, who wanted her artists' books to be used in medical education – and although, like Spence, he defines himself as a cultural worker rather than just an artist – Guillermo Gómez-Peña has not used his performances to reach medical professionals. His work has been examined so far in terms of race, border studies and postcolonial theory rather than the medical humanities, which raises the question of what we bring into medical education and why. In envisaging him as an interloper I want to suggest that his work can enrich the medical humanities not only because it adds another artistic form or medium into the field. Rather, as the quotation above shows, and as this chapter goes on to explore, his performances encourage us to open up narrow understandings of the medical and at the same time to counter instrumental educational practices through the development of a more critical or radical pedagogy. While Hall's work has begun to articulate some of these issues – for example, through her commitment to dialogue and critique of superficial forms of empathy, and through a pedagogy of touch – I want to consider here performative/pedagogical encounters that move beyond the clinical setting and individualised conceptions of health. These encounters also address more explicitly questions of social justice, democracy, human rights and community care which are often missing from medical ethics/humanities discussions.

The reciprocity between performance and medicine that Gómez-Peña posits in the above statement is not new. Narrative medicine has been supplemented with work that exemplifies that it is not only literature, but also the visual and the performing arts, that crucially inform medicine: performances, whether this refers to medical dramas on television and on stage or body-based performances such as Orlan's surgical operations, engage with medical themes. In turn, medical humanities scholars have drawn attention to the everyday rituals medicine involves, some of which entail a larger degree of theatricalisation (for example, ward rounds where medical students play roles as both actors and audience), to the hospital as a theatrical space (this is clear in the term 'operation theatre'), and to the value of performance skills within medical education for exploring doctor-patient interactions (rehearsing how to communicate bad news or show empathy).[2] However, Gómez-Peña's statement is not limited to such models of reciprocity. He has crossed many borders in his life and career, starting with the Mexico–United States border in 1988, which gave birth to his most famous performance persona, 'Border Brujo', in the eponymous work dealing with border identity. His statement can be therefore read as yet another crossing of a dangerous border: one that maintains that the culture of medicine is divorced from the broader culture. What he is articulating is not merely that performance artists play a useful role in society; he is not simply acknowledging that every kind of work has value. Rather, given that the terrain shared by artists – especially performance artists – and doctors is the body, like medical practitioners, performance artists can produce knowledges about the body and mind as well as 'treatments'[3] for individual and social well-being that demonstrate performance's pedagogical and political value.

Gómez-Peña is often described as 'a shaman who lost his way' (33), but in my consideration of the ways performance art can amplify the meanings and concerns of medicine in this chapter, I want to encompass much more than alternative healing methods or the mixture of medicine and spirituality that characterises shamanism.[4] Borrowing Ludmilla Jordanova's definition, which she uses in a different context, Gómez-Peña's work can be read as *medical* 'in the general sense that it addresses pain, suffering and death' and 'in a more precise and intense sense' around his own illness and recovery (2014: 52–3), although I will show that these two levels are productively blurred throughout his work. The first two sections of the chapter deal with the radical pedagogy and content of some of Gómez-Peña's famous body-based performances, in collaboration with members of the performance art troupe La Pocha Nostra. I return to surgery and the medical gaze, which were important topics in Chapters 1 and 2, but this time I am interested in a series of gazes and 'invisible surgeries' (Gómez-Peña 60) that denude and wound bodies. These discourses and practices are associated with anthropology and the popular media as well as with medicine, and engage with fields such as border and disability studies (both concerned with questions of physical and political accessibility) with which Gómez-Peña's work is in dialogue. Examining broader cultural representations of dehumanisation and disempowerment confirms that suffering 'is not a raw datum – not a natural phenomenon we can classify and measure, despite its links with biological processes – but a fluid social state: a status that we extend or withhold' (Morris 1998: 216). Subsequent parts of the chapter analyse two spoken-word performances (one still in progress) which draw on Gómez-Peña's own experiences of disability and illness and which, on account of their formal and thematic complexity, broaden the scope of the medical humanities by expanding the current pool of illness narratives.

Performance and radical pedagogy

In 'The Arts and Medicine: A Challenging Relationship', Paul Macneill argues that 'provocative' performance art such as the work of Stelarc and Orlan can provide an antidote to the existing instrumental framework of the medical humanities (2011: 85). This is not only because such works generate controversy and debate about the body and the use of technology in medicine/art (an aspect I discuss later in relation to Gómez-Peña's performances), but because they do not presuppose particular or single answers, and are less pre-digested for students and teachers than the 'classics' that are used for specific predetermined purposes (88). While not explicitly examining this dimension when assessing the value of the arts for medical education, Macneill's diagnosis of their instrumental use opens up the important issue of critical or radical pedagogy and the ways it is linked to politics. Gómez-Peña's interest in critical or 'radical pedagogy' (95) developed in the mid-1990s from a need to resist neoliberalism, commodification and the backlash against politicised art, and as a natural extension of his collaborative, democratic and risk-embracing performance practices. He cites influences such as Paulo Freire and Augusto Boal even though the pedagogical practices he has developed also borrow elements from Chicano culture. Performance art as 'a place where contradiction, ambiguity and paradox are not only tolerated but encouraged' (22) and where 'authoritarian hierarchies and specialized knowledge' are challenged (79) becomes an important site of critical pedagogy for Gómez-Peña which replaces technical mastery and instrumental logic with interdisciplinary dialogue, imagination and opportunities for increased individual and social agency.

The presence of undemocratic hierarchies and intolerance of ambiguity have been diagnosed as some of the most dangerous ills of medicine, leading to poor communication/teamwork, medical errors and lack of true empathy. These aspects can be addressed through a more critical medical humanities that builds on the arts' democratising power. Bleakley affirms that medical education needs to engage 'with values-driven ways of being' rather than simply instrumental skills (2014b: 502), a key component of critical/radical pedagogy, as well as with context and culture-specific values that become increasingly important to debates within global health and medical ethics. Central to the project of the democratisation of medicine is the 'dispersal of the medical gaze', greater public and patient involvement in medicine, interprofessionalism and better collaboration, as well as a more critical engagement with difference, and they can be fostered by the distinct pedagogical and political methods of the humanities and the arts (Bleakley 2014b).

Gómez-Peña's and La Pocha Nostra's polyvocal and dense performances, which also take the form of video and radio projects, installation, poetry, journalism, and cultural theory, are allied to what was described in the Introduction as 'emergent narratives'. Their embodied and improvised aspects differentiate them from published narrative texts as well as from theatre, which is still the most common performing art form discussed in the medical humanities. The script is just a blueprint for action for the majority of performance artists, and the performance is never 'finished'. This means that the script (if there is one) need not be memorised and rehearsed in the traditional sense, and that no performance event is identical to another. Another factor that contributes to this process of constant reinvention is that La Pocha Nostra is an 'ever-changing community' (Gómez-Peña 79) of artists and intellectuals, and its performances encourage collaborations across national borders and generations. While traditionally plotted drama has a beginning and an end (this is also true of many experimental plays), Gómez-Peña and La Pocha Nostra 'choose a portion of [their] process and open the doors to expose the audience to it' (35). Rather than locating the 'transformative power of performance' in the finished piece, 'incorporating other artists and audience members in the process of co-creating the piece' and developing new models of thought and action is the 'ultimate project' for them (Gómez-Peña 2011: 125). This emphasises the process of teaching, learning and sharing, envisaged here as deeply democratic and political.

La Pocha Nostra's performance rituals create a complex web of meaning around fantasies and cultural stereotypes – in particular Anglo-American visions, desires and fears of Latino/Latina bodies – that force spectators to actively try to understand and relate to the performances.[5] Even though audience participation may be dangerous or may not be accompanied by the amount of reflexivity that the performers would wish for, Gómez-Peña justifies participatory practices on the basis that they create situations in which participants face democratic dilemmas similar to those they would face in real life. If we read Levinas' face-to-face encounter, situated at the core of his philosophy, as a concrete experience that can occur in ordinary everyday life,[6] in facing their participants Gómez-Peña and his fellow performers often make ethical and political demands for crossing dangerous borders and divisions. As in the case of Hall's artists' books, even the choice not to interact made by some audience members is therefore meaningful, in that it illuminates aspects of the relation between performer and audience that the interactive performance has opened and seeks to examine. Failure to interact does not automatically mean, then, that the performance has failed. La Pocha Nostra's 'performance ethics are situational. It's a case-by-case situation.' Even though there is a larger 'ethical backdrop' for what they do, they are aware of the danger of reproducing 'authoritarian models' or reducing complexity (2011: 137). The exchanges between performers and audience create provisional communities (they last as long as the performance does) or 'temporary utopian spaces' (2005: 96) that can identify new forms of agency to be put into practice outside the performative space. This is a way performance can be linked to 'a pedagogy of intervention' (Giroux 2011: 144), activist politics and radical democracy.

As Gómez-Peña further explains, 'It is precisely in these raw interstices of tolerance/intolerance where we can really further a dialogue on intercultural relations, instead of pretending that hollow gestures of sympathy and "empathy" can transform human condition overnight' (83). Although this comment addresses the ways performance can open a space to engage with cultural, racial and political difference, the acknowledgement of the limitations of empathy resonates well with criticisms around some of the more reductive or instrumental uses of the arts to 'humanise' medicine.[7] It is a more radical theorisation of empathy we are presented with here: instead of relying on role-play – often used in clinical training, especially medical simulation that encourages students to keep a 'script' and can therefore become artificial (Brodzinski 2010: 135–6) – the performances, as well as the pedagogical workshops that have emerged from them, create 'various pathways, trajectories and unsuspected intersections that are mostly discovered/learned through the body and later circulated through language and action'. As Gómez-Peña adds, 'this is where the true political power of the work lies' (83). Such a radical pedagogical approach can reinvigorate notions of education as synonymous with job training, and of success being assessed through measurable standards, as well as more specifically counter phenomena of 'empathy decline' and 'the pervasive cynicism within medical culture' observed when 'idealistic students meet the realities of clinical work' (Bleakley 2014b: 503). It can do that not only by embracing dialogue, discomfort, uncertainty and open-endedness, but also by mobilising hope and a militant utopianism that imagines how things could be different and then tries to effect change.

It is not only the pedagogical philosophy underlying La Pocha Nostra's performances but also, more practically, the workshop methods they have devised that can bring changes to medical education's currently 'counterproductive pedagogy' (Bleakley 2014b: 503). La Pocha Nostra's workshops integrate students from art, media, theatre, anthropology and literary studies, building the most interdisciplinary group possible (99). Though they have not addressed medical students yet, their workshops can challenge the kind of learning done 'in the bubble of the simulation' or based on protocols that often brackets complexity. Bleakley notes that 'medical students are rarely taught about the dynamics of erotic transference and countertransference' in professional communication (2014b: 503), and the same thing could be said about the dynamics characterising cross-cultural encounters, either between patients and medical professionals or medical student groups. Many of La Pocha Nostra's exercises, such as 'poetical ethnography' and 'creating tableaux vivants' (living pictures) and 'human murals', teach participants how to work together by learning 'to negotiate other people's aesthetic and conceptual decisions' (115) – an important goal when considering medical errors that happen due to poor communication or intolerance of difference. For example, 'poetical ethnography' could be productively compared to peer physical examination (PPE), a common teaching method within the medical curriculum, which seeks to teach medical students basic clinical skills by examining their peers and allowing their classmates to examine them. The majority of studies have used quantitative methods to explore students' attitudes and comfort levels towards PPE, but there needs to be a more in-depth analysis of the kinds of gendered, sexual and cultural meanings attached to bodies, and how students are instructed to negotiate them in their interactions with their peers.[8] This is where La Pocha Nostra's exercises could be very useful in addressing head-on such meanings.[9] Unlike many role-play situations where professional performers are employed to work as patient simulators, 'which puts them at an advantage in the performance stakes' (Brodzinski 2010: 137), 'poetical ethnography' challenges expertise and hierarchy; the partners involved (the ethnographer and the specimen) embody or inhabit these roles[10] without acting or former experience, and the ethnographer's gaze is reversed halfway to allow mutual examination and reflection on these roles.

Some of the aforementioned exercises can also reshape debates about cultural competence in medical settings by encouraging participants to cross borders they cannot or will not 'cross on a daily basis' (Gómez-Peña 135), and to examine cultural difference both theoretically and through their bodies. The term 'cultural competence' is used to refer to the professional capacity to understand how diverse cultures and belief systems perceive health and illness and might affect diagnosis, treatment and care. The fact that such competence is often reduced to a technical skill or 'a series of do's and don'ts that define how to treat a patient of a certain ethnic background' (Kleinman and Benson 2006: 1673) has generated controversy concerning what is the best way to teach medical students about cultural difference and cross-cultural communication. While narrative, and specifically literature, has been marshalled to such service, many have criticised the simplistic or didactic use of certain texts in the medical education curriculum or questioned whether readerly empathy can lead to social empathy.[11] The fact that Gómez-Peña views the performance and workshop space as an extension of the social world can perhaps make that transition more palpable. Arthur Kleinman and Peter Benson have proposed what they call 'a mini-ethnography' in order to redress the focus on technical skills and put the emphasis on the individual patient rather than a case or stereotype (for example, the Mexican or the Chinese patient). The advantage of ethnography, according to them, is that it fosters 'imaginative empathy' with the lived experience of patients (1674). Gómez-Peña's performance work engages with ethnography, but complicates straightforward models of empathy and understanding by exploring power dynamics and who has control in encounters between an ethnographer and his or her specimen (as we saw with his 'poetical ethnography' workshop).[12]

Many of his workshops push the boundaries of 'ethnographic' work, and even entail risk. For example, 'impersonate your favorite subculture' (117), during which participants dress up according to their projections and fantasies and spend an entire day inhabiting a different identity outside the workshop environment, has helped his students acquire first-hand understanding of racial and sexual difference and of the power of stereotypes. This is important in countering what Gómez-Peña calls 'the mainstream bizarre', a phrase he has coined to refer to a pervasive atmosphere of stylised hybridity or 'corporate multiculturalism' (48). I return to this phenomenon in the following section of the chapter, but it is important to stress here how the workshops and pedagogical methods La Pocha Nostra has developed over the years expose a central limitation of current engagements with cultural difference; as medical humanities critics Claire Hooker and Estelle Noonan have crucially observed, a commitment to respect differences that is akin to superficial inclusion of multicultural works can reify cultural difference and even become 'a form of Othering'. This is why the field needs not only an emphasis on ' "receptive" but also more critical encounters with difference' (2011: 83, 82).

The spectacle of the mainstream bizarre: extreme bodies and invisible surgeries

Gómez-Peña's and La Pocha Nostra's work, like that of other contemporary performance artists, engages with the human body and its various meanings, as well as with medical images. Performance artists such as Donald Rodney, Franco B., Ron Athey, Kira O'Reilly, Stelarc and Orlan use skin markings, actual body fluids like blood, body parts and medical instruments in their work. Such performances cannot be strictly seen in a medical context but need to be placed within broader cultural discourses around feminine beauty, prosthetics, AIDS and others. Body-based performances involving alterations or extensions of the body beyond cosmetic surgery, such as Stelarc's technological augmentation of his body through a prosthetic arm and Orlan's facial surgeries, generate controversy that can challenge prevailing metaphors in medicine such as the 'mechanistic' view of the body and raise ethical questions about new technologies and their use in either art or medicine. As Petra Kuppers argues in her study on medical performances and contemporary art, what she calls 'bodily fantasies' (such as the cyborg and the monster) can draw on medical visions to 'create revisions of body functions, life experiences, and ways of being in the world' (2007: 53). Their generative potential can therefore open up dominant knowledge systems such as Western medicine. Spence's *tableaux* of her body, discussed in Chapter 1, are closer to performance rather than static portraits and deploy such a notion of fantasy (1995: 105) through the help of phototherapy. Some of them have striking links with Gómez-Peña's performance personas – for example, *Cultural Sniper*, created with David Roberts in 1990, uses the metaphor of the 'sniper, terrorist, freedom fighter' for solidarity across oppressed groups (163).

Gómez-Peña's position towards the body (including the altered body) is influenced by the body artists of the 1960s and 1970s, such as Marina Abramović, and performance artists such as Stelarc and Orlan. It is also informed by other histories including pre-Columbian spirituality and imagery, even though the latter is often fused with multiple traditions to show the syncretic nature of Latin American culture. Although his performances do not centrally feature in such work, recent scholarship on the intersection of disability studies and Chicano/a studies serves as a timely reminder of the ways conceptions of disability, illness and pain, as well as understandings of the body, vary across cultural contexts.[13] Stelarc's challenging and technically sophisticated performance actions since the late seventies, in performances like THIRD ARM and MOVATAR, have led to debate concerning the viability of the human body, tapping into his audience's anxieties, but also fantasies about unlimited power and disembodied immortality. In his commentary, Gómez-Peña confesses to being captured by the performer's body rather than the technology used:

> When we witness Stelarc demonstrating a brand new robotic bodysuit or high-tech toy, after fifteen minutes we tend to pay more attention to his sweating flesh than to his prosthetic armor and perceptual extensions. The paraphernalia is great, but the human body attached to the mythical identity of the performance artist in front of us, remains at the center of the event. Why? I just don't know. (25–6)

As Gómez-Peña himself is aware, such a stance towards technology risks being equated with a theoretically discredited humanism (we can recall here Herndl's invocation of the posthuman in her response to Lorde in Chapter 1) or technophobia. The latter stems from a mythology that Mexicans and Latinos, 'caught between a preindustrial past and an imposed modernity', have an 'understanding of the world [that] is strictly political, poetic, or metaphysical, at best, certainly not scientific or technological' (Gómez-Peña 2001: 84). However, when Stelarc created his famous robotic arm, Gómez-Peña came up with his own version – his 'robo-garra'. Even though they look similar, Gómez-Peña's arm does not come with the sophisticated technology of the former. Rather, in his work he is interested in what he terms 'imaginary technology': 'Since Latinos don't have real access to new technologies, we imagine the access. All we have is our political imagination and our humor to interject into the conversation' (250).

In light of this difference, Gómez-Peña's recent performance photography portfolio *No Portraits: A Bizarre Tribute to Joseph Beuys, Frida Kahlo, Stelarc, Orlan, and Other Artists*, which includes the portraits *Not Stelarc* and *Not Orlan*, makes much sense.[14] The first portrait features Gómez-Peña with his robo-garra. The second portrays Gómez-Peña who, instead of undergoing proper surgery, is simply shown pulling his face with his fingers so that his face and mouth look deformed or operated upon. Though not restricting his argument to this genre, Macneill has suggested that performance art involving alterations and extensions of the body and bioart making use of new biological technologies are two powerful ways of countering the 'quiescent notions of the arts' (2011: 85) that are prevalent in the medical humanities. Gómez-Peña's work is relevant to these debates as well as to the urgent need for a global, rather than a Western, medical humanities.[15] Given his version of the ethno-cyborg body and the aforementioned self-portraits, his work can be used to expand our notions of what counts as radical/provocative art and address some of the inequalities that arise when specific kinds of material – for example, work that engages with cutting-edge technology – are considered to be more central to medical humanities concerns and debates.

In addition to engaging with bodily fantasies that can open up medical understandings of the body as well as intervene within Western constructions, many of Gómez-Peña's performances attempt to establish connections between the individual body and the larger socio-political body – a link that is not new,[16] but that

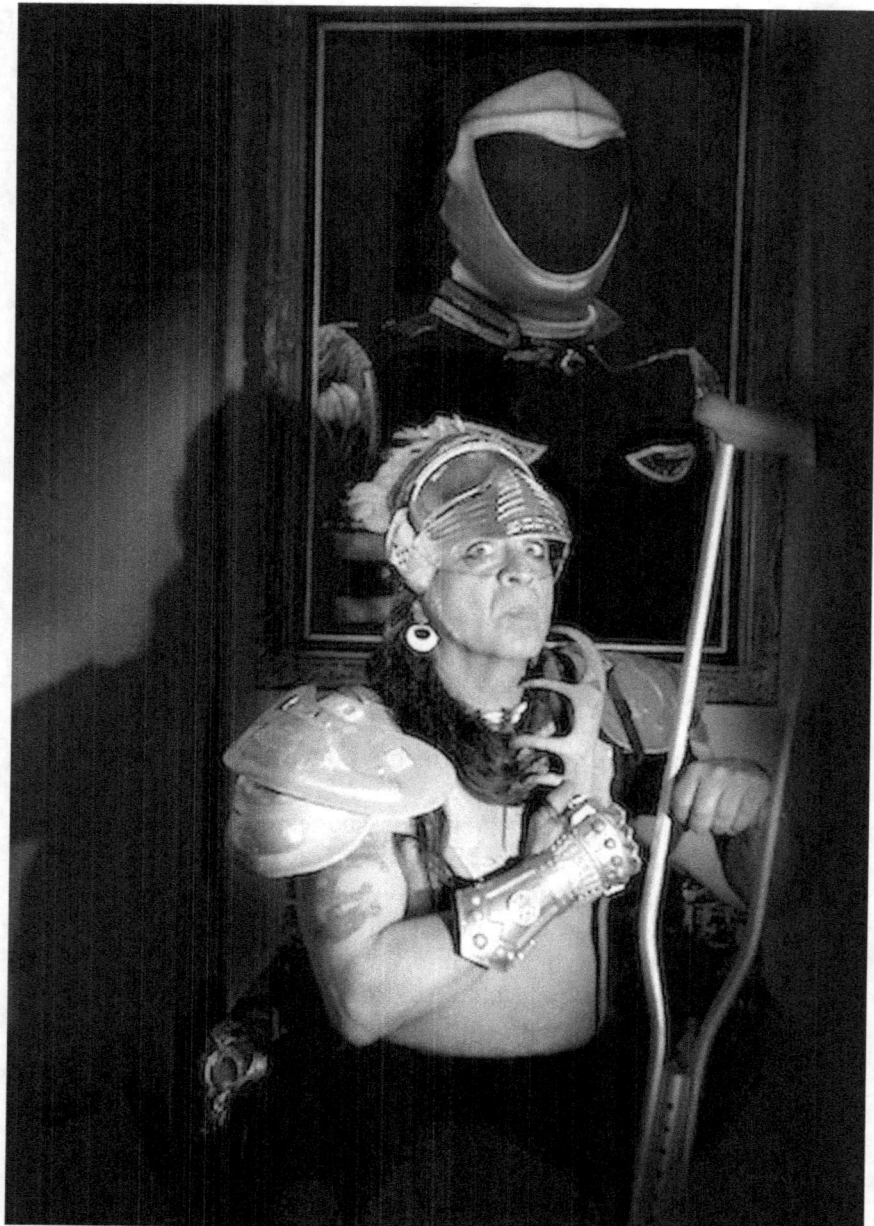

Figure 3.1 Guillermo Gómez-Peña, *No Portraits: Not Stelarc,*
© Guillermo Gómez-Peña and La Pocha Nostra.

greatly impacts definitions of medicine and medical ethics as they both become infused with questions of social justice and politics. The environments he creates for his audiences reference a number of histories and contexts including the early modern anatomy theatre, the *wunderkammer* (or cabinet of curiosity) that was popular in Renaissance Europe and the freak show. His collaborative project with Coco Fusco, *The Guatinaui World Tour* (various locations 1992), involved the artists exhibiting themselves for three days in a cage as authentic indigenous people recently discovered. Even though the performance was supposed to challenge the ethnographic gaze and deconstruct the image of the colonised other, Gómez-Peña and Fusco were shocked to discover that the majority of their audiences believed that the exhibit was real and did not do anything about it. Rosemarie Garland-Thomson (1997) and Rachel Adams (2001) have discussed the cultural work of freak shows in nineteenth- and twentieth-century America and the ways in which such spectacles of the non-normative (disabled or racial) body brought together scientific analysis, entertainment and aesthetic contemplation. *The Guatinaui World Tour* reveals how foreign bodies continue to remain vulnerable to the spectacle and violence of the 'freak show' and to be deciphered according to audiences' needs and desires. But in placing the embodied encounter of individual performers and members of the audience at the centre of the performance, such work challenges the kind of distance and disinterested knowledge typical of anthropology museums.

Discourses of enfreakment resurface in moments of cultural stress and Gómez-Peña's most recent work, especially after the 9/11 terrorist attacks, returns to ideas of commodification of the body to explore such a process. In these performances, the ethnographic/medical gaze is substituted by a no less pervasive gaze, that of the media. In *The New Barbarians Collection*, first performed in November 2007 in Bristol, Gómez-Peña appropriated the format of an extreme fashion show and engaged the audience with a variety of fashion-inspired stylised performance personas stemming from problematic media representations of foreigners, immigrants and social eccentrics. In the format of the fashion show Gómez-Peña found the perfect objective correlative for the culture of 'the mainstream bizarre', a culture of a radical but thoroughly apolitical type of multiculturalism that fetishises otherness (50–2). The 'show' is not really about clothing, but it is about bodies that become fashionable and then unfashionable (especially post–9/11), imitating the way fashion works in cycles. By the end of the fashion show, the exotic/fashionable 'models' who have been displaying themselves along the catwalk to the sounds of ethno-electronica have become the global evil others or 'the new barbarians'. They re-enter the stage naked for the conclusion of the performance, namely, their public execution.

The link between the individual body and the body politic in Gómez-Peña's work is further pursued through the imagery of the cartographic body in body-based performances that are equally about marking or inflicting pain on the body and the violence surrounding global geopolitical events. *Mapa/Corpo* (2004), a response to the invasion of Iraq, for example, is described as 'a poetic, interactive ritual that explores neocolonisation/decolonisation through "political acupuncture" and the re-enactment of the post 9/11 "body politic"' (Gómez-Peña 2011: 343). During the performance, which was censored in the United States prior to 2005 but toured in Latin America, Europe and Canada, the audience is confronted with a female performer's nude body lying on a surgical table covered by the flag of the United Nations. Above the body, an acupuncturist dressed in a lab coat prepared for surgery lays out forty needles (a small flag is attached to the tip of each needle). As Gómez-Peña delivers a multilingual poem dressed in one of his 'shaman in drag' personas, the acupuncturist exposes the body and methodically inserts each of the needles into it. The audience is then asked to decolonise the body/map (*mapa/corpo*) by carefully removing the flags with the assistance of the acupuncturist. The body becomes a site of public debate, and

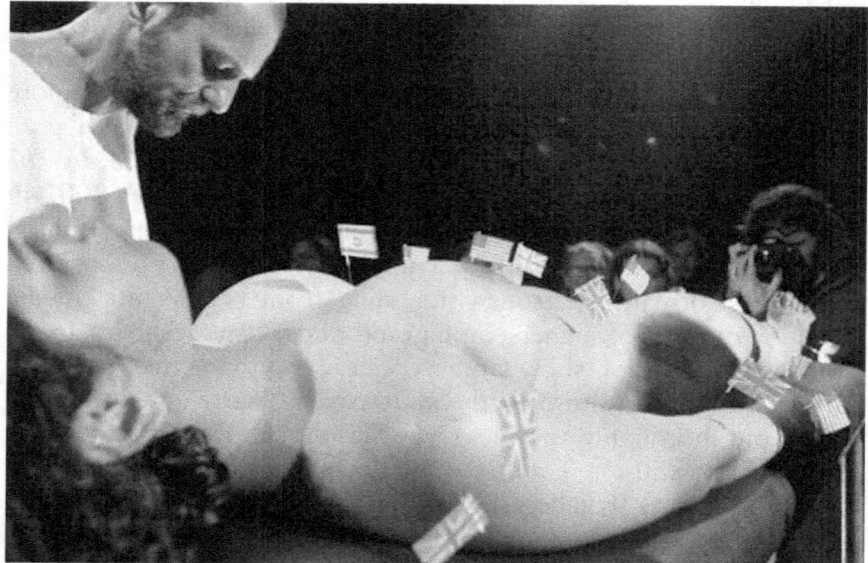

Figure 3.2 Colombian performance artist Maria Alejandra Estrada and 'acupuncturist priest', *Mapa/Corpo*, Buenos Aires, 2007, © Guillermo Gómez-Peña and La Pocha Nostra.

touch, with all its healing qualities, as discussed in Chapter 2, stages intimate pedagogical/political moments of witnessing and solidarity that can be transferred outside the performative space. Many members of the audience who took part in *Mapa/Corpo* during its various tours described the ritual in ways that uncover the tenderness and caring that it involves rather than simply an instance of extreme behaviour on stage, making it clear that they came into contact with something powerful and persuasive.[17]

As part of the same show on another station, Gómez-Peña's collaborator Roberto Sifuentes has his body shaved and washed by a curator as if he is being prepared for a burial, representing 'the brown body of "the universal immigrant"' (Gómez-Peña 2011: 345). Once this cleansing ritual is complete, his body becomes a canvas for the audience members to inscribe it in such a way so that his lost humanity is restored. Clearly this gesture is not the same as medical or racialised markings on the body even though it evokes them, like Spence's performative re-enactments in her phototherapy projects; in his statements about the performance, Gómez-Peña alludes to a different kind of surgery but, like Spence, devises an alternative kind of treatment grounded in the potential of performance art to heal. In what can be read as a more radical version of Frank's analogy between illness narratives and post-colonialism (1995: 13), he explains:

> We try to offer to the audience the sacrifice and the spectacle of our brown bodies distorted and exaggerated by the media ... in the hope of triggering a serious process of reflexivity ... Our formidable challenge is how to rehumanize, repoliticize and decolonize our own bodies wounded by the media and intervened upon by the *invisible surgery* of pop culture. (Gómez-Peña 60, emphasis added)

Even though wounding and surgery are employed as rhetorical strategies here, this does not reduce the urgency of Gómez-Peña's critique against what he calls 'extreme bodies', namely proliferating images within popular forms of entertainment that humiliate people of colour, women, the working class, foreigners and disabled people. As he explains, what characterises the new areas of interest in an 'extreme body' is 'the "bizarre" combination of pathology and Eros, of implied violence and high style, of the medical and the criminal realms. It is the morgue, the surgical table, the biogenetic lab, the forensic dossier, as well as the "extreme" sex club, tabloid TV, and the porn websites with their myriad subcategories' (59). These are examples of glamorising suffering without taking on board its ethical and political demands or the fact that the world includes people whose lives are shaped and constrained by such destructive images. Medical humanities scholars have interrogated images of patients and doctors in medical dramas showing how they can create false impressions for medical students and undermine the public's trust in medical practitioners.[18] However, as indicated in the passage above, there is a host of problematic quasi-medical representations that circulate through various media and forms and need to be explored through the lens of both the medical humanities and the visual/performing arts. In this sense, Gómez-Peña's interrogation of the sensational display of 'extreme bodies' and the commercialisation of suffering[19] should equally be the province of the arts and the medical humanities, especially when the goal is to bridge strict understandings of the body and pain within medicine with broader cultural representations of suffering and dehumanisation. If we accept that the medical humanities shares with cultural studies an attempt 'to limit interventions that are needless, pointless, irrational and ultimately inhumane' (Squier and Hawkins 2004: 253), this is an important goal.

The conjunction of the medical and the criminal that Gómez-Peña finds striking in contemporary popular representations of the body is not new when we think of the shared history of medicine and the arts. The medical humanities has been primarily concentrating on telling the story of how the arts can humanise medicine, but looking to the past, there are other stories that should not be overlooked: artistic representations of dissections from the sixteenth up to the eighteenth century, such as Rembrandt's *The Anatomy Lesson of Dr Nicolaes Tulp* (c.1631) and *The Four Stages of Cruelty* by William Hogarth (1751), show how the dissection of a corpse was more commonly 'perceived as the final act in a drama of retribution and punishment' (Sawday 2006: 4). In *The Reward of Cruelty*, the last of the four engravings by Hogarth, we see the overseer-surgeon seated on a raised chair, like a judge passing sentence. Such works have a place in medical history, but also in the closely allied histories of punishment and poverty, as before the Anatomy Act of 1832 it was initially executed convicts and later unclaimed poor – that is, economically vulnerable people – who were transported, amidst a violent crowd, to the executioner's scaffold and after that to the anatomy theatre for dissection. Jonathan Sawday is right that if these images 'reflect the growing "medicalisation" of the body, they also emerge from a world in which they were held to serve a wider moral purpose. Moral didacticism was as important [as] any commitment to a rational understanding of the body's functions' (2006: 3). Such connections can be pursued anew in each generation; if the contemporary medical detachment towards patients has been read as a development of the idea of 'necessary inhumanity' that eighteenth-century surgeon–anatomist William Hunter urged his students to gain,[20] I would suggest that moral didacticism has changed into a kind of political scapegoating, as this is demonstrated in Gómez-Peña's work addressing the aftermath of 9/11. Even though the 'spectacle' is framed differently, the vulnerable people have remained the same: poor, immigrants and people of colour, especially women.

Wounding does not only take place in the media but also in real settings such as borders (and border cities), airports, detention centres and streets, where migrants and foreign-looking people are subjected to ethnic profiling, humiliation and violence – even though his work does not address them explicitly, we could add scientific/medical experiments that exploit the most vulnerable.[21] Immigration and healthcare are undoubtedly two of the highest-profile and most contentious policy issues in the United States. The US–Mexico border in particular, seen as a free-trade zone as NAFTA came into effect, is now even more literally '*una herida abierta* [an opened wound] where the third world grates against the first and bleeds' (Anzaldúa 1999: 3), given its militarisation through the Border Protection, Anti-terrorism, and Illegal Immigration Control Act of 2005 and the Secure Fence Act of 2006. The relationship between the dehumanising ways immigrants are treated in the media and even in places like hospitals was made apparent in Mónica Novoa's article about a Chicago-area hospital discharging a critically injured young Mexican national, Quelino Ojeda Jimenez, and without his approval, transporting him to a less-equipped hospital in Mexico in 2011. Some of the reactions by commentators to this story reveal how attaching the illegal immigrant label becomes a convenient way of stripping people of their basic human rights, including the right to healthcare: 'Would it have been cheaper just to pull the plug than to fly him back to Mexico?' 'So nice we absorb the expense of his crime of coming to America illegally' (Novoa 2011). While deportation decisions are not the jurisdiction of hospitals, as this story shows, often there is a lack of advocacy on the part of the poor and sick from doctors.

Drawing connections between different punitive histories of the body, Gómez-Peña's work invokes descriptions of the anatomy theatre as not merely an auditorium but 'a temple of mortality, in which the human form – itself understood as a "temple" fashioned by God – was gradually dismembered' (Sawday 2006: 12). His rituals of political surgery, such as *Mapa/Corpo*, have been described as 'performative temple[s] where the sacred and the profane intertwine with racy contemporary issues' (Gómez-Peña 2011: 348); and, we could add, in whose interior we witness the dismemberment of the citizen – his or her humanity and rights taken away. At the same time, however, through these performances that focus on the martyred flesh we also partake in the attempt to re-member, de-criminalise and re-humanise those bodies, or at least bury them properly. Writing about migrant deaths and border violence such as femicides in border cities like Juárez, Julie Avril Minich observes that it is precisely because of the state neglect from both sides of the border that such dispensable bodies are only mourned and accounted for in literary narratives. Such sites, to which we could add performance art, are not only means of expressing trauma and memorialising victims but also of exposing the disregard for human bodies and seeking justice (2014: 101).[22] This is how we could interpret Gómez-Peña's assertion in *Brownout 2* (discussed in the next section of this chapter) that 'when you don't have access to power / poetry replaces science / and performance art becomes politics' (213). Rather than a merely romantic or utopian statement, it affirms the ability of performance to enact 'cultural critique within multiple public spheres' (Román 2005: 3) and create solidarity among various marginalised groups.

While Gómez-Peña's work does not address medical communities or questions of health directly, the ills of the globalised world he diagnoses resonate with pressing issues in conversations about global health and social justice. Physician–anthropologist and activist Paul Farmer, who is often in dialogue with such communities, has argued for the need of a new medical ethics that goes beyond the individual patient, and that is not divorced from questions of social rights and differential standards of care across nations:

> What is defined, these days, as an ethical issue? End-of-life decisions, medicolegal questions of brain death and organ transplantation, and medical disclosure issues dominate the literature ... These are quandaries of the fortunate. But in working for the health of the poor, we are faced with a different set of moral issues. Will this patient get any treatment at all? Will her survival be considered less precious than a fourteen-dollar savings in basic medicines? (2005: 174–5)

One of the key problems Farmer has identified is resistance to ground medical ethics in 'contextualising disciplines' such as political economy, history, anthropology and sociology (2005: 204) that would 'develop a broader view of who gets sick and why' or 'who has access to care and why' (207). As he stresses, 'without a social justice component, medical ethics risks becoming yet another strategy for managing inequality' (201). While the arts do not explicitly feature on his list of disciplines that could help socialise ethics, it is clear from the previous analysis that performance art can become a radical form of pedagogy and politics. Farmer's commitment to pedagogy and democracy is evident every time he encourages medical professionals but also policy makers and other cultural workers to '*reimagine* equity' in order to transform global health (2013: xxiii). He often delivers presentations and speeches to these groups, especially students; like Gómez-Peña, but in the more specific context of public and global health, he exposes the kind of 'anesthesia' that leads to what he calls 'failures of imagination', a failure to imagine an alternative 'to the way things are' (5) or, more concretely, to the kinds of health programmes that are deemed 'cost-effective' (60), and puts forward his own utopian vision founded on: partnership and collaboration with the people who are in need of better healthcare rather than just relying on experts; openness; 'accompaniment' instead of aid (234); and 'willingness to tackle what may seem to be insuperable challenges' (246) by 'building' and continuing to build 'a social movement' that will bring this alternative and more hopeful vision into being (221). If medical ethics and bioethics, as Farmer is right to suggest, as well as the current conceptualisation of the medical humanities, have ignored dimensions of human rights, the politics of health, imagination as a form of political praxis and the importance of radical pedagogy by becoming professionalised, Western-centric and narrow, the critical medical humanities can usher in a bolder chapter by embracing some of the more experimental and risky aspects found in performance art.

Brownout 2 as palimpsestuous illness narrative

Many of the contemporary performance practices that involve bodily markings and other 'extreme' interventions risk being seen as self-indulgent or aestheticised responses to bodily difference when measured against real experiences of illness and disability. In *Carnal Thoughts* Vivian Sobchack examines a series of representations in films and other media alongside the discourse of postmodern theorists and medical researchers that offer fantasies of 'beating the meat'. Countering these through the 'lived body', including her own experience of having a prosthetic leg, she writes 'that there is nothing like a little pain to bring us back to our senses, nothing like a real (not imagined or written) mark or wound to counter the romanticism and fantasies' that characterise the current discourse on the techno-body (2004: 167). Similarly, examining the rhetorical significations of the wheelchair in Gómez-Peña's performances, Kuppers notes: 'The wheelchair's cultural history of "suffering" collides with Gómez-Peña's unsuffering live presence, a man in his wheelchair but in control and clearly having fun' (2001: 84). What happens then to a performer and their performance practices or most iconic images of the wounded, marked and 'ethno-cyborg' body when they experience disability or illness first-hand?

In addition to considering some of the problems that stem from the representation of disability in Gómez-Peña's work, in this part of the chapter I am interested in the broader conversations that derive when illness confronts certain theoretical models about bodies or identity formation prevalent in academia as well as professional practices across disciplines and art forms. We have seen in Chapter 1 how Herndl contextualises her choice for breast reconstruction in relation to feminist responses to the body and to posthumanism; she notes that 'all the theorizing about the body that I've ever done didn't prepare me for how I'd choose' (2002: 149). In contrast, Sedgwick has revealed that her experience of breast cancer, while scary, was also '*sheerly* interesting with respect to exactly the issues of gender, sexuality and identity formation that were already on my docket' (1994: 12) and has famously described it as 'an adventure in applied deconstruction' (12); one that demonstrated in the most immediate and visceral way the 'instability of supposed oppositions that structure the experience of self' (12). Illness narrative scholars have paid attention to what happens when a doctor becomes a patient – in particular how this experience often requires that doctors rethink aspects of their profession, most crucially the doctor-patient relationship and its power dynamics.[23] However, illness (both temporary and prolonged) poses challenges to other professionals too.[24] What happens, for example, when a performer's bodily and mental faculties, which are crucial to their ability to perform, break down?[25] What are the conversations between illness and performance that arise? Can limitation and loss be converted into gain or read as an enabling condition for creative practice? As well as exploring the politics of illness, as in some of his body-based performances, Gómez-Peña's solo work begins to articulate such matters.

Brownout 2 (2000–3),[26] one of Gómez-Peña's most ambitious and personal solo pieces, was written while he was recovering from a serious illness contracted while touring in Brazil in 2000. In the performance script he names it *'esteatosis'* – steatosis, more commonly known as fatty liver disease or FLD, in English. Having no medical insurance, he was hospitalised in Mexico. His recovery took eight months and the doctors forbade him to perform or rehearse. The script was subsequently staged as a sort of 'hospital-bed soliloquy' and intertwines two discourses: a 'poetic/political account of the times' and the artist's 'inner hell during the recovery from [his] liver crash' (Gómez-Peña 2011: 341). Doctors and nurses, together with relatives and several of his performance personas, are invoked in this polyphonic and multilingual political manifesto that masquerades as illness narrative (or perhaps it is the other way around). The props range from hospital mask and 'Mr Clean' bottle filled with Gatorade to Spanish dagger, rubber heart and hand-made 'lowrider' prosthetics and braces, all of which are consistent with his idea of 'imaginary technology'. While these props exaggerate and ridicule the medical setting, they also bear similarities to the props used in other performances and reference certain styles of Chicano art.[27]

The title 'brownout' has multiple significations, both serious and more playful or risqué: it suggests a partial loss of power similar to a blackout and cleverly references Gómez-Peña's interest in the 'brown' Chicano body but also alludes to 'the extreme emotional distress caused by the tremendous urgency to defecate'.[28] The number 2 of the title points to another performance with the same name, *Brownout: Border Pulp Stories* (2000); Gómez-Peña has described this earlier performance as a 'palimpsestual' performance (quoted in López 2003: 4), overlapping and juxtaposing radio commentaries for Public Radio, duets with his co-performer Roberto Sifuentes and notes from performance diaries, combining and presenting them as a monologue. *Brownout* part 2 certainly operates in a similar way, not only reworking Gómez-Peña's familiar themes but also reproducing whole sections of part 1, reframing them through the story of his illness. Recycling images and texts, reformatting and recontextualising them into multiple media is a favourite methodology of La Pocha Nostra, and many of the performances remain works in progress, to be revised and reframed. *Brownout 2* is also pieced together from pre-existing material, recalling the process of *bricolage*. This material encompasses: a blessing or prayer; advertisements and news updates; a geography lesson; a poem in 'robo-esperanto'; reworked Latino songs; and a series of 'exercises in political imagination' through which Gómez-Peña pretends to be a politician turning parts of his performance into a political campaign.

Among scholars who have explored the theoretical adaptability of the term palimpsest, Sarah Dillon proposes a form of palimpsestuous reading that 'traces the incestuous and encrypted texts that constitute the palimpsest's fabric'. Since those texts bear no necessary relation to each other, 'palimpsestuous reading is an inventive process of creating relations where there may be none at first sight; hence the appropriateness of its epithet's phonetic similarity to the incestuous' (Dillon 2005: 254). *Brownout 2* can be viewed in this way given that the imagery of illness creates a vast network of homologies and interrelations. Gómez-Peña's precarious and contingent health becomes an instrument or prism allowing him to look at the social body and reveal hidden pathologies. It triggers memories and a backward look towards what led to his present situation, and it is exploited purposefully in order to reflect on the nature and mission of performance art as well as Gómez-Peña's fears for the future. It is this complex relationality between the body and the body politic, illness in the individual and in society, and personal and cultural death that makes this piece so powerful in its address to the audience. Unlike the prevalent conception of illness as biographical disruption, the performance shows how Gómez-Peña's illness experience fits into the larger tapestry of his work as a Mexican-American performance artist. Considering this multiplicity of images and narratives that incite rather than 'calm the imagination' (Sontag 1991: 99), *Brownout 2* offers an example of how one's illness story need not be merely inscribed within the boundaries of clinical experience or one's 'personal tragedy', but can extend far beyond the medical encounter to encompass other kinds of histories – in this case, personal and collective histories of immigration and border crossings. Attending to these multiple narratives of illness can challenge both the dominant utilitarian sensibility with which illness narratives continue to be approached as well as frequent criticisms that target their individualistic, solipsistic and voyeuristic nature.

Wearing the complete attire of either 'El Travelling Medicine Vato' or 'El S/M Zorro' – in other words, of one of his shaman-personas in drag – as the stage directions inform us, Gómez-Peña appears on stage as 'an existentialist *mojado*', translated as 'wetback'; a derogatory term for an illegal immigrant to the United States (179). In the introduction to the piece he explains why the particular performance is more challenging than usual:

> it's quite a challenge, my dear friends,
> for I've been stripped by airport security
> of all my robo-baroque paraphernalia,

> my ethno-technobilia ye-ye,
> which means,
> no more hand-made lowrider prosthetics,
> no mariachi robotic bodywear,
> no cheesy fog machines,
> no hanging dead chickens, nothing,
> not even a voice-effect processor
> to help me get rid of my accent.
> Just one costume,
> and a bit of make-up
> to protect myself. (179)

In many of his other performances, Gómez-Peña uses costumes as a central method of exploring the performativity of the racialised body – his props, make-up, body paint and other cultural artefacts are used to comment on ethnic stereotypes and intercultural relations. However, the experience of illness peels off the various layers of costumes and make-up, and brings about a more radical form of exposure which Gómez-Peña attempts to understand through an analogy to the illegal immigrant or 'wetback'. The suggestion is that immigration and serious illness both expose their victims to surveillance and physical or metaphorical stripping.

Though being stripped can be taken literally (he has written extensively about his adventures with airport security, especially post–9/11, when he is almost always detained and searched),[29] stripping in the context of serious illness conjures the spectre of death. This becomes apparent when Gómez-Peña describes the script as his 'uncertain fate' (182) and invokes the figure of La Pelona 'staring down my own death'; 'this time she looked serious' (180).[30] While his illness is known by medical linguists and medieval poets as 'esteatosis', he describes a more intimate encounter with death, personified as a lover (195). In *The Labyrinth of Solitude*, Octavio Paz offers a theorisation of death in Mexican culture. He argues that European notions of death tend to provide euphemisms or a certain reticence that implies an avoidance of the subject (the word death 'burns the lips', as he puts it,) whereas in Mexico death is approached in a more direct and 'truthful' way: 'The Mexican ... is familiar with death, jokes about it, caresses it, sleeps with it, celebrates it; it is one of his favorite toys and his most steadfast love' (1961: 57). While *Brownout 2* draws on this perception of death in Mexico, popularised through *El Día de los Muertos* (Day of the Dead), the performance also subtly undermines the romanticised and essentialist idea about the culture's embrace of death, that is, the inherent ability of

Mexicans to confront mortality 'face to face' through humour and 'impatience, disdain or irony' (Paz 1961: 58). Testing his microphone at one instance, Gómez-Peña says in Spanish, 'Estoy muriendome en voz alta y nadie se da cuenta, probando' (203).[31] Even though the testing of the microphone suggests that this is a performance and the comment can be taken as a humorous remark, it is likely that the boundary between performing and being really ill was hard to distinguish in some of his performances of *Brownout 2*.[32] As with his body-based performances that are critical of 'extreme bodies' and of the culture of the 'mainstream bizarre', Gómez-Peña here recognises the risk that his intentions, including his illness story, may be misunderstood by audiences; not only by monolingual viewers, who will most likely not understand the above words, but also by those accustomed to consuming such performances, using them to simply try on and off different fashionable and even marginal experiences.[33]

Brownout 2 is divided into seven days and also consists of an introduction and a postscript. Each day section includes a fragment marked in bold (the directions state that it should be delivered in a nasal voice) and the contents of that directly refers to Gómez-Peña's health condition. Day 1 sets the scene and explains how he landed in **'a Mexico City hospital bed / hooked up to some retro sci-fi looking *maquina*'** (180). This experience forces him to look at some of his performance creations in a new light:

> So, they connected me to a myriad more IVs
> and made me look precisely like one
> of my Mexi-cyborg performance characters,
> like some kind of cheesy self-fulfilling prophecy
> featured on the sci-fi channel *en español*... (201)

Contrary to *The Museum of Fetishized Identities*, where disability accrues meaning and stands for 'the paralyzing effects of colonizing fantasies' (Kuppers 2001: 84), here it points to actual immobility. Similarly, the artist who metaphorically found himself 'on the other side of the Mexican mirror' when he crossed the border to the United States and started the process of 'de-Mexicanization' (Gómez-Peña 6), now looks at himself and sees a pale, skinny man with a frail gaze. The Border Brujo's ritual was all about deconstructing wholeness and purity; a reminder to his audience that the site of the border is representative of such realities as migration and globalisation that attest to cultural exchange and hybridity, and that we all contain a multiplicity of voices and selves, some even contradictory. The Brownout's ritual, years after, involves crossing another border between health and illness that despite being invested in similar concepts such as fragmentation is described differently: 'I am the most other and fragmented I've ever been. / I'm *literally* talking to this Other self / on the other side of the mirror' (204, italics added). Here we have the kind of confrontation that Sedgwick writes about in *Tendencies*, as Gómez-Peña examines how his illness fits earlier models that helped him make sense of his experiences of border-crossing, cultural loneliness and identity reinvention.[34] If Sedgwick is interested in exploring connections between the performativity of gender, which is central to her earlier work, and that of grave illness, as well as the kinds of cross-identifications and politics that come with it (in her case, with gay cultures and AIDS activists),[35] *Brownout 2* promises to explore similar connections in relation to race and the politics of migration and national displacement.

The mirror imagery in the above quotation is pertinent since, though a monologue, the performance consists of a series of dialogic or mirroring encounters with Gómez-Peña's multiple selves, both past and future; in the performance, he revisits his 'original sin', that is, his decision to leave Mexico for California (197) and some of his most well-known performances, and dreads the possibility of a bland future without the ability to perform:

I'm back in San Francisco
learning how to be a laptop intellectual, *coño*!
I miss the road, the troupe,
our dangerous crossborder adventures.
I badly miss Myers rum and Marlboro reds. (210)

In as much as his illness prevents him from travelling, a central aspect of his performance work, Gómez-Peña views the experience of rethinking his artistic practice as an abandonment of his political responsibilities, a reduction of his self. His image of the 'laptop intellectual' is consistent with his critique of academia and universities as merely 'reservoirs for thought' rather than 'laboratories for social action'; in other words, as divorced from social reality and less radical than performance, a criticism which he has subsequently revised (95).

Although the equation of illness with passivity is problematic, as it implies that activism or art cannot take different forms and shapes, Gómez-Peña is at least critical of one particular dominant discourse surrounding health and illness in America. He takes issue with his doctor's advice, '**Guillermo, you need a total change of lifestyle**' (210).

Even though there is a general view that all liver disease is self-induced and alcohol-related, *Brownout 2* does not comment on such stigma, which may be shared by members of the medical community. Instead, Gómez-Peña considers the implications for his work – work that is political – when it is dismissed as a certain kind of unhealthy 'lifestyle'. Being a performer definitely takes a toll on one's health and body. As he says, 'I've got forty-five scars accounted for, half of them produced by art, and this is not a metaphor' (186). He then goes on to list some of his most political (and dangerous to his health) performances: 'Living inside a cage as a Mexican Frankenstein / crucifying myself as a mariachi to protest immigration policy' (186).[36] The doctor's words, in this sense, are indicative of a neoliberal discourse of personal responsibility for one's health. It recalls Lorde's response in *The Cancer Journals* to a doctor's claim that no happy person gets cancer: 'Was I wrong to be working so hard against the oppressions afflicting women and Black people? Was I doing all this to merely avoid my first and greatest responsibility – to be happy?' (1996: 59–60).[37] But in the end, rather than embracing such a superficial idea of happiness, she opts for 'the rewards of self-conscious living' (3). Another instance in *Brownout 2* that suggests that Gómez-Peña's performance work runs the risk of being seen as 'pathological' is a statement that both recruits and deconstructs this stereotype: he notes that he has been performing to 'avoid ... mental hospitals, / to justify intellectually my sociopathic tendencies' and 'to exercise my freedoms' (192).

The US–Mexico border and immigration are central threads throughout *Brownout 2*. In an alternative anatomy or cartography of Gómez-Peña's body towards the start of the performance, each body part is 'examined' in relation to the experience of crossing the border. He starts with his '*casa*, my head', then proceeds to his '*cuello*' [neck], described as 'going North', and his '*piernas* [legs], the journey north continues'. Similarly, his '*espalda*' [back] evokes (through its aural echoes) the word 'wetback' that follows it (184). The analogies between the regulation of the body and of the body politic are pursued further, often placing in dialogue seemingly unrelated forms of social critique. But the fact that the text does this through its palimpsestuous nature is important as it encourages connections between bodily displacement and medical regulation on the one hand and cultural/national dislocation and structural violence on the other. *Brownout 2* positions experiences of disability/illness and illegal immigration next to each other so that the medical and the political are able to comment on each other. One image, for instance, moves from the scene of Gómez-Peña's body in hospital, invaded by a sound scanner, to that of the United States sponsored by white hands but actually maintained by brown hands, 'their undocumented fingers / deep inside America's sphincter' (184). Like the wheelchair, invasive medical technologies have rhetorical and metaphorical value to which Gómez-Peña wants to hold on, even when he has had direct experience of these technologies through his actual illness.

It could be argued that in the above image disability is used as a metaphor to express immigrants' outsider status and alienation from the national body, rather than put in the service of political work that benefits people with disabilities.[38] As Minich states, 'The US–Mexico border is discursively tied to disability in ways that are both theoretically generative and politically dangerous.' The question of accessibility (physical or political) with which both border and disability studies are concerned creates opportunities for linking struggles across marginalised groups, but many immigration campaign debates 'rely upon disability and pain for their rhetorical impact' (2014: 25). Even though this dynamic in Gómez-Peña's work and its limitations are evident, following Minich, I want to read his performances in ways that 'provide *a starting point* for imagining accessible political communities' (4, emphasis added) and for drawing connections between medical humanities and political activism. A clear example is when Gómez-Peña confronts an audience member: 'Hey, do you know your genetic code? / Do you know your civil liberties? / How many have you lost so far?' (206). Once again the continuity may not be apparent – it is easy, as he encourages his audience throughout the performance, to attribute his strange juxtapositions to his 'delirious psyche' (180) or side-effects of his medication. But the juxtaposition between one's genetic code and civil liberties acts as a provocation to notions of self and what it means to know who you are: the decoding of the human genome in 2000 has been presented as one of the most important scientific projects; is the increasing loss of civil liberties a darker, but no less successful, experiment whose consequences we are beginning to understand?

Similarly, the imaginary political speeches interspersed within *Brownout 2* are parodies that provide a sharp critique of the indifference to human pain across diverse sites:

> We politicians have total disregard for human pain, for the homeless, the immigrants from the South, our elders and teens, the artists, the enfermed, the crazy ones, like you. (199)

In 'Defense of Performance', Gómez-Peña mentions his strong 'spiritual affinity' for 'hookers, winos, lunatics, and prisoners' and adds that 'our empathy for social orphanhood expresses itself as a visceral form of solidarity with those peoples, communities, or countries facing oppression and human rights violations; with those victimized by imposed wars and unjust economic policies' (27). Lumping together different 'marginalised' groups of people is an indication of the often romanticised approach Gómez-Peña takes, even as he offers images (for example the sexually deviant cripple) that are not positive. He has also been forced to acknowledge the problem of speaking on behalf of subaltern others – in his own words, people who 'drown' in deeper waters than him (27). The emphasis on spiritual affinity in the above statement suggests that Gómez-Peña is not necessarily concerned with the day-to-day matters of actual disabled or mentally ill people, and to my knowledge his work has not explicitly addressed disability issues (or even the intersection of race/ethnicity and disability).[39] However, it offers that 'starting point' to imagine and forge alliances across these communities and their struggles.

Brownout 2 also alludes to a historical tradition in which disease is characterised as a foreign invader. Immigrants have often been feared as carriers of disease.[40] Gómez-Peña encodes this fear of the foreigner/ diseased body aesthetically too, through the use of many hybrid languages that appear like a virus running through the performance, threatening linguistic and cultural purity. In one of the poems included in the performance, written in what he calls 'robo-esperanto' – a language pieced together from five different European languages, Latin, Nahuatl[41] and Chicano slang (188) – he asks what would happen if you opened your computer and found a message in a '*lingua poluta*', that is, infected language (189). In his draft manifesto 'Remapping Cyberspace' he expresses his, and other Chicano artists', wish to 'brownify' virtual space, to 'Spanglishize the Net', and to 'infect' the lingua francas. His coined term 'Webback' (in analogy to wetback) shows how cyberspace is not a neutral territory that gives equal access and opportunities for belonging to all: if images of disability and disease are used to conjure the threat of (illegal) immigration to the healthy national body, such imagery recurs with descriptions of the cybermigrant, described as '*el nuevo virus virtual*' (the new virtual virus) (2001: 91). But, appropriating such imagery, Gómez-Peña demands that the new cultural presence of the Webback and the many new or hybrid languages spoken online be acknowledged as 'healthy' or legitimate.

In the performance's postscript, entitled 'Millennial Doubts', Gómez-Peña posits his work as a necessary form of politics for those who 'don't have access to power' (213). At the same time, recalling Hall's statement 'I make books so I won't die' discussed in Chapter 2, he affirms how necessary performance is to the continuation of his life: 'I thought maybe I might have one more chance / to make a deal with my personal death. / So, I wrote this script' (214). For those who cannot tolerate the cacophony, Gómez-Peña's response is unequivocal:

[*I grab the megaphone*]
Locos and *locas, perdonen*
But if I stop moving, performing, talking back ...
I simply die. (193)

Illness and artistic practice

Years after *Brownout 2*, in 2013, Gómez-Peña had another health crisis, a viral infection of his spinal cord (transverse myelitis), through which he was faced with the possibility of permanent neurological damage. The experience of his slow recovery, social isolation and frustrating attempts to regain his capacity to write despite his unreliable memory led to another performance script (still in progress) with the title 'Gómez-Peña on Illness, the Human Body, Performance and Quantum Physics: A Psychomagic Script for a Hard Recovery'. This text, 'his most personal' one to date (2014: 152),[42] bears some similarities to *Brownout 2* in that both scripts explore 'a larger artistic and philosophical struggle' (151) rather than merely experiences of illness and recovery, and use the method of recycling previous material for their composition. Once again, Gómez-Peña notes the ironic contrast between his exploration of the 'frail and eccentric body' in his performance *El Cuerpo Diferente* (which he was presenting at the time of this new health crisis) and the actual reality of inhabiting such a body (151). Like *Brownout 2*, this performance reflects on the politics of health and illness and challenges discourses that pathologise specific emotions and actions, most notably those that threaten the status quo: 'I had no idea I was even stressed. I thought existential fatigue was just a normal way of being in the world – a socially and politically stressful world ... Doesn't everyone feel this way?' (152) Gómez-Peña not only laments the fact his illness prevents him from being physically active but also, like Lorde, how certain understandings of health and illness even dictate our feelings in the name of preventing the risk of illness: 'Some people I know have been arrested for protesting ... I'm pissed because I can't go visit them in jail since I have no immune system. Actually, I'm not even supposed to be worrying about them because my liver is ill. What the @#$%!+ ?' (155)

'Gómez-Peña on Illness' explores the potentially healing dimensions of performance art more explicitly than *Brownout 2*. Gómez-Peña imagines himself re-enacting his most dangerous performances and even though he objects to nostalgia as a form of escapism, he resorts to it in order to facilitate his recovery. He realises that performance has similarities with quantum theory and that during the course of his performance he can choose to be perfectly healthy in 'the parallel reality of [his] imagination' even if his physical body contradicts that (160). Dwelling on the past, especially on the apparent invincibility of his youthful body and some of his most physically challenging performances, provides him with a sort of refuge where the present losses can be displaced. But the danger of self-indulgence is lurking: 'I suddenly realize I'm being too self-centered ... It's my mother, scolding me: "Guillermo ... You seem to be obsessed with an imaginary illness. You are a hypochondriac ... You're becoming Americanized. Get a grip! I miss your madness"' (154). Even though Gómez-Peña attributes such a response to his mother's dementia (or 'sacred amnesia', as she calls it), her comment is indicative of the ways in which illness is often understood differently across cultures. Diedrich has explored the possibility that narratives of illness reflect 'contrasting national attitudes and/or ideologies' about conceptions of the self and illness or death (2007: 61). Although she does not address Mexico and acknowledges that she is diagnosing stereotypes or fantasies of national character, we can approach the response of Gómez-Peña's mother in a similar way. Her words in the performance draw on the idea that the confessional mode (dismissed as self-indulgent and even hypochondriac) is an American import by simultaneously appealing to the notion of communal identity as what distinguishes Mexico from the valorisation of individualism in the United States. Through her statement we also glimpse here the essentialist cliché of the Mexican who is fearless of death (sketched in Paz's influential study *The Labyrinth of Solitude*), and naturally equipped to face it with humour or disdain.

Unlike Gloria Anzaldúa and other Chicana writers who have turned to the models offered by Coatlicue (the Aztec goddess of creation and destruction whose headless body incorporates snakes) and to Mexican philosophical frameworks to find culturally grounded meaning for physical pain, Gómez-Peña does not discuss disability/illness in a Mexican or Latino context as extensively in his solo performances.[43] This performance, however, features a humorous description of Doña Cristina, an indigenous witch doctor who gives him a cleansing ritual followed by a very strong massage. Doña Cristina leaves with 'some herbs with written instructions on the table' and Gómez-Peña is advised not to tell his own doctor, as he will not accept her treatment (161). More serious is Gómez-Peña's allusion to the Chilean filmmaker and performance artist Alejandro Jodorowsky, who coined the term 'psicomagia', a type of self-styled ritual performance meant to break the behavioural patterns that lead to pain, frustration or illness. *Psicomagia*, or psychomagic in English, has affinities with both psychoanalysis and art (specifically drama) therapy. Unlike the former, it is not enough for Jodorowsky to make patients aware of the specific issue that is causing distress, but also to prompt them to perform concrete actions. Jodorowsky does not call himself a shaman, but shamanism is something that he has been interested in throughout his life: 'The shaman carries out theatrical acts and imitations of powers; by imitating powers, he produces the effect because it opens the doors of the mysterious thing that we are' (Jodorowsky 2010: 235). Similarly, even though Jodorowsky does not call his psychomagic acts pieces of performance art, they can be viewed as works of art in themselves. Gómez-Peña asks: 'Is this clumsy attempt to recapture my ability to write an unconscious form of ritual healing; using my own aesthetic and philosophical willpower as medicine?' (154). In as far as the answers to these questions are positive, he suggests that his writing 'is a psycho-magic script for healing in the best Jodorowskian tradition' (155). The script that we have in front of us is an integral part of Gómez-Peña's treatment programme.

In addition to individual acts of healing, this performance also acknowledges the importance of community and lists a series of artists and friends who, in sharing their experiences with heart disease and breast cancer subsequently turned into art projects, help Gómez-Peña to endure his own. He admits that in the past acknowledging the role of a community in this way would have been 'too sentimental or cliché', 'but the thing is, back then I didn't know anything about this' (158). Compared to *Brownout 2*, then, this performance is more open to experiences of vulnerability and crucially pursues connections across different kinds of illnesses. Like Lorde, who, writing from the West Indies in *A Burst of Light*, hears the sea echoing her 'mothers' voices of survival from Elmina to Grenville to Harlem ... resounding inside [her]' (1996: 305), Gómez-Peña acknowledges the contributions that a bigger community of care and movements for political change – from the Spanish *indignados* to Arab Youth and the Occupy movement – make to his healing:

> **Tonight I am standing on the ruins of globalization. I am reentering the world,** a witness to the collapse of the global economy and the emergence of myriad citizen movements against authoritarian regimes worldwide. ... Everywhere I turn, I see imaginative and brave citizen actions. I feel humble and temporarily hopeful. (159, emphasis in original)

While *Brownout 2* ends by affirming Gómez-Peña's commitment to continue performing, 'Gómez-Peña on Illness' ponders the more specific question of what kind of performance artist Gómez-Peña will be in the future as his ageing body might continue to face health-related challenges. He notes that during his recovery he continued as much as it was possible to do 'small creative tasks such as revising old, half-baked, unpublished texts' and 're-writing the photo captions on my blog' (153). In light of his social isolation and diminishing endurance, the Internet becomes an important vehicle of communication as well as a way of continuing his performance work. Engaging in his 'Twitter Poetry Project' is more manageable than a large performance script: '(I can manage 2 or 3 lines at a time). *Verbigratia: Tweet: 'Reenactment #12: Remember? Remember me? I used to be ... Mexican. There used to be a Mexican inside this body, but something happened in the process*' (153). There is currently much discussion as to whether illness or death should be the subject of live-tweeting (a question I address in this book's Afterword), but here the 140-character poems, building blocks of a performance script, provide an important form of authority and freedom as well as community, for the patient/performance artist.

Even though Gómez-Peña knows that his illness will not affect his commitment to 'continue making art against violence for communities that are experiencing it first-hand' (160), he wonders in what form this may be possible in the future: 'if in fact I do have permanent damage, will I have the courage to reinvent myself and continue to do performance? Can I create performance art without making much physical effort ... maybe only for video?' He playfully adds, 'is it time for me to become a German minimalist ... or a Canadian conceptual artist?' (153). The performance script ends with a series of unanswered questions that will be revisited as he performs his recovery and as his recovery prompts him to reflect on his performance practices:

What will be the new role and shape of my body in my performance work? Will my artwork change considerably from now on? In what ways? Who will I be when I settle into my new 'normal' self? Will I ever be able to forget this chapter of my life? Should I? Raising questions, more questions, never ending questions. After all, that's the fate of a performance artist, *que no*? (162)

Illness as a lesson often leads to cliché-perceived statements of enlightenment, or at least to the more open question of what illness is trying to tell someone, and is posed by many of the artists considered in this book. In the documentary *I Make Books* Martha Hall (2004) explains, for example, that she understood her cancer recurrence as a message that she could not continue competing with the 'big boys' in corporate America; she was missing a more creative part of herself that eventually led her to become a book artist. In addition, many narratives outline how ill people develop an ability to live in the present by modifying expectations of the future. Gómez-Peña's performance takes this further by exploring what a series of other artists are doing;[44] namely, renegotiating existing practices that cannot continue due to illness, which, in addition to their therapeutic intentions, also have implications for artistic practice: 'I'm probably not coming back as Gómez-Peña, the extreme bohemian. *A ver que pasa!* Let's see if we recognize each other next time you see me. DEFINITELY TO BE CONTINUED ...' (162).

On provocation

Performance art, as we have seen in this chapter, encompasses much more than what performance studies scholars mean, including anthropology, popular culture, pedagogy and politics. As Gómez-Peña has clarified: 'Performance artists spend the bulk of their time "scanning" rather than "focusing", as theorists do, settling on one spot and then pulling out the binoculars' (21–2). Scanning, as described here, is to be distinguished from the kind of precision associated with the word in the medical context (MRI and imaging technologies) or even in literary study, where scanning a line of poetry requires meticulousness. I would suggest that in addition to the close reading (advocated by narrative medicine, and complemented by the intimate touch or caress of artists' books, as discussed in Chapter 2), this alternative meaning of 'scanning' is important for the critical medical humanities; rather than the focused clinical gaze or even the specialist gaze of many academic practices, which excludes what is considered not relevant, 'scanning' makes connections and forges conversations. As such it is both an interdisciplinary and political method, necessary for a field that needs to stay polyvalent and create bridges between different disciplines and methodologies.

When La Pocha Nostra describe themselves as 'radical pedagogues' whose 'place is the world and not just the art world' and as 'active citizen[s] immersed in the great debates of our times' (78), they voice a message to which the medical humanities should adhere if it wants to remain a broad and dynamic movement. Taken together, their performances act as important provocations for medicine too. Medicine and the health professions are often perceived in heroic terms, 'unlocking nature's secrets with promises of laboratory grown organs from our own cells, pushing the limits of human finitude, and rendering the secret codes of our genes open to scientific code breakers who promise to eradicate cystic fibrosis and diseases of old age' (Macneill 2011: 88). If Gómez-Peña's work responds to the need to meet these provocative images 'with equally strong images and responses from the arts' (2011: 88), his performances do not do that merely by offering us 'extreme' images of the body that may cause discomfort (especially when placed against 'softer' images in the medical education curriculum). This is precisely what he objects to – a series of depoliticised, stripped of their context, so-called radical images. His 'Mex-Terminator' performance persona, featuring the robo-garra that is reminiscent of Stelarc's prosthetic arm, may fit this description, but it is one layer of his performances. Like the artists in Chapter 1 who use photography to reconstruct the scarred female body, Gómez-Peña invites his audience members to embrace 'a new form of radical faith' with the help of his performances: faith that 'the art process can serve as a personal and political force and that the human body can become a site of change against a backdrop of global despair and war' (2011: 348). This can be approached as an alternative kind of provocation: to the mechanistic image of the body in medicine *and* to the perception of the humanities as romantic and naïve – in other words, as incapable of enacting political critique.

Crucially, what differentiates the 'radical faith' Gómez-Peña posits in the above statement from the faith in medicine as the solution to many problems which medical students often uncritically embrace is that such a project is open to uncertainty and the possibility of failure. As he acknowledges, the interest in the extreme body within mass entertainment has created a true ethical dilemma for performance artists: in the age of the 'mainstream bizarre' and corporate multiculturalism, 'what certainty do we have that our audiences won't misinterpret our "radical" actions and our complex performative identities as merely spectacles of radicalism or stylised hybridity' (52)? The danger is exacerbated by the fact that if this happens, then performance artists like him are becoming complicit in perpetuating images of marking and wounding the body outside of context; it is a variation of the risk discussed in relation to Spence's work in Chapter 1, namely that her kind of photography draws attention to violence even as it reclaims agency from a coercive medical system.[45] However, it could be argued that unlike photography, and especially mainstream media representations, the living body of performance avoids the risk of being reduced to a particular kind of body or icon. Moreover, Gómez-Peña's answer to 'corporate multiculturalism' is provisional. He hopes that the rituals and interactive 'games' of his performances, even though they mimic mainstream culture in many ways, will 'trigger a long-term process of reflexivity in the psyche of the viewer, which hopefully leads to deeper ethical and political questions' (83–5). Performance, like a pill, slowly begins to act, whether on a personal or activist level – provocative images stay with or even haunt the audience after the performance is over, and feelings experienced originally in the body can become translated into language and action. This outcome cannot be guaranteed, of course. Yet it is precisely this acknowledgement of difficulty, also found in Gómez-Peña's solo performances, that makes such work relevant to the medical arena, an environment with little tolerance for uncertainty and ambiguity.

The next two chapters continue looking at the unpredictable trajectories that open up through a vision that engages with inadequacy, failure and reworking, as well as with hope, and the ways it could be useful to different communities of professionals. They turn, though, to illness narratives that address not only the representation of serious and contested illnesses, but also the ethics and challenges of collaboration.

Notes

1. Unless otherwise indicated, all subsequent quotations by Gómez-Peña are taken from *Ethno-Techno* (2005). Only page references will be given in brackets.
2. See for example Rossiter et al. 2008, Shapiro and Hunt 2003, Mienczakowski 1997, Brown and Gillespie 1997, Deloney and Graham 2003, Bates, Bleakley and Goodman 2014 (section 4, 'Performance'), Brodzinski 2010 and the UK programme *Performing Medicine*, <http://performingmedicine.com/> (last accessed 27 July 2015).

3. For 'treatment' as an interdisciplinary tool/methodology, see Diedrich 2007.
4. Even though Gómez-Peña's work engages with spirituality, his critique of commodified bodies and fetishised identities in the era of 'corporate multiculturalism' makes him wary of so-called alternative spirituality, where everyone gets to be 'shaman for a weekend' (62).
5. See, for example, the installation performances *The Temple of Confessions* (1994–6) and *The Museum of Fetishized Identities* (1999–2002).
6. See Morgan 2011: 42–3.
7. See Smajdor, Stöckl and Salter 2011, Garden 2007, Shapiro 2007 and 2008, and Wear and Zarconi 2007.
8. See Reid et al. 2012 and Auton 2013.
9. For a detailed description of these exercises, see Gómez-Peña 2005, particularly Chapter 6.
10. *Being* as opposed to *acting* is also a central distinction between performance art and theatre (Gómez-Peña 110).
11. Jurecic surveys some of the less generous responses to Anne Fadiman's *The Spirit Catches You and You Fall Down: A Hmong Child, Her American Doctors, and the Collision of Two Cultures,* which was published in 1997, shortly before the Association of American Medical Colleges' Liaison Committee on Medical Education introduced standards for cultural competence (2012: 117).
12. Also see his term 'reverse anthropology' (25).
13. See Bost 2010 and Chabram-Dernersesian and de la Torre 2008.
14. The portfolio can be seen at <http://www.artpractical.com/feature/no_portraits/> (last accessed 27 July 2015).
15. See Hooker and Noonan (2011) and their call for the inclusion of non-Western and non-Anglophone examples in the field. Describing English as 'the official language of science, information, and international communications' (2001: 87), Gómez-Peña adds that 'hopefully one day I won't have to write in English to have a voice' (2001: 91).
16. See, for example, Sontag 1991.
17. See YouTube video 'La Pocha Nostra Performance in Norway', September 2007, <http://www.youtube.com/watch?v=qhkxwn7rAic> (last accessed 27 July 2015).
18. See Brodzinski 2014.
19. The commodification of death and commercialisation of dead women (specifically artists such as Frida Kahlo, who were largely neglected while alive) within Latin Catholic culture has been explored in the work of Cuban-American interdisciplinary artist and writer Coco Fusco. See for example her 1997 project *Better Yet when Dead* for which she appeared as a corpse in a coffin (2001: 22–5).
20. See Richardson 2000.
21. See, for example, Veracity 2006.

22. Of interest here is the work of Mexico City-based art group SEMEFO (Forensic Medical Service), founded in 1989 and dissolved in 1999, who referenced death and violence in urban life during the 1990s by using materials such as remains of unclaimed bodies or victims of crimes and their personal effects. One of its members, Teresa Margolles, even established a relationship with the staff of the real SEMEFO morgue that enabled her to participate in dissections and learn more about corpses and their preservation (Fusco 2001: 75).
23. See Diedrich 2007, Chapter 4.
24. A good example is the study *The Body Silent: The Different World of the Disabled* (1987) by anthropologist Robert Murphy, which has been described as an 'autoethnography' (Couser 1997: 206).
25. These questions concerning the impact of disability upon the performing arts (including theatre and dance) are important to the field of disability studies. See Kuppers 2003 and Linton 2006.
26. I cite from the script as published in *Ethno-Techno* (2005), but the work is still in progress.
27. For example, *rasquachismo* (see Townsend 2011).
28. As defined in the Urban Dictionary, <http://www.urbandictionary.com/define.php?term=brownout> (last accessed 27 July 2015).
29. See Sections 21 and 22 in Gómez-Peña 2005.
30. Among the names used for death in Mexico are *la calaca* (the skeleton); *la pelona* ('baldy'); *la flaca* ('skinny'); and *la huesada* ('bony').
31. In English this can be translated as 'I am dying aloud and nobody notices, testing.'
32. Gómez-Peña acknowledges, for instance, that when he first performed *Califas 2000*, a performance opera that was written around the same time and drew on the same experience of illness as *Brownout 2*, 'most of the audience didn't even know that the wheelchair and IV weren't props' (2014: 158).
33. On the radical pedagogical and humanistic role of learning a foreign language, see Giroux 2011: 179.
34. See Gómez-Peña's essay 'On the Other Side of the Mexican Mirror' (2005: 5–18).
35. See Sedgwick 1994 (specifically pp. 252–66), Diedrich 2007 (Chapter 2), and Hawkins 2006.
36. The first refers to *The Guatinaui World Tour*, discussed earlier, and the second to *The CruXi-fiction Project* (1994).
37. For a critique of 'the cancer personality', see Sontag 1991.
38. For the use of disability as a metaphor for wider social ills, see Mitchell and Snyder 2000.
39. See, however, Kuppers' article for the ways Gómez-Peña's performances deny 'the possibility of any single reading of disability's presence' (2001: 84).
40. See Sontag 1991, Kraut 1995 and Wald 2008.

41. Nahuatl is a group of closely related Uto-Aztecan languages (an American Indian linguistic stock) that includes the speech of several peoples (such as the Aztecs) of central and southern Mexico and Central America.
42. All quotations from this work in this section refer to this publication. Only page numbers are given in brackets.
43. See Bost 2010. Even though Anzaldúa's writing about diabetes has been approached through disability studies, she does not identify as disabled (see Keating 2009, Part 4).
44. One example is Spence's practice of reinterpreting material from her archive rather than creating new images due to the exhaustion brought by leukaemia discussed in Chapter 1 (her 'slide-sandwich' technique prefigures the digital tool Photoshop). See also the work of American performer Peggy Shaw after her stroke (her 2001 one woman-show *Ruff* requires technological accommodations given her inability to memorise her script); and the Scottish artist Chris Dooks (<http://www.dooks.org/>, last accessed 27 July 2015) whose chronic fatigue forced him to reinvent himself as a 'fragmented filmmaker', pursuing 'small clusters of audio, music, writing and photographic works' and developing 'a bricolage methodology' (Dooks 2013).
45. See Gómez-Peña 2011, especially pp. 300–1. Like Gómez-Peña, Spence was concerned about the appropriation of radical work by the mass media and advertising industries (1995: 103).

Chapter 4

Collaborative Film as Terminal Care

Filmmaker Jon Jost's response to *Nick's Film/Lightning over Water* by German director Wim Wenders, filmed in April and May 1979 in the last few weeks before Nicholas Ray died of lung cancer, is indicative of reactions to artwork that deals with sensitive issues such as terminal illness and death. In his review of the film, 'Wrong Move', Jost writes:

> The film business has long been noted for cruelty and harshness. In his last months Nick Ray needed something for himself, though perhaps he didn't know what that was. It certainly wasn't this movie, which clearly he did know. What Ray needed, simply, was love. Instead he got a crew who seem to perceive life only through the mechanical devices of film. They rolled over him with a movie-making machine, and now they even choose to display the carnage. (1981: 96)

Comments such as this about the legitimacy of using illness as the basis of art are familiar to many illness narrative and cultural critics. One of the best-documented controversies on this topic is, as mentioned in the Introduction, Croce's 'non-review' of Bill T. Jones's performance *Still/Here* in the *New Yorker* in 1994. Another much-debated case that provoked disagreement among viewers, readers and reviewers over the tensions between voyeurism and empathy is Annie Leibovitz's photographs of her life with Susan Sontag in *A Photographer's Life, 1990–2005* (2006). This book includes pictures of Sontag hospitalised and hooked up to machines, receiving chemotherapy at home, recovering from bone marrow transplant, dying and finally dead, elegantly dressed for burial. As death functions indexically rather than symbolically in photography and non-fiction film, and is thus experienced as real by viewers, the violation of such a visual taboo in our culture is often accompanied by the need to justify it. This is especially pressing in the case of the representation of another person's experience where consent may be an issue, as well as in collaborative narratives where one person (the healthy party) often finishes the joint work. With reference to Leibovitz's photographs of Sontag, a number of reasons have been suggested for making them public that show the ways illness and death narratives cannot be divorced from broader questions of personal and cultural trauma, mourning and memorialisation as well as issues of political visibility, witnessing of trauma and wider cultural attitudes to death.[1]

One of the difficulties with illness narratives is that, even for those readers who can keep reminding themselves that what they have in front of them is not an unmediated personal experience but a representation, it is difficult or perhaps ethically problematic to bracket the fact that behind these stories and images are real people who are suffering or dying. But if the writing and reading of such narratives can be construed as an act of self-indulgence or voyeurism, these stories demand to be witnessed in some way, even when the accounts they provide may be unreliable or cannot be trusted. Cinematic representations of illness and dying are not excluded from such predicaments. Sobchack writes of the 'unsettling, epistemological ambiguity' and the 'ethical outrage' that may ensue in the case of films with an undecidable status – for example, when an audience finds it hard to discriminate between fiction and reality (2004: 265). Wenders' *Lightning over Water* is characterised by such ambiguity: on the one hand it bears a likeness to spontaneous revelation in an immediate situation through its present-tense narration and documentary feel, and on the other hand it foregrounds the strategies of its own composition in a number of ways.

Its uncertain generic status becomes apparent in various published comments Wenders has made about this film. When he offers a categorisation of all of his films in a talk given at a colloquium on narrative technique, he notes 'I'm not even sure that [*Lightning over Water*] counts as a film at all, so let's leave that one out' (2001: 214). He calls it 'a mistake' in the same talk, implying perhaps that it has failed to qualify as a film, or at least as the kind of film Ray and Wenders wanted to make when they first started working on it. In an interview, Wenders further clarifies: 'in my mind *Lightning over Water* counts much more as the *experience* we went through together, Nick Ray, myself and the crew. It still amazes me that you can actually watch it. We would have done it without film in the camera' (2008a: 2, emphasis added). Wenders does not say we *should* have done it without film in the camera, but the question of whether the 'experience' should have been made public lingers both in contemporary reviews and in responses by audiences today who often feel they are being forced to gaze at a sick old man's death. As Wenders notes in one of his conversations with Peter W. Jansen, 'the whole film is like one long answer to that question' (2001: 332).

Alongside this, another question remains open: that of failure. Atul Gawande, a surgeon, writer and public health researcher, has written of his shock at 'seeing medicine *not* pull people through. I knew theoretically that my patients could die, of course, but every actual instance seemed like a violation, as if the rules I thought we were playing by were broken. I don't know what game I thought this was, but in it we always won' (2014: 7). Are artists equally bound by the rules of their respective 'games' – or, conversely, more open to the prospect of failure? Exploring failure in art practice, Sara Jane Bailes argues that such a discourse 'has mapped a vibrant counter-cultural space of alternative and often critical articulation, in which conventional standards of virtuosity are challenged and methods of practice scrutinised and re-worked' (2011: 2). The value of failure lies not merely in foregrounding inadequacy, even though inadequacy should be acknowledged in a study that deals with narratives of serious illness, but also in the ways 'it can lead to unanticipated effects ... establish an aperture, an opening onto several (and often many) other ways of doing that counter the authority of a singular or "correct" outcome'. In this sense, and as we have seen for example through Herndl's interrogation of her initial sense of failure as a feminist theorist in Chapter 1, failure can be understood as 'generative' (Bailes 2011: 3). *Lightning over Water* may fail as a film (in its strict definition) or in terms of what we would expect to find in an homage to the American director and his career, but in risking failure and asking of its audience to witness the failures and losses it enacts, it succeeds in doing something else altogether.

A discourse of failure is relevant to medical practice, which is prone to accident and errors, as discussed in Chapter 2, as well as to ongoing attempts to enlarge existing conceptions of medical professionalism which are often assessed through checklists and other quantitative methods.[2] Its generative potential is evident in Diedrich's exploration of failure and loss in medicine, the body and language. Drawing together the 'multiple idioms' of medicine, literature, philosophy and politics, she opens the way for the invention of new methods that can reorient medical thinking and practice (2007: 159).[3] From her own perspective, Whitehead, building on Kathryn Montgomery's argument that medicine is 'a practice' despite its reliance on scientific knowledge,[4] suggests that literature, especially texts that attend to moments of narrative discontinuity, 'can fruitfully intersect with medicine in opening up the uncertain and contingent' (2014: 116). These efforts within the critical medical humanities, as well as within critical pedagogy as seen in Chapter 3, to challenge discourses of mastery can be expanded to encompass other media so as to examine how knowledges and practices among different professionals – in this case medical communities and filmmakers – can be productively translated and used to forge closer and more critical conversations across disciplines.

'It didn't rest in peace': the editing history of *Lightning over Water*

Wenders' confession that 'we would have done it without film in the camera' is striking not only given that ultimately the decision was to film *Lightning over Water*, but also because the camera or cameras (the crew filming Ray and also a porta-pak video camera held by Tom Farrell, another close co-worker of Ray's) are persistently present in the final film. What is the point of flaunting the constructedness of this experience if having film in the camera was not important? Michele Aaron reminds us that self-reflexivity can be both transgressive and conservative. Self-reflexivity reveals what should be covered up; like Bertolt Brecht's distanciation technique in the theatre, it questions 'the spectator's mythic distance and safety, the irresponsibility or neutrality of looking on' (2007: 97) that perpetuates cinema's voyeuristic–scopophilic look.[5] But it can also naturalise such artificiality, or even make it aesthetically pleasing, a more conservative gesture. What is certain is that self-reflexivity, as the following chapters also show with respect to theatre and animated documentary, is intimately connected to the issue of responsibility and the implicatedness of the spectator in the film they are watching.

Lightning over Water is self-conscious not only in the sense that the ubiquity of cameras makes us aware of our position as spectators, but also in that it refuses a stable viewing position for the audience from which to look at the dying man Ray. There is a range of techniques mixed together in the film: cinéma vérité (the spontaneous video segments documenting the process of creating the film, such as rehearsals between Wenders and Ray, but also a sequence of Ray in the hospital); staged documentary (the scripted conversations with Ray in his loft, and the sequences when Ray lectures at

Vassar College and rehearses an adaptation of Kafka's *Report to the Academy* with Gerry Bamman), filmed with a 35mm camera in their greater part; and staged fiction (fictional or dream sequences, artfully lit and shot in a studio, in which Ray and Ronee Blakley, Wenders' wife at the time, imitate King Lear and Cordelia, and Wenders finds himself in the hospital bed). There are also clips from the body of Ray's own cinematic work in black-and-white and in colour, as well as snippets from his diary superimposed on the film in some of the images. Finally the sequence of the boat in New York Harbour sailing under a bridge – a reference to Ray's dream of sailing on a Chinese junk, in search of a cure for cancer – directed by Wenders after Ray's death, appears at intervals throughout the film, but most prominently in the titles and in the epilogue. The epilogue also includes conversations among the film crew as to the difficulty of finishing a project once the subject is no longer alive. Wenders' voice-over commentary at the start and at various points serves to orient the viewer in this disorienting film that shifts between reality and fiction and between different levels of both.

To approach the question of what this self-consciousness and formal complexity serve we need first to consider the film's editing history. *Lightning over Water* underwent two processes of editing as Wenders was unhappy with the first version shown at Cannes film festival in May 1980. As he explains:

> Peter Przygodda who was responsible for the [initial] editing saw the material as a succession of certain events that took place over a three-month period... He edited the film as if it were a documentary, feeling it his duty and responsibility to find the 'truth' behind the images. But in this process something else almost got lost, our story, Nick's and mine, the world of fiction into which we constantly tried to transfer our reality. We hadn't intended to make a documentary. (2008b: 10)

The only thing Wenders was certain of, invoking the unfinished nature of the project, is that the 'film [and we are tempted to add Ray too] did not "rest in peace"' (10). While the original version of the film is no longer available and as a result a more detailed comparison cannot be pursued, the second and definitive one (November 1980, Internationale Filmtage, Hof) contains the video segments as well as Wenders' voice-over narration. The latter turns the third person or objective documentary into a more personal testimony – a film that resonates with the diary or essay-like documentaries[6] through which

Wenders reflects on his tools as a filmmaker, such as *Tokyo-Ga* (1985) and *Notebook on Cities and Clothes* (1989). As a hybrid form the 'essay film' has a complicated history, but has taken a middle position between feature film and documentary as it pushes both genres in unexpected directions (Alter 1997: 136). Moreover, it breaks away from chronological sequence and has an intense self-reflexive aspect, often marked by the incorporation of different media such as photography and video. In *Lightning over Water*, the choice of a mixed form that Wenders was wary of before producing his subsequent diary documentaries is not arbitrary. Rather, it is suggestive of the way neither a narrative film nor a 'conventional' documentary can adequately capture the uncertain and 'messy' aspects of illness and dying that are the subjects of this film.[7]

Wenders does not dismiss the documentary genre entirely when he takes the film back into the cutting room: 'Of course the film was guided by our reality, but we had made a big effort to produce a fiction or at least to make our story seem fictional' (2008b: 10). *Lightning over Water*, in its second version, is intensely aware of its border status between document and fiction, its struggle to come into being as a film at all, and this self-consciousness affects us as viewers, as we constantly have to negotiate ways of looking and responding to it: does the film in its self-reflexive combination of forms and mixing of narratives prompt us to respond to it as a film (an aesthetic representation) or as a record of a painful experience undergone between Wenders, Ray and the crew? What would it mean to prioritise one over the other in our responses? What are the accompanying ethics of spectatorship, which, following Elizabeth Bronfen, we could split into 'aesthetic' and 'moral' spectatorship (1992: 45)? Finally, if both medicine and filmmaking, in their own ways, rely on discourses of mastery or a certain 'professionalism', can the experience of losing control or embracing uncertainty and difficulty in one field (that of filmmaking) help to orient medicine towards a similar direction? All these questions not only qualify Jost's condemnation of the film, with which this chapter opened, but also move beyond narrow 'bioethical' approaches that revolve around a set of codified principles or prioritise *what* occurs in the film, aiming for clarity and closure.[8] The critical medical humanities approach that I adopt here is more attentive to form and encourages 'interdisciplinary messiness and open-ended exploration' (Pattison 2003: 35). Attending to formal and structural issues is not an activity divorced from questions of ethics and politics; indeed, as all the case studies of this book demonstrate, such issues are integral to these questions. In the case of *Lightning over Water*, their interrelatedness can be best seen by modelling reading practices of critical interloping that can enrich both illness narratives and film/documentary studies.

'Would you kill someone for a great shot?': documentary gazes

The ethics and challenges of collaboration have been given ample attention within life writing. In 'Making, Taking, and Faking Lives' Thomas Couser (1998) explains that in addition to the factor of consent, which is not always straightforward, collaborative projects often involve relationships characterised by inequalities and asymmetries. Differences of race, gender, class and age matter, and so do, in the case of narratives of illness or disability, those pertaining to health/able-bodiedness. Wenders has noted in interviews that the question of whether to switch on the camera 'was never off the table. And sometimes we didn't shoot, for instance when Nick had had to take too many painkillers and wasn't really in control' (2001: 332). The power imbalance latent in narratives of illness and disability is perhaps most problematic in those cases when the completion and publication of the narrative devolve upon a survivor who narrates another's terminal illness. Ray died on 16 June 1979, while *Lightning over Water* was being made. Although the film lists both Ray and Wenders as directors, the circumstances of its production raise the question of whose property the collaboratively-produced life story is. *Lightning over Water* is a film largely created in the cutting room, given that it went through two different processes of editing. Which version Ray would have liked (if any) is something we will never know. In the epilogue of the film, after Ray's death, the crew gathers together to fulfil his final wish: to sail out to the ocean on a Chinese sailboat, which we see moving past the skyline of New York City. In some ways, the final party for Ray, similar to an Irish wake, seems disrespectful. In the boat people are joking and drinking next to the urn containing Ray's ashes: 'Here we are: Nick is dead and all we can do is talk about film. We're all film junkies.' The camera, bolted to the top of the boat, carefully revolving in a circular fashion, showing at random frames of the river, the Manhattan skyline and the boat, continues filming the absent/present Ray (the urn with his ashes), pushing the limits of (auto)biography beyond the closure of death. One member of the crew jokes about setting fire to the boat because they have no images of him being cremated: 'It's a great shot.

I would burn this boat down.' Yet the last clearly audible line before the concluding scene is Farrell saying, 'Would you kill someone for a great shot?'

This question presents an ethical dilemma that reverberates across the film. In 'Ten Propositions on Death, Representation, and Documentary', Vivian Sobchack outlines the phenomenology of five gazes in documentary films (and raw nonfictional footage) that engage with death and dying: 'the accidental gaze', 'the helpless gaze', 'the endangered gaze', 'the interventional gaze' and 'the humane gaze' (2004: 249). She also adds a sixth one, 'the professional gaze' that is 'marked by ethical ambiguity' (255). The latter seems to be invoked in Farrell's question, 'Would you kill someone for a great shot?', and *Lightning over Water* interrogates where one's duty as a filmmaker lies. As Ray struggles to meet the demands of filmmaking, Wenders agonises in the voice-over narration that accompanies the film: 'All I knew was that Nick was in immense pain, that it might be better to stop shooting but that nothing might be more painful for him than that.' Tending to the dying and writing do not occur simultaneously; or as Sontag writes, referring to the practice of photography, 'the person who intervenes cannot record. The person who records cannot intervene' (1979: 11–12). Wenders is torn between his 'professional' role and that of being simply a friend: 'I was more and more under the pressure of making "a movie," and found myself ... preoccupied with the work itself and the sheer mechanics of setting up shots and deciding upon schedules rather than being concerned with Nick.' Wenders' concern resonates with a more generic predicament: the replacement of personal closeness with technological intimacy that also characterises modern medicine and has led to a deterioration of empathy in medical students.[9] Like the medical gaze that places 'in parentheses' the patient (or the human body) in order to ironically render disease visible (Foucault 1989: 7), the cinematic gaze effectuates a similar kind of bracketing of what is before the camera.[10] The film constantly gives voice to Wenders' ethical qualms about the project but does not necessarily resolve these moral questions. Wenders' voice-over narration, for example, serves contradictory purposes. His constant doubting as to whether the project should continue given Ray's deteriorating condition shows his awareness of the responsibility he has throughout the shooting of the film. However, given its compulsive nature, it can be also taken as a way of eliciting the audience's complicity; the constant threat of interruption creates suspense and a desire to continue documenting, and this is exactly what Wenders does. Moreover, the fact that the voice-over narration has been added after the shooting (the decision has been made to switch on the camera, irrespective of the doubts) makes us even more sceptical of these comments.

Another way the film inscribes the fear of manipulation is through some of its dream/fictional sequences. These sequences, which resemble psychodrama, are entirely scripted and are highly stylised, as indicated by the choice of studio set and expressive use of lighting. In one of the scenes, following an argument Wenders has with Farrell concerning whether Ray is a father figure to the two younger directors and whether they should continue filming, Wenders is in the hospital bed and Farrell is shooting with a video camera. After that he walks over to Wenders and tries to strangle him. Even though the argument between Wenders and Farrell has been noted for its Oedipal associations, the sharing of the hospital bed by Wenders also captures his (murderous) proximity to the dying friend/director: a proximity that risks infecting him too. The scene and its subsequent versions, approached by some critics as examples of the film's anti-Oedipal spirit,[11] are contained in a dream. The ritual that takes place during this dream sequence could be situated on a continuum between what Diedrich has described as 'the fantasy of identification' and the 'fantasy of empathy', using Abraham Verghese's and Rafael Campo's doctor narratives respectively. Exploring their relationship with the AIDS patients they treat and write about in their memoirs, Diedrich suggests that 'Verghese's fantasy is that he can get close enough to know his patients' stories, but not so close.' Instead, Rafael Campo's fantasy is that 'his patients' stories are his own, that they are, in fact, *about him*' (2007: 110). In either case, such 'compensatory fantasies' (105) undermine the goal of feeling empathy or experiencing true sharing. However, the fictional sequences are only one form through which Wenders' generically mixed work attempts to treat the difficult subject of dying and the relationship between him and Ray.

Lightning over Water enacts the process of trying and discarding different ways of looking at illness, revealing the inadequacy of single forms to the task and the necessity to keep on trying despite the difficulties. If the stylisation and self-indulgence of the fictional sequences discussed above deflect from reality, a similar danger the film confronts, and according to Timothy Corrigan exposes, is that of 'narrative murder', the 'murderous displacement of the body which the image-play of the filmic narrative usually accomplishes' (1985: 13). The two directors' motivation, as we find out at the start, is the shooting of a fiction film under the name *Lightning over Water*, which Ray asks Wenders to help with: 'I knew that he wanted to work, to die working,' Wenders says in the film. His wish to regain his self-image or self-esteem by creating a final film (meanwhile Ray's last film *We Can't Go Home Again*, material from which is shown in *Lightning over Water*, was still being edited, remaining unfinished) alludes to both his outsider position from Hollywood and his experience of dying.[12] In many ways Ray, like Broyard in *Intoxicated by My Illness*, seeks to develop 'a style' for his illness and way of dying (1992: 63), in this case expressed through his love for filmmaking and films. *Lightning over Water* includes conversations between Wenders and Ray about the film they set out to make: its story, its different scenes and how it would end. Wenders had secured some funding but he required a script, also known in cinematic language as a 'treatment'. One scene has Ray sketching a storyline that recalls Wenders' film *The American Friend* (1977), where Ray also played a part, about a terminally ill painter who forges his own paintings and sails off in a Chinese junk festooned with red flags in search of a cure for cancer (the scene that Wenders directs after Ray is dead). If *Lightning over Water* expresses the need for alternative treatments – indeed, the collaborative film becomes a form of 'terminal care' that challenges medicine's power to largely define how to live one's final days[13] – it equally poses the question of what kind of treatment it should become. How should it 'treat', in its cinematic, medical and ethical meanings, its dying subject?

Ray's proposed scenario to Wenders closely resembles *The American Friend*: the story of their film, Ray tells Wenders, is of a painter who needs both to make money and 'to regain his own identity as fully as he can before he dies'; fatally ill with cancer, he would consequently steal and forge his own work.[14] 'He's been living with his present lady for five years. He's forty years her senior,' the script continues, closely following Ray's reality while displacing it within a fictional story. Wenders confronts him directly: 'why make the detour of turning him into a painter', he asks, 'why isn't he you, and why isn't he making films instead of paintings? It's you, Nick. Why take the step away?' While *Lightning over Water* does not share the lexicon for cinematic dying – in the context of the mainstream terminal illness film, this lexicon includes self-sacrifice, saintliness, triumph, self-discovery, painlessness, stoicism, futurism, beauty and the good death (Aaron 2014: 104) – it confronts, rather than entirely resisting, gestures of distortion and displacement of dying as well as those following metaphorical/allegorical trajectories.[15] If conventional signifiers of cinematic dying in Hollywood are conservative and often violent, so is rejecting the displacement of dying altogether. Wenders confesses this fear to Ray when he arrives in his loft: 'I was afraid to come ... I was aware that I would see you in weakness and that you might be worried about being seen [or filmed] this way'. As he adds, he is more afraid of the possibility of finding himself 'attracted to [Ray's] weakness or to [his] suffering', and if this were to happen he would have to leave, because it would be as if he were betraying Ray. In that scene, Ray responds with the assertion that this will not happen, and then the conversation stops. But in the scene where Wenders confronts Ray with the question, 'why not turn the film into one about you', Ray replies with the words 'Then it has to be about you, too,' suggesting that he will have to expose himself as well[16] – that is, account for his subjective/affective investment in the project. Wenders replies: 'I guess we just go on making this film, huh?'

Rather than a 'traditional' documentary claiming a privileged relationship to reality, *Lightning over Water* becomes, as it unfolds, a 'great lesson in modesty' (Wenders 2008a: 2). This is how Wenders conceives of the documentary, distinguishing it as well from another genre that demands mastery: the fiction film. Part of his growing attraction to the documentary is the fact that 'you're confronted with a reality of a situation and you have to find the form for it. You "react" as opposed to a fiction film where you "act" or invent' (2008a: 1). As he clarifies, in a documentary 'you look at whatever reality you have in front of you, and then you let that reality dictate how it wants to be captured'. Not being 'in control of the "content"' does not mean an abandonment of involvement or responsibility: the content 'is there, and you try to be there at the right time and in the right place to witness it' (2). The documentary therefore can become an exercise in modesty and response-ability in the sense of letting go of one's control or presumed knowledge and approaching the other with the sole intention of responding to him or her. However counterintuitive to the reality of healthcare and medicine, this is a valuable lesson; there is, or should be, room for similar non-narrative moments of witnessing (when 'doing' stops) within the action of medicine and the plotting of diagnoses and treatments, and films like *Lightning over Water* provide an opportunity to experience these kinds of moments.

Early on in the film, we observe the intersubjective space opened by the collaborative project: 'I have one action, which is to regain my self-image,' Ray tells Wenders, referring to his (and his character's) goal.[17] 'You have to select your own action.' Wenders replies, 'My action is going to be defined by yours, by you confronting death.' The symmetry in the dialogue resonates with what Susanna Egan calls 'mirror talk' to foreground the emphasis on intersubjectivity, dialogism and relational selves in a wide range of contemporary (auto) biographical projects focusing on crisis and the body. She explains that the mirror in 'mirror talk' 'is more constructive than reflective of the self. It foregrounds interaction between people, among genres and between writers and readers of autobiography' (1999: 12). As Ray replies to Wenders' acknowledgement that he is there to respond to his action, 'that would mean you're stepping on my back. Which I don't mind. Hell, that's all I'm here for.' It becomes clear from this exchange that if both directors are struggling at first to find out what the film is about and what it will contain, the answer will emerge from a series of joint actions rather than a predetermined script. Crucially, medicine, in the narrowest sense of treatment and doctors, rarely enters this space of experimentation and joint reflection on how to do a film about dying; as Gawande has forcefully suggested, treating mortality as merely a 'medical concern' (2014: 128) fails to recognise the priorities of ill people and, more specifically, how 'the chance to shape one's story is essential to sustaining meaning in life' (243). What sustains and gives meaning here without providing a cure is the collaborative project between the two directors and friends, including its challenges.

Their interaction is also expressed visually through the sharing of or exchange of the camera: when we see Wenders in the film, it is Ray behind the 35mm camera, and vice versa, though not with all scenes. Michael Renov describes such exchange, often found in what he names 'domestic ethnography', as an instance of 'sharing textual authority' that happens when the subjects behind the camera share intimate relations (1999: 146).[18] During the course of the film, such authority sometimes shifts to Wenders (for example, when he reads from Ray's diary, and after Ray's death, when he has to finish the film). Ray, for his part, gradually relinquishes himself to Wenders; in the hospital sequence he tells Wenders: 'I wanted you to be able to feel free to go, go, go, wherever you could. And I started out as strong as I could and then there was a great relief when I surrendered more and more to you. And that was fine. I was very comfortable in those days.' In a sense, the film includes some of the characteristics that Sobchack attributes to the 'humane gaze': there is 'an agreed-upon *complicity*' between the two subjects, the camera engages with 'the direct gaze of its dying subject, who looks back', and it inscribes 'intimacy', 'respect' and 'sympathy'. Sobchack draws attention to collaboration by describing films that exhibit the humane gaze as 'a ritual' organized by the dying person himself, who presides over

Figure 4.1 Still from *Nick's Film – Lightning over Water* (BRD 1979, Director: Wim Wenders), © Wim Wenders Stiftung.

it and knows its protocol' (2004: 253). While Ray surrenders some aspects of the project to Wenders, the final scene of the film can be approached as such a ritual; conceived by Ray and executed (that is, continued) by Wenders once Ray is no longer alive: 'How is our film going to end, Nick?' 'I'm going to hold out for a Chinese junk, just pulling out, all festooned with red flowers. On the Hudson? On the Hudson, going out to sea.'

'That's the mess I'm in': cinema and video

The humane documentary gaze 'settles in' as opposed to fixing itself, and inscribes images through the use of a steady camera placed at a distance; when zooms occur they are controlled, and 'vision is purposefully framed and clearly focused'. All of these, insofar as they indicate planning and technical preparation, are signs of '*permission to be there*' (Sobchack 2004: 253). In the case of *Lightning over Water*, however, Wenders doubts whether such 'professional' images that provide distance and respect their subject can show much 'truth'. This realisation becomes apparent through the alternation of the 35mm camera with the video shots of Ray, which betrays the film's refusal to settle on one way of looking at the dying subject.

The video images function as another defamiliarisation technique for the audience, especially when they are first introduced, raising once more the question of aesthetic and moral spectatorship.

Wenders used video for the first time in the very rudimentary applications that technology allowed in 1978. The video segments that are incorporated into the film, either directly (through cuts from the 35mm to the video) or by being replayed on a monitor and watched by Farrell and Wenders at night without Ray being present, are intentionally very rough – we have out-of-focus shots and handheld camera movements, as well as surrounding sounds (for instance, radio or TV from an adjacent bed in Ray's hospital sequence) that affect the overall sound quality of the film. 'Those lousy VHS images', Wenders has noted, 'became something like the cancer inside the film' (2008a: 1). Cancer is here aestheticised and used as a metaphor to convey another kind of death; in the same way that a tumour is killing Ray's body, the video images have penetrated the cinema and threaten its future. In other words, Wenders projects his apprehension about the decline of a certain kind of cinema onto this new technology. Later, during the Cannes film festival in 1982, he would invite a group of film directors to sit in a hotel room in front of a camera, and more crucially next to a television set projecting throughout the duration of each response with the sound off, to answer his question 'Is cinema becoming a dead language, an art which is already in the process of decline?' These responses were collected in the film *Room 666*.[19]

Despite Wenders' feelings about the video images at the time of making *Lightning over Water*, they turned out to enrich the film. As he explains, the video images of Ray 'contained more truth and showed our common experience with more clarity and honesty than the 35mm film' (2008a: 1). Here we can further note that it is the combination of the two modalities that brings such a realisation about their different points of view or visual languages. But what do the electronic images show exactly? At one point in the film, Farrell and Wenders watch a TV monitor with a talking head soliloquy by Ray, taped by Farrell weeks earlier. The film cuts between the film image of Wenders, Farrell and the video image of Ray (at one point we only have his disembodied head against a black backdrop). Wenders then reflects to himself about the terrifying representational gap the video has suddenly exposed:

> I was very confused. Something was happening each time the camera was pointed at Nick, something that I had no control of. It was in the camera itself, looking at Nick through the viewfinder. Like a very

precise instrument, the camera showed clearly and mercilessly that time was running out. No, you couldn't really see it with your bare eyes, there was always hope. But not in the camera. I didn't know how to take it. I was terrified.

Even though they are more 'real' than the film sequences, the video images have an otherworldly quality that evokes death, and, as in other case studies of this book, it is the clash between the two media that makes this apparent. Wenders seems to experience 'the technological uncanny' or 'collision between science and the supernatural' that, according to Laura Mulvey, is brought by a technological novelty. Developments such as photography and the cinema (here it is video) 'made visible forces that existed, hitherto invisible, within the natural world (or by the naked eye)', thus opening 'questions not usually confronted such as around the passing of time and death' (Mulvey 2006: 43). Wenders' description of the camera as 'a precise instrument' penetrating the human body also alludes to the ties between radiography and the cinema, discovered in the same year, which are not readily acknowledged in either histories of the cinema or medicine/science; in other words, to the ways both technologies have been implicated in the disciplining and managing of the human body.[20]

In his documentary *Notebook on Cities and Clothes*, where he pursues an extensive analogy between the arts of fashion and the cinema, Wenders notes that video is 'ephemeral until transferred to celluloid'.[21] Even though both film and analogue video retain an indexical relationship to the object they represent, the special physicality of the former, evident through the chemical processing of film, which generates a palpable and material object, is sacrificed with the shift to electronic (in this case analogue) images; apart from the image transmitted on a monitor, no other image is available in the case of a videotape.[22] If the cinema, like photography, disrupts the flow of time and the decay it brings by preserving or 'embalming' its object (Bazin 2005: 14), video has a sense of impermanence. This is problematic when death is the subject of the film. In *Lightning over Water*, cinema's ability to immortalise its subject – unlike photography, cinema creates a stronger sense of presence because it is able to show an object through its 'duration' or 'change mummified' in André Bazin's figurative definition (15) – is questioned on several occasions. In one scene, played on the TV monitor, for example, we see a video image of Ray (from his lecture at Vassar, filmed in both 35mm camera and video) answering the question 'What is the film about?': 'The film is about a man who wants to bring himself all together before he dies. A regaining of self-esteem.' However, while the words convey one intention, the flickering image exposes the fragility of this project.

Another image with a similar function, though not a video image, is when Wenders, Ray, Farrell and Ray's wife Susan watch footage from Ray's film *We Can't Go Home Again* in Ray's loft. Ray shuffles to the bathroom and stops next to the screen to watch a close-up of a younger, healthier and more energetic Ray. Two different times are presented here with this doubling, exposing the temporal difference that cinema tries to suppress and challenging Bazin's idea of 'change mummified'. Unlike the extended flashbacks focusing on their protagonists' attractive younger selves in many mainstream films of terminal illness that privilege youth and beauty (Aaron 2014: 105), this scene from Ray's own autobiographical archive foreshadows a third, unseen image: that of Ray in death. In this sense it is similar to Spence's resignification of older photographs in *The Final Project*, mentioned in Chapter 1.

Despite his ambivalence towards video at the time of making *Lightning over Water* and some of his subsequent diary documentaries, Wenders acknowledges the advantages of this medium: its intimacy, closeness and ethical call.[23] Unlike Sobchack, who is sceptical about the ethical vision of electronic images, described as removed 'from the materiality of the real world' (2004: 154), Wenders shows how video and new technologies – which, in his view, have also enriched the documentary as a genre – can re-embody their subjects and bring filmmakers closer to 'the real world' (2008a: 4). In one of the video scenes taking place when Ray is in the hospital, Wenders confesses: 'I had this thing – this Oedipal feeling that this film might kill you.' He explains that 'all the confusion and the subconscious fear' led him to 'making images that I didn't like ... The film, whatever we did, looked very clean, pretty – like licked off. And I think that is a result of fear. And then you try to show it beautiful.' One example of the temptation to present something more tangible or secure rather than deal with difficulty is the opening scene, in 35mm film (a rehearsed scene, as we find out after the titles through the video images that have documented it and expose the presence of the crew). Once he is inside Ray's flat, Wenders lies down on a couch, and in the distance we see Ray lying in bed. He coughs and yells in pain, so at this point his sick body is displaced to aural perception. As a reviewer rightly notes about this opening scene, 'There is nothing so immediate in a film as the ambivalence of that moment, of the desire to identify with the suffering and to be distant from it, to see the pain, but to *know* that the sight can be avoided' (Burnett 1981: 12). The gaze,

Figure 4.2 Still from *Nick's Film – Lightning over Water* (BRD 1979, Director: Wim Wenders), © Wim Wenders Stiftung.

both Wenders' and ours, is averted. But later, when the film bridges some of the distance and shows Ray for the first time, we have a carefully crafted and well-framed image; of Ray's sore body, and of the difficulty he has lying down on his bed in the background, while in the foreground his healthy and much younger wife Susan is executing difficult yoga poses on the floor. A series of oppositions between healthy and ill bodies are established through the images comprising that opening: Susan's suppleness set against Ray's brittleness; her yoga against his smoking; his shouting against her silence (even when spoken to). Moreover, Ray's bottomless physique, and the intimacy of a rear shot of him where he keeps leaning forward to reveal his nakedness, contrasts with another mildly sexualised pose in which Farrell opens the door to welcome Wenders – his virility signified by his bare chest. Wenders acknowledges in an exchange during the making of the film that in filmmaking, 'making images instead of people work is an easy way out. I'm doing that' (Ray et al. 1993: 210).

The distance created by these 'clean, pretty' or aestheticised images is overcome through the video segments in a gesture that anticipates what Laura Marks calls 'analog nostalgia', 'a sort of longing for analog physicality' experienced today by those working in the high-fidelity medium of digital video who import 'images of electronic dropout and decay' into their productions (2002: 152–3). The handheld camera work, the jerky movements, rough sound and low-level light generate an effect of 'embodied immediacy' (Hallas 2009: 31). If the previous images were watched with detachment, the video images mark a shift in viewers' affect as they witness what is happening in the here and now – especially in the hospital sequence, filmed exclusively on video. Ray's admission to hospital interrupts the shooting of the film. The scene before the video sequence shows Wenders and Farrell wondering where Ray and his wife are going as they catch a glimpse of them in a taxi. They were preparing a new scene, but once they return to the loft, the crew informs them that Ray did not feel well and insisted on going to the hospital. One of the crew members notes that Ray dictated an addendum to his will before going. Even though the scene is constructed (surprise is feigned), the interruption, signalled as well by the shift from film to video, underlines the conflict between a professionally planned shooting schedule and the live, personal reality that no such schedule can contain.

The video disappears about three quarters of the way through the film. Catherine Russell argues that the video images are contained by the dominant 35mm camera in an effort to repress the difference they articulate and sustain 'the illusion of cinema's triumph over time' (1995: 85). Even though Russell asks the question of how Ray's cancer fits into the film, her focus, like that of other film critics, remains on a largely allegorical[24] reading that also pays attention to the relationship between New German cinema and Hollywood. The 'narrative mortality' of Russell's book title is 'the allegory of the dialectic of cinematic realism and narrativity', and stands for the mortality of a certain idea of European art cinema in the 1980s that Wenders is bent on salvaging from the commercialisation of 'art cinema'. The effect of the film, and of Wenders' desire for a cinema with all the aura of Bazinian realism, can be approached as either 'melancholic' or 'redemptive' (68). While this reading appears too specialised, it resonates with broader concerns in the fields of illness narratives and the medical humanities. In particular, we can turn to the unresolved tension between images and narrative in the film, a topic many film scholars continue to debate,[25] which can be resituated to place illness and death at the centre rather than treat them as metaphors or allegories. Writing about consolation in illness narratives, Diedrich asks what happens when its structure 'breaks down and something else – beyond consolation – is glimpsed?' What are the implications for ethics when life's messiness or suffering cannot be redeemed through art? Her answer is that 'consolation is a conservative gesture, not an inventive one' as it 'implies a comfort in old, familiar forms' (2007: 140). In its experimentation with different forms and productive tension between visual and narrative technologies, *Lightning over Water* offers such glimpses. The film registers both the desire to redeem death through some of its more consolatory images and fictions *and* the ethical call not to displace Ray's embodied presence (and biological decay), even as this risks challenging cinema's life-preserving function. This is similar to the aesthetic collision between image and caption discussed in relation to breast cancer photographic narratives and the feminist politics of visibility in Chapter 1. As Wenders writes in 'Impossible Stories':

> I totally reject stories, because for me they only bring out lies, nothing but lies, and the biggest lie is that they show coherence where there is none. Then again, our need for these lies is so consuming that it's completely pointless to fight them and to put together a sequence of images without a story – without the lie of a story. Stories are impossible, but it's impossible to live without them. That's the mess I'm in. (2001: 218)

'Don't cut, CUT'

Even as the video images gradually disappear, a new medium of embodied immediacy penetrates the film: Ray's handwritten diary, which Susan gives to Wenders before he leaves for Los Angeles to meet with the production team of the film *Hammett* (which he was also shooting at the time). Wenders reads segments from the diary – an act of ventriloquism or appropriation that some critics have read as 'an authorial dissolve from one "director" to the other' (Margulies 1993: 60) and in line with the Oedipal framework of the film. Ray's writing at one point is superimposed over the image (including over aerial views of New York City), a graphic representation of the materiality of writing, as if the writing is on the film stock. Is this an acknowledgement of the superiority of writing over the visual image, perhaps an attempt to redress the act of appropriation and reassert Ray's presence via his writing? Instead, we could argue that what is emphasised here is an affinity between writing and cinematic language, their shared aura, their precious singularity threatened by the proliferation of electronic images in the case of cinema, and other technologies of writing, in the case of handwriting. Sobchack describes handwriting in terms of leaving 'marks on the world as an existential assertion of presence' (2004: 123), and the same could be said of cinema; Wenders has described it as 'a heroic act ... The camera is a weapon against the tragedy of things, against their disappearing' (2001: 160). Sobchack further notes that 'writing's relation to existential style is most materially figured in the eccentricity and "personality" of one's handwriting' (2004: 117). Despite the auratic quality that binds them to the cinematic image, the concrete shapes of the letters – in particular, the unsteady or laboured list of words in one of the pages of Ray's diary – functions as a continuation of the jerkiness of the video images and their embodied immediacy; they both draw attention to a body in crisis.

The content of the diary confirms this; the sections are the closest we get to Ray's reflections on his illness and how he is preparing himself to face death. Previous mentions of his condition (through the voice-over narration at the start) were reduced to references to his treatment of radiation and a dangerous surgery entailing implanting radioactive seeds to shrink the lung tumour – an 'adventure', according to his surgeon, that Ray, the eternal adventurer, did not hesitate to have;[26] and staged scenes, reminiscent of Spence's reconstruction of family gazes through phototherapy, such as the scene loosely adapted from *King Lear* in which Wenders' wife plays the role of Cordelia looking after her sick father Ray. This scene, in as much as it revolves around Ray's illness, attests to the ways in which, as Wenders comments in the film, 'reality was stronger than the fiction that we wanted to turn it into':

> Ray: The first time they opened me up they sewed me right back again. They thought no chance. So I moved out of that hospital and went to another one.
> Blakley: That was brave of you. What happened at the other one?
> ...
> Blakley: Did you lie [to mother]?
> ...
> Ray: Telling the truth becomes very dull, except sometimes not. Sometimes telling the truth becomes very exciting, because you never expect to tell it. Not all of it. And then when you find out you're up there, your face in front of God and everybody – and you're telling the truth. Hey, what am I doing? And you're exposing yourself. I mean this kind of truth.

The diary passages provide a first-person perspective that strikes us with its sincerity, given the former self-consciousness and textual fragmentation of the film: 'I want to live because I'll miss breathing. Must be very uncomfortable. Makes me angry if I can't breathe, taste and say hello ... I'm spitting blood and it panics me this morning with sadness. It's a gut and head panic I've never had before.' Death here becomes experienced as 'the visible cessation' of a lived body's 'intentional and responsive behavior' (Sobchack 2004: 235). Another entry that Wenders reads refers for the first time to a dialogue Ray had with his doctor:

> Today Susan asked Dr B., how does one overcome fear? Was she asking for her or for me? Dr B. looked at me and said, by confrontation. Vague enough – implying, I suppose, confronting that which you fear head-on. Hardly a remedy for the pain. How about love? Battle fear with love. Even the want to love will help. Even acting as if you do can help.

The theme of acting is given more space in the diary. Ray writes that 'to experience death without dying seemed like a natural goal for me'. This can be linked to symbolic deaths he has suffered in his films (two in the unfinished *We Can't Go Home Again*, for example). Those who are familiar with Ray's films will probably recognise several of his own heroes in *Lightning over Water*, especially their intention to reach to the very end of their powers, like Ray's best-known character in *Rebel without a Cause* (1955). But the experience of terminal illness also allows Ray to ironically perfect method acting, to which he remained tied as a director and actor. Ray tells Wenders in an earlier passage, 'An actor has to work from a character whose needs are his greatest needs – his greatest personal needs,' and in the diary he writes that 'an actor must speak each line as if it were the very first or the very last time it will ever be said by him'. In the context of Ray's dying of cancer, these statements acquire an added poignancy. As with the difficulty of drawing a clear distinction between an event's real or fictional status in performance art, the boundary between performance or acting (that is, art) and real life is extremely blurry in *Lightning over Water*. In this sense the film has affinities with Gómez-Peña's performances, despite their differences in terms of content. In one of the early scenes when Ray verbally expresses his pain, he asks Wenders, 'Does it seem like acting, Wim?' Wenders replies, 'No, not at all.' In the epilogue, one of the crew members marvels at the fact that Ray was 'acting the whole time, that's what was pretty amazing', but another member responds, 'I think he was hurting also.'

The boundaries of performance are stretched to their extreme in a long-held close-up of Ray – the last time we see him on camera. This moment is one of the rare occasions in the film when 'real' and 'represented time' are collapsed (Russell 1995: 79) and we are experiencing the sheer here and now of illness and even, it seems, of dying. The long take starts by showing Wenders in the hospital bed in what is clearly a studio scene, a continuation of the preceding Cordelia fictional sequence; but unlike the previous scene, which undoubtedly was scripted, here there is uncertainty as to what we are witnessing. Ray wearing an eye patch (like the one we had seen his double wearing in clips from *We Can't Go Home Again*) is seated next to Wenders, whose comments are heard off screen during the whole of the scene. Ray is shot frontally centre-frame, occasionally turning towards Wenders on the right of the frame. At one point Ray tells Wenders: 'You're making me sick to my stomach. You realize that? You are. I don't know why', and continues 'I'm sick. And not with you and not because of you.' It is an uncomfortable scene that implicates us as spectators even more as it is not Wenders who is fixing his gaze on Ray, but us, the viewers. The comment 'you're making me sick' followed by the contradictory clarification 'not with you and not because of you' returns us to the same ethical questions the film has been revolving around: are we voyeurs of Ray's dying, or is the film's refusal to avert its gaze from ill people a brave act, given the various ways the cinema is often implicated in displacing death? Is Ray sick in the sense of being disgusted by the pleasure we are taking from this spectacle? Or is he referring to literal nausea as a result of his illness? In any case, our sense of separation, despite the mediation of the camera, is compromised. The terminally ill body threatens to erupt, in this case to throw up before us, or even worse, die, confronting us with the vulnerability of our own mortality: 'I have to go now. I'm beginning to drool. Ah, *merde*.'

The viewers' desire at this point is to abject the diseased body and regain the distance erased by this scene. We are offered a kind of release through the 'cut' that eventually comes, even though delayed, and relieves us from the pain of watching. Ray says, looking directly at the camera: 'Don't cut, CUT'; this is his last living action on film, followed by the black leader that represents what cannot be represented – in other words, his death. The words 'don't cut', coming from Wenders and later from Ray, could be approached in terms of Garland-Thomson's account of staring in *Staring: How We Look*. Paying attention to the position of the 'staree' and *how* starees are stared at, as opposed to *whether* they are stared at (2009: 185), Garland-Thomson suggests that 'we become ethical starers by being conscious in the presence of something that compels our intense attention'; rather than forbidding us to stare, the stareable sight disturbs 'not just the visual status quo but the ethical status quo as well' (187–8). Writing in the more specific context of the role of theatre within medical education, Kate Rossiter argues something similar about performances that break the fourth wall and address their audiences directly. Their power lies in the ways they ask their viewers to witness, hear, see and notice without presuming to know the other's experience or being able to act to relieve such suffering. These moments may be particularly agonising for medical students, who are most of the time encouraged to respond to their patients through the immediate recourse to 'fix' them (2012: 14). We can recall here the Levinasian distinction between 'caress' and 'palpation' discussed in Chapter 2; how Hall's artists' books demand to be 'examined' in a radically different way that unsettles her doctors' usual routine. Likewise, the long take in *Lightning over Water* compels a special kind of attention, 'an ethical staring' that exceeds any models of empathic care or action which would aim to quickly close down the moment of witnessing opened by the scene.

The long take cuts to the Chinese junk sailing to the sea. The ribbons of 35mm film blowing in the wind from the camera bolted to the top next to the urn of Ray's ashes paradoxically evoke both Ray's immortality through his films (the power of cinematic technology fetishised) and the inability of cinema to preserve human life. Many critics have argued that the junk sailing to sea becomes a symbol of transcendence, timelessness and beauty that eludes death. It is noteworthy that this image comes directly after the long take in order to replace the terminally ill body in an attempt to contain death's violent unspeakability. Moreover, Ray's dream of a cure for cancer, captured in this image, offers a romantic view of cancer that fits Sontag's description of tuberculosis: 'The TB sufferer was a dropout, a wanderer in endless search of the healthy place. Starting in the early nineteenth century, TB became a new reason for exile, for a life that was mainly traveling ... There were special places thought to be good for tuberculars' (Sontag 1991: 34). Travelling, with its sense of irresponsibility (found in the romantic myth of TB), and exile or homelessness are of course dear to both Wenders' and Ray's films.

In the epilogue of the film, the crew inside the boat debate the different meanings of the junk:

> Becky Johnston: The whole thing with the junk was always between being a funeral boat and being a boat that was taking you to a cure for what you're dying from.
> Eddie Lachman: I never thought that he saw it as a cure ... a cure to something.
> Johnston: In the beginning it was – he was going to go off and find the cure to cancer ...
> Tom Farrell: He would have died sooner if it wasn't for this film ...
> Stephan Czapsky: He was looking for a solution to death in film that didn't exist in life.

The scene with the junk, and the film project more generally, is the remedy or treatment for Ray; not a cure in the literal sense, but, like Hall's artists' books, life-sustaining. The suggestion by some film scholars, as reflected in the above conversation between the film crew members, that deep down Ray knew all along that making a new film or finding a cure were 'fantasies' (Rosenbaum 2014: 16) reproduces the narrow medical view that all that matters is repairing one's health, and misrepresents the work of illness narratives: namely, how the representation of illness involves not only depicting being a cancer patient but 'world-making' (Radley 2009: 42). The idea of world-making encompasses the process of giving shape and form, which does not exclude mess, to experiences and feelings that cannot be communicated in any other way by either the person who is ill, or others who bear witness to their experiences. By executing the scene conceived by Ray, rather than seeing with Ray's own eyes, Wenders conjures a fragment from Ray's 'world of illness' (Radley 2009: 188) and invites the crew and the film's viewers to participate in that figured world.

The final words of *Lightning over Water* come from Wenders, who utters Ray's name – 'Nick. Nick. Nick' – while the image of the writing from his diary (superimposed on the film) includes Ray's signature at the end. The author's signature is meant to identify a work, to mark its singularity, but in a project that documents the death of the author, signing something with one's proper name (in order to own it) becomes especially poignant. The signature is not only signing the diary (where it is originally found) but also the film, which would have remained unfinished without Ray. As the crew stress in the epilogue, 'He made us finish. The only way he could do it was to die' – and they proceed to call his dying 'his last directorial assertion'. However, the signature, as Derrida reminds us, is never uniquely and purely one's own. It gains its power (for example, that of legal signatures) from the assumption of presence – the person who signs is present at the moment of the signature's production – but because it is repeatable, it can be detached from the signatory and his or her intentions, as in the case of this final scene, when the signature is superimposed on the film by Wenders. 'Corrupting' the signature's identity or purity, or 'dividing its seal' (Derrida 1977: 20) may raise the danger of counterfeiting, but could also be approached here as a condition for *sealing* the collaborative project between Ray and Wenders. *Lightning over Water*, like the signature that cannot give assurance of its intentions, does not resolve this ambiguity but affirms the need to continue creating new ways of looking at, and responding to, the experiences and relationships portrayed in the film.

Notes

1. See for example DeShazer 2013: 156–74.
2. On medical professionalism and professionalism in medical education, see ABIM Foundation, ACP-ASIM Foundation, European Federation of Internal Medicine 2002, Cohen 2007, Ludmerer 1999, Shapiro et al. 2009, Bleakley, Marshall and Brömer 2006, Charon 2006, Coulehan 2007 and Swick et al. 1999.
3. See also Shapiro's formulation of 'an ethics of imperfection' (2008: 10).
4. See Montgomery 2006: 3.
5. See Mulvey 1975.
6. Couser also uses the terms 'documemoir' and 'cinematic memoir' when considering the intersection of memoir with visual media (2012: 37; 28). A clear example of the former also characterised by generic multiplicity is Jonathan Caouette's *Tarnation* (2003).
7. The film's self-consciousness could be approached in relation to what Stella Bruzzi has described as 'performative documentary'. The performative documentary has 'an alternative honesty' as it does not seek to mask its inherent instability, including its relationship with fiction (2006: 187). Also see Scheibler 1993.
8. See Alarcón and Aguirre (2007) for using cinema to address palliative care and bioethics. The article makes a passing reference to Wenders' *Lightning over Water* suggesting, but not exploring, its relevance to bioethical questions.
9. For an overview of empathy in medical education see Shapiro 2012.
10. For the affinities of the cinematic and medical gaze in the field of medical education and humanities see Darbyshire and Baker 2012, Friedman 1995, Self and Baldwin 1990, Clark 2005, and Reagan, Tomes and Treichler 2007.

11. The son shares the father's hospital bed rather than the marriage bed and achieves empathy (see Corrigan 1985). Given the complex role of American influences in Wenders' work, many film critics explore (Oedipal) conversations between Wenders and other contemporary European directors who came to prominence in the seventies, and their American cinematic patrimony.
12. It is not accidental that *Lightning over Water* is interested in another unfinished or difficult film: Ray's project about the situation and emotions of youth in America at the start of the 1970s, which came to be worked (and then endlessly reworked) into an experimental form using multiple screens.
13. I have borrowed the term 'terminal care', also used in the chapter title, from the film's description on the Wim Wenders Stiftung website, <http://wimwendersstiftung.de/en/film/nicks-film-lightning-over-water-2/> (last accessed 27 July 2015).
14. *The American Friend* describes the odd pact that develops between the American entrepreneur Ripley and the Swiss-German craftsman and terminally ill Jonathan, whom Ripley involves in a series of murders. For the visual and aural echoes of this film in *Lightning over Water*, see Geist 1981–2.
15. See also Corrigan 1985.
16. Wenders had never been in a film before.
17. Influenced by director Jerzy Grotowski, Ray emphasises the importance of the actors (finding their 'action') when it comes to executing a scene rather than framing or lighting (Ray et al. 1993: 209).
18. A more faithful example shot exclusively with a handheld video camera is the 1993 documentary *Silverlake Life: The View from Here* directed by Peter Friedman and Tom Joslin, which documents the couple's final months of living with AIDS.
19. When, twenty-six years later, Wenders appeared in *Back to Room 666* (a film by Gustavo Spolidoro, who asked him the same question), his answer – this time next to a laptop rather than a TV – is that he could not believe the cultural pessimism that he and others felt in the early 1980s. In his view, the cinema today is more alive than ever, and can only gain from the undiscovered possibilities of digital technology.
20. See Cartwright 1995.
21. A film that tries to merge systems together can only be monstrous, Wenders adds in this film, recalling the analogy between cancer and video images in *Lightning over Water*.
22. Given, though, that electrons and photons constitute the electronic image, it has its own materiality or 'body'. For a materialist understanding of digital media, see Marks 2002.
23. In *Notebook on Cities and Clothes*, Wenders offers a similar revelation in the middle of the film: 'Suddenly, in the middle of a Tokyo street, I realized that the image proper to this city could very well be an

electronic image and not only one of my so-called "sacred" celluloid images. In its own language, this video camera could seize this city in an APPROPRIATE way. I was amazed' (2001: 126).
24. See also Burnett's view that 'Ray, the outsider of Hollywood despite his early success, is dying and with him one age of cinema is in terminal decline because it has excluded him' (1981: 12).
25. See Cool and Gemünden 1997.
26. See Ray et al. 1993: 297. Nick had two lung and one brain surgeries in 1977–8. The diary entries in this book that draw on his illness experience contain an intriguing dream which, according to Ray's interpretation, communicates something about the appropriateness of his lack of fear. Many of the entries confirm his will to be able to 'function' for as long as possible and 'do the things I can do within the limitations under which I must work' (Ray 1993: 166–7).

Chapter 5

Messy Confrontations: Theatre and Expert Knowledge

Acquiring a vaudeville-style education among performers such as Deb Margolin, Peggy Shaw and Lois Weaver when she moved to the East Village in the 1980s, Lisa Kron, an American performer known for her edgy autobiographical one-woman shows, developed a very dynamic connection to her audience. What her solo work tries to create is the impression that the performer is not dissimilar from a storyteller, appearing herself in front of an audience and speaking to them directly as if for the first time. The production notes of her autobiographical performance *2.5 Minute Ride* (1996) describe the atmosphere she aspires to create: 'The sense should not be that the performer entered the room with every word planned out, but that the energy exchanged by the teller and the listener is building the story in the moment and taking it in unforeseen directions' (Kron 2001: 4). Even plays like *Well* that draw on more traditional theatrical conventions seek to create the kind of 'presence' and the sense of an event's unavailability for re-presentation (even as it can be re-staged several times) that gives performance art its unique power. Like Wenders' film *Lightning over Water*, which negotiates the tension between documentation and narrative in the representation of Ray's illness and dying, *Well* uses a mixture of forms to explore questions of health and illness drawing on Ann Kron's story, and relies on the collision between autobiographical performance and theatrical convention to interrogate the criteria of its successful treatment of these questions.

Well, directed by Leigh Silverman, received its world premiere at the Public Theater in New York on March 16, 2004 and opened on Broadway at the Longacre on March 30, 2006. Unlike Margaret Edson's 1993 play *Wit*,[1] widely used in medical curricula, with which it shares some similarities (for example, the use of humour and metafictional elements), Kron's play is not as familiar to medical communities. This fact returns us to the question that many of the chapters of this book have posed: what do we bring into medical education and medical humanities, and why? In advancing what I have called critical interloping I have shown that it is important not only to introduce a diverse range of material, but also to engage with different critical and interdisciplinary methods, in order to prevent the field from becoming in the future what Stephen Pattison has described as a 'paramedical academic discipline' (2003: 36). Addressing topics such as end-of-life treatment, the doctor-patient relationship and the ethics of initiating or avoiding a resuscitation attempt after a patient's death is what has established *Wit*'s relevance for medical ethics and narrative medicine programmes. While the inclusion of experiential pedagogical methods such as performance complements more traditional ones, bringing something new to medical education, it also risks reproducing instrumentalising engagements with the play that focus merely on content and its direct relevance to particular medical issues.[2] The Wit Educational Initiative notes that 'although postperformance survey responses [shown in their publications through various charts] may not reflect the play's long-term impact, we regard the play's success at eliciting strong emotional responses [in trainees] as encouraging'. Their emphasis on establishing 'a supportive and *noncritical* environment' where medical students can experience emotions in a safe context (Lorenz et al. 2004: 485, emphasis added), while doubtless important, conceptualises the medical humanities in purely humanistic rather than critical terms as well. The use of 'noncritical' in the passage above, it could be countered, means an environment that is not negative or counterproductive; but this is precisely the point. As demonstrated in the preceding chapters, we need both receptive/supportive and critical encounters with difference that do not shy away from discomfort and difficulty. In both form and content, just as Wenders' film does, *Well* addresses several wider questions about professional competence, artistic practice and the politics of health that intersect with medical concerns while resisting the current drive towards a narrow and measurable relevance.

Well is structured on the basis of a series of oppositions that are deconstructed and debated as the play progresses. The first of these is between the personal and the universal. At the start of the play, Lisa, Kron's theatrical alter ego, tells the audience that the play they are about to see is not about her mother and herself. Instead, it is a play that deals with 'issues of illness and wellness' (2006a: 11).[3]

As Lisa continues, the play asks 'universal' questions such as, 'Why are some people sick and other people well?' Why do some people stay sick whereas others get better? The urgency with which Lisa repeatedly emphasises throughout the play that it is '*not* about my mother and me', or about why her mother has been sick for years while she got better, is enough to convey the opposite to the audience, notably that the play is also about these things.[4] But, as Lisa puts it, reading from the note card she is holding, the play 'uses those things as a vehicle for "a multi-character theatrical exploration of issues of health and illness both in the individual and in a community"' (12). Already the other oppositions at the heart of the play are revealed: health and illness, and illness in the individual and the community. The former is dramatised through the division of the stage: one portion, Lisa's world, is flexible, allowing for the other scenes (the Allergy Unit and the Neighbourhood scenes) to assemble and disperse, whereas her mother's portion is cluttered with tables, shelves and drawers filled with books and magazines, crammed into a claustrophobically small world that Lisa has escaped. Lisa's preamble also draws attention to the division between art and reality: the play the audience is about to see will consist of another play, or intended play, for which Kron has hired characters. The opposition between art and reality is contained within a theatrical (in other words, fictional) structure, of course. Nevertheless, it is foregrounded, ushering the audience into the world of metatheatre.

With the insistence that *Well* is about more than just her relationship with her mother, Lisa reiterates Kron's view that 'the goal of autobiographical material should not be to tell stories about yourself but, instead, to use the details of your own life to illuminate or explore something more universal' (2001: xi). Given the confessional trend characterising our contemporary context, this is perhaps a way to anticipate common criticisms against memoirs, 'misery literature' and life narratives across different media, more broadly. Such an attempt is precarious, as indicated in one of the less favourable reviews of the play:

> For 100 navel-gazing minutes [*Well*] seems about to expire from an overdose of therapy-speak and terminal cuteness ... Lisa is quite vehement that this is a show about 'universal themes' and not about her relationship with her mum, yet ... [t]his is drama as therapy (only it is the audience who pays for it), dressed up in a Pirandellian box of tricks that does not bear close examination. (Gardner 2009)

When a story, even an experimental one, participates in recognisable structures, conventions and genres such as the mother–daughter narrative, it is difficult to counter the powerful hold of certain assumptions and expectations that are created.

Lisa's opening statement, irrespective of whether the play achieves this goal, could be read as an invitation to the audience not merely to consume another personal story but to critically reflect on the kind of broader issues the playwright wants to raise. This Brechtian appeal to reason rather than simply emotions continues every time Lisa, breaching the fourth wall, explains to the audience the mechanisms behind the play. She notes, for example, that she intends to look 'at some scenes back and forth from the neighborhood and from when I was in the Allergy Unit to see if we can find some resonances and some parallels between those stories of healing' (18). Breaking the identification with the characters and the theatre of illusions through this gesture bears similarities to the stories Kron told about her Holocaust-survivor father and her Jewish family in her earlier and better-known play *2.5 Minute Ride*. She has described these stories as serving 'as a template, a framework into which audiences project their own relationships and experiences' (2001: 3). This is indicated, for instance, by Kron's choice to use an empty slide frame, that is, not show the photographs of her grandparents that she describes verbally to the audience during the performance, thus prompting a practice of witnessing that goes beyond recognition, as described in Chapter 2. Even though this choice prevents the passive consumption and mythologisation of the Holocaust, by not showing the images and letting the audience project their own, her grandparents' individual experiences are in danger of being erased. A similar danger haunts *Well*, bringing the tension between the particular and the general, and the ethics of witnessing, to bear upon the more specific questions of health and illness.

'A solo show with other people in it': relational narratives of illness

The intention to tell a story of wider significance and encourage a public discussion about health and illness, though laudable, is fraught with risk. This is because Kron draws on her mother's own experience with long-term allergies for this story. In reality, as Deirdre Heddon notes, Kron interviewed her mother for this play and 'according to

Kron a lot of the words in *Well* are her mother's' (2008: 155). In this sense, the play is not far from verbatim theatre, also known as theatre of testimony or documentary theatre. This kind of theatre is often described as giving a 'voice to the voiceless' (Heddon 2008: 128) and as a democratising force.[5] However, given that verbatim theatre uses actors to perform auto/biographical testimonies of other people, it also raises the kinds of questions that have been debated in relation to life writing and illness memoirs (by both patients and doctors): Which stories of illness get to be told, and who tells them? Moreover, who is the protagonist of these stories? In contrast to her previous one-woman shows, *Well* features other characters, so the mother has the opportunity to intervene in the process of telling her story. This is not Kron's actual mother (even though, as reported by Kron, audiences frequently think that it is her actual mother who is on stage).[6] In the play Ann, or rather the actor who plays her, wants to know who Lisa is 'using to explore' the topics of health and illness. Lisa's defensive response, 'I don't know what you mean by "using"' (16) shows her awareness of her responsibility towards her mother, and is a way the play begins to expose the problematic structure of documentary theatre even as it participates in this genre.

The problem with what, following Paul John Eakin, we could call 'relational' narratives (1999: 43) – that is, narratives by a proximate other (a parent, a child, a sibling, or an intimate) – is that it is difficult to decide whether a specific incident or story from someone's biography belongs only to them. In the case of *Well*, unlike *Lightning over Water*, Ann's illness is as much a part of her own life story as it is of Lisa's; Lisa also got ill and, as the play unfolds, we find out that she blames her mother for her inability to get better while she was staying at home. Does this give her the right to tell or draw on this story, or would this violate her mother's privacy? Relational narratives are interesting precisely because the ambivalence of their writers towards their projects demonstrates how difficult it is to provide a simple answer to such a question. I would agree with Eakin that the genre 'seems to embrace, conceptually, the reality of relational identity, the structuring bond between self and other, but the desire for ... authorship persists' (1999: 181). This ambivalence is expressed in theatrical language in *Well* through Kron's paradoxical description of her play as 'a solo show with other people in it' (16).

Even though Kron is primarily known for her performance work within the women's theatre collective the WOW Café, she has always been interested in experimenting with form and extending her autobiographical performances. *Well* brings together traditional theatre, memory play (through the use of flashbacks, and in particular the scenes of the Allergy Unit and the Neighbourhood meetings that become assembled on stage) and autobiographical performance. In her preface Kron describes it as developing out of an 'aesthetic collision' between solo performance and more traditional theatrical structure (ix), which means that other characters need to be used, a tension that the play dramatises and uses for various effects, as I will show. The paradox of 'a solo show with other people in it' is acknowledged towards the end when Lisa, exasperated by the interruptions of her play, admits: 'I was a solo performer for a long time, you know. It's a lot easier to do your own thing than dealing with a bunch of "characters" criticizing what they don't really know anything about' (67).

After her initial dialogue with her mother, Lisa steps into her 'special light', 'literally a square of isolated light', as described in the stage directions (8), and speaks confidentially to the audience. The fourth wall has already been breached with Lisa's opening remarks and especially when Ann, seeing the audience for the first time, throws them packages of chips and cookies at the start of the production. The special light is meant to create a double opaque wall isolating Ann from both Lisa and the audience, even though later this wall is pierced too. Addressing the audience, Lisa admits that she is exploring some 'emotionally touchy topics' that she hasn't discussed with her mother. Appealing to the audience to become almost complicit in this exploration, she reveals that there are some issues she and her mother do not agree upon but promises that this play is not going to be a 'messy "confrontation"' with her. Instead, the particular staging decisions and conventions she will follow will allow her to explore these issues in 'a professional, theatrical context' even though her mother, not being 'a theater person', cannot appreciate them (17–18). With this confidential dialogue Lisa, as the narratorial agent, dictates the shape of the play and manipulates the spectators' reactions, and Kron introduces the theme of *expert knowledge*. This theme does not only apply to the world of theatre but also, as we will see, to issues of health and illness as well as to politics.

The 'professional theatrical structure' Lisa defends at the start of the play progressively reveals its fissures as the intended play becomes interrupted by both Ann and the characters in a clear Pirandellian conceit.[7] The stage directions describe this in the following way: 'As the play continues, we see their standard actor show-must-go-on ethic erode as they ... start to find Ann a more compelling source of information, entertainment and warm human connection' (7). This is a mechanism through which, as we also read in the preface of the play, Kron and her actors can 'flip back and forth in their relationship with the audience from being a performer on stage to being a person in a room with many other people' (xi). Even though the audience is not implicated in the same way, this picture is not altogether different from what we encountered in Chapter 4, where the experience, rather than the film with the name *Lightning over Water*, matters more for Wenders. In other words, both works are characterised by a mixture of authenticity and theatricality. The climax in *Well* comes when the actor who plays Ann (Jayne Houdyshell in the Broadway production) breaks her character and demands that Lisa rewrite her ending because it is 'small', 'trite' and 'not right' (73). At the end Lisa is left alone on the stage, questioning her project and the original shape she desperately tried to give it. This outcome is not just the result of a self-indulgent experiment, even though some reviews have approached it in this way by missing the significance of Kron's turn to the metatheatrical. Instead, I would argue that it has the capacity to raise a number of more serious questions about the role of 'the professional' in theatre, the opposition between the general and the particular, and the place of uncertainty and failure within performance.

Professional structures and expert knowledge

Lisa's chosen approach, as she insists throughout the play, will allow her to explore issues of health and illness 'in a professional, theatrical context. And it will also make the process much easier on [my mother]. Because she's not a theater person, you know, so she doesn't quite get that there's a plan in motion here' (18). With this condescending tone, Lisa asserts the need to draw on her superior knowledge of theatrical convention to tell her mother's stories. Like Edson's protagonist Vivian Bearing in *Wit*, a scholar of poetry who revels in John Donne's witty approach to life and death only to find her expert knowledge lacking in the end, Lisa tries to hide under complicated dramatic conventions. However, inserting her mother's stories within a theatrical structure involves ruthless editing and simplification, as Ann's interruptions gradually but persistently reveal. This is one mechanism through which *Well* witnesses and thus criticises its tendency to inflict symbolic violence. For example, when Lisa has finished rehearsing one of the Neighbourhood meeting scenes, Ann responds, 'That seemed awfully compressed.' Lisa once more falls back on her expert knowledge and counters that it was a 'montage'; rather than all the details, she is 'aiming for the overall effect' (25). Condensing, simplifying, generalising and leaving important things out is the result of the desire to impose sense or coherence, to 'make all the parts fit together', as Lisa puts it (74), in order to give comfort and shield oneself from the messiness of life. In *Lightning over Water* a similar desire confronted by the film often took the form of displacing reality into fiction by both Wenders and Ray.

Kron's treatment of her mother's story is transferable to the context of the clinical encounter. Like *Wit*, which establishes links between medicine and academic life, *Well*'s critique of expert theatrical knowledge connects, albeit more implicitly, to ongoing discussions about performance, power inequalities and the exercise of distance and impersonality within medicine. Due to lack of time and the need to conserve energy, the difficulty of responding to suffering as well as the 'spirit of abstraction' that characterises medicine (Shapiro 2008: 4), a number of dimensions of the patient's experience that are not directly relevant to the diagnosis have to be left out (as we have seen in Chapter 2). As Johanna Shapiro writes, 'modern medicine promotes a kind of *scientific* altruism ... ('cognate professionalism') that still encourages approaching the patient, albeit as an object of interest, rather than a sympathetic subject. The fear and vulnerability underlying withdrawal are addressed by efforts at mastery and control' (4). Lisa's frustrated interruptions of her mother's attempts to provide detailed information thus resonate with doctors' efforts to redirect their patients' conversations so that they furnish only 'relevant' information, and in some cases, to force patients to accept their authoritarian version.[8]

Similarly, the scenes where Lisa withdraws into 'the special light' to confide in the audience, without her mother being able to hear, draw attention to the 'othering' effected by 'professional' or expert theatrical conventions. This becomes apparent if we move from the aesthetic representation (the play) to social drama (the clinical encounter).[9] The theatrical device of the fourth wall, more specifically its different positions and didactic functions for communication training, has featured among the topics of medical education. One of the positions examined in such work, which uses a role-play model that imitates a theatrical performance and incorporates Brechtian and Boalian techniques, is similar to the double opaque wall created by the special light in *Well*. In the medical role-play, Lisa's discussion of her mother with the audience would be the equivalent of a doctor's (or medical student's) discussion of his or her patient with the audience/medical team '*as if* [the patient] *was not there*, even though she was sitting among them' (Jacobsen et al. 2006). Through this exercise, students can be reminded that in real life they should never talk about their patients without taking notice of their presence. In *Well*, Ann breaks this double opaque wall forcing the audience and Lisa to reflect about the ethics of such a situation:

> Ann: You get out of that ... special ... light and stay here and deal with me.
> *(A stunned pause).*
> Lisa: Can you hear me?
> Ann: Yes, of course. It's a spotlight, not a sound-proof booth.
> *(The special light dissolves, leaving Lisa exposed in every way).* (70)

The professional structure Lisa defends throughout the production, whether this illuminates theatrical or medical practice, also takes us to the case, which medicine, psychoanalysis, law, the humanities and the sciences are founded upon. Even though Kron is not strictly approaching her mother as a case (more like 'an example'), Lauren Berlant's thoughts on this genre elucidate the situation we are presented with in *Well*. Berlant notes that the case is always 'pedagogical', promising to 'generate an account of a situation that is recognizable enough that people can debate about it' (2007: 665). She describes it as 'a genre that organizes singularities into exemplary, intelligible patterns ... a professional genre' (670) and interrogates 'the fate' of singularity 'in exemplifying narratives and expert commentary' (672). Lisa's argument with Jayne about the questions the play is asking covers similar ground:

> Lisa: The play is asking really hard questions.
> Jayne: I think they're the wrong questions.
> Lisa: They are the whole point! You don't think every person sitting there has some personal relationship to these questions? There are people out there who are sick – there are people there who are taking care of someone's who's sick. We can't jerk them around. They want to know; Why are some people sick and other people get well? ... The purpose of this entire endeavor was to give coherence to things that are really confusing. Because otherwise it's too messy. Otherwise it's too overwhelming.
> Jayne: You mean she's [your mother] too overwhelming.
> Lisa: ... She's overwhelming to me. That's why I wrote a play. But you're right. It doesn't work. She doesn't make any sense. She doesn't make a bit of sense as a character. (74–5)

Jayne suggests that Lisa is hiding behind the play; in other words, the 'professional structure', even though it is justified persistently for raising broader questions, serves as a shield that allows Lisa to keep her distance from her mother. She has become a project or a character (and even then her singularity is not important) rather than a human being. Jayne reminds her what Kron has herself admitted in reference to *2.5 Minute Ride*: namely, that she began to forget that her father was a real person. 'I had to remind myself [to] stay actively engaged with this person. He's not just a character in your play. He is still this real person' (quoted in Heddon 2008: 147). Lisa's previous statement that her mother 'doesn't know the rules of theater' brings to mind the distinction between professional and amateur theatre that was intriguing to both Brecht and Walter Benjamin. As Bailes describes it, 'In contrast to bourgeois theatre, the forcelessness and weakness of amateur performance can illuminate the ideological re-enforcement mastery performs, whilst work that falls below certain standards and criteria can indicate alternative versions of the world that do not re-enforce the dominant image of the world' (2011: 35). The mother's interruptions can be construed as indexes of amateurship, which do not lack in power and authority as gradually the actors find Ann's stories more interesting than Lisa's intended play. Even though they do not expose the economy of value and exchange in the bourgeois theatre, as in Brecht's epic theatre, they function as alienation effects that break the integrity of the 'professional structure' and expose the ways the universal themes treated through this vehicle elide problematic questions of power and responsibility.

Ann's interruptions are also linked to her chronic illness. Every time her mother interrupts the plan to draw attention to simplifications, Lisa becomes frustrated and more afraid; there is a parallel between Lisa's fear of becoming like her mother – even though she has managed to escape her illness, sick people like her mother, with their beliefs in sickness, 'pull her down' (69), she reveals later – and her resistance to have the professional structure become 'infected' by someone who does not know the rules of theatre. In some ways, the mother's interruptions in *Well* function like the interspersed video images in Wenders' film – in other words, as a source of infection. What both Kron and Wenders are called upon to decide is whether they are going to allow their own agendas and visions to be affected (and infected) by such alternative treatments of their stories. We have seen in Chapter 4 that Wenders incorporates such technologies, which allow him to continue recording even when the professional shooting has to be interrupted but also interrupt the kind of bodily displacement that characterises the dominant iconography of death in the cinema and ensures its life-preserving function. Kron also suspects from the start that the professional structure she has chosen will not sustain enough pressure. As Lisa says earlier in the play when the actors rebel, 'this avant-garde meta-theatrical thing will just bite you in your ass!' (68). This is an example of the play's mocking of the very same conventions it uses; something that the audience realises much earlier than Lisa's character. *Well* ends with a more serious realisation, namely that integration (both in the community and in a play) means 'weaving into the whole even the parts that are uncomfortable or don't seem to fit' (76). Like Wenders, Kron's alter ego learns to accept generic multiplicity and 'incoherence' as necessary to the story she is trying to shape. Rather than sources of infection, these features become emblems of 'wellness' and end up enriching her work, despite her initial intention of maintaining authorial agency and a particular pattern.

Kron's work has been described as concentrating 'less on the success or failure of endeavor than on the striving – the places where human beings stumble – where we are derailed by awkwardness, grandiosity, pretentiousness, vanity'.[10] Ultimately, *Well* is not driven by who knows the most about theatre, or by a conventional 'show-must-go-on ethic' on the part of the actors. Jayne's interruption when she breaks character to challenge Lisa's ending, as she is about to 'wrap it all up and tie it together' (73), promotes a different kind of ethic resulting from the failed attempt to make sense through art; as Lisa says, '[Ann] doesn't make sense as a character … I can't make her make sense' (75). Rather than a failure, this turn of events is as much about the volatile process of telling a story, the limitations and difficulties when things do not go as planned, as about the need to continue telling the story. As Bailes writes about failure, it 'has the capacity to sustain desire even as it thwarts it' and is thus linked to 'hope', which turns it into 'a driver in the attempt to continue' despite interruption (2011: 12). We have seen before how the fourth-wall convention, and the way it is breached in the play, allows reflection on what is ethical or unethical that could be instructive in the context of medical education. Outside the more conventional field of communication skills training, *Well* can be 'useful' to medical communities in terms of exploring uncertainty, or 'the striving', as Kron puts it.

Building on Bailes' interest in the discourse of failure within artistic practice, Emma Brodzinski has gestured towards the need to explore what performance theatre, especially the work of experimental companies interested in vulnerability, fragility and failure, can offer to the medical humanities.[11] As she argues, 'highlighting the shortcomings of a performance' can help reconfigure the idea of 'the professional' or how successful performance can be measured not just for performers and their audiences but also for medical practitioners (2014: 182–3). Healthcare provision is assessed through a number of performance indicators and criteria. The focus is on delivering results, but following the work of many performance companies, this emphasis can be resituated so that it falls on process rather than product (Brodzinski 2010: 158–9). In *Well*, promises of coherence are made in the play at different points, but at the same time the performance's shortcomings are emphasised both in terms of the exchanges between characters and the ways of acting such scenes. The actors' ability to perform their roles is not left untouched by the events that unfold on the stage between Ann and Lisa. As the stage directions explain, once an interrupted scene is resumed, 'Lisa's anger over A's [one of the actors designated in this way] betrayal and A's vulnerability from the quiet catharsis she's just had with Ann, color the way they play this scene with each other' (45). As Lisa's exchanges with her mother become more uncomfortable to witness, the actors apologise to the audience: 'We don't really have anything to do with it. We were just hired to be in it' (64), while after they leave, Lisa reassures them that 'this whole thing is gonna come together' (68). Ultimately the play comes together not by providing neat answers to the questions it asks, but by making room to express the difficulty and uncertainty surrounding these questions.[12]

These aspects which the performance foregrounds can open up productive ways for medical students to prepare for clinical uncertainty and accidents arising from team miscommunication in their own professional lives. Like Gómez-Peña, Kron shows her commitment to more critical pedagogical methods that replace blueprints with a language of possibility. As she has stated in an interview, when she teaches her students she asks them to 'reconstruct events' and 'to remember what the experience was before it was organized into a narrative' (2006b). She adds, 'I want them to learn to be innocent of the conclusion; in life, none of us have any idea what the next moment is going to bring. And that's the effect that must be achieved in drama – even in autobiographical solo shows.' Perhaps if medical students were to explore uncertainty and the challenges of the live event in dialogue with performance actor students, it would be mutually beneficial in encouraging both groups to think more broadly and creatively about distinct aspects of their profession. It might, for example, help turn the focus away from some of the prevalent genres within the culture of medicine such as 'the epic, dark comic and tragic'. The epic is associated with medicine's heroic interventions; tragedy characterises 'acute', 'emergency' and 'intensive' care; and the comic genre, 'the medical profession's long-standing secret', where staff let off steam behind their patients' backs, is now 'publicly advertised as a common theme for medical television soap operas' (Bleakley and Marshall 2012: 51). The dominance of such genres overshadows and closes off other possibilities – one such alternative, which emphasises care rather than cure, is Bleakley and Robert Marshall's 'lyrical' genre. To this alternative we could add a hybrid genre, like the one presented by *Well*, that confuses neat categories and in drawing attention to the fragility of joint/broken narratives shows how difficulty, inadequacy and the will to scrutinise and rework existing 'professional' practices can generate *other* ways of performing.

In the preface to *Well*, Kron writes that 'both the form and the content of the play have all along been about making room enough to allow life to spill over in all its contradictory messiness' (xii). I have considered so far the formal aspects of *Well* and specifically the ways the professional structure breaks open to reveal something not planned; this is both theatrically exciting – 'it makes the audience feel the electricity of something happening right now in this moment in this theater' (Kron xi), something that solo work cannot deliver – and instructive (in a broader, rather than utilitarian, sense) for both performers and medical practitioners. The unplanned or 'authentic encounters' that erupt, though not involving the audience to the degree that Gómez-Peña's interactive performances do, raise ethical questions and make room for uncertainty or difficulty. I want to turn now to the content of the play, namely its alleged preoccupation with universal questions of health and illness. The statement above that the content of the play, like the form, had been all along in the service of making room for life to 'spill over' runs the risk of suggesting that health and illness were merely pretexts for creating dramatic conflict. This would signify another level of betrayal to the mother's real story; rather than addressing important questions about health and illness, it has been aestheticised and used to create tension or entertain the audience. What does this play reveal, then, about the experiences of sickness and wellness in the individual and the community?

Illness and wellness in the individual and the community

As we have seen, *Well* opens with Lisa's statement that the play she is about to present to the audience deals with issues of illness and wellness. The choice of the word *wellness* rather than health, and the title of the play (why not *unwell* instead?) are significant. Does the play judge those who cannot become well – like Kron's mother, a member of 'the remission society' (Frank 1995: 8) – or point to a state of well-being that goes beyond strict medical understandings of health to encompass other spheres of life? Kleinman's classic definitions of disease and illness in *The Illness Narratives* are complemented by a third term, 'sickness', defined as 'the understanding of a disorder in its generic sense across a population in relation to macrosocial (economic, political, institutional) forces' (1988: 6). Even though Kron's use of 'sickness' does not strictly follow Kleinman's description, the play moves away from the narrowly medical and shifts the conception of the patient from the individual to the collective sphere through the theme of racial integration. Kron's mother was involved in long efforts to integrate their neighbourhood during the fifties and sixties, and was the president of the West Side Neighborhood Association. When this theme is first introduced in the play through the Neighbourhood meeting scenes, the neighbourhood where Kron lived in Lansing, Michigan is described as 'terminally ill' (23). Even though her mother, Lisa tells us, was not able to 'heal' herself, she managed to 'heal a neighborhood' (11). From the outset, then, and through the alternation of the Allergy Unit and Neighbourhood meeting scenes (the same actors play the characters in both environments), the play strongly suggests that hospitals are not the only places where treatment takes place and that allergies are not the only ailments that need cure.

Well explores not only treatment in the individual and the community, but also different kinds of individual treatment through the mother and daughter's distinct responses to their ill health. In this way, *Well* foregrounds the many narratives of illness both in terms of form, as discussed earlier, and content. Lisa's attitude to health and illness can be gleaned at the start of the play, when she says that even though she got well, she is not able to help her mother: 'But then when you get home, what you realize is that your parents live in an alternate universe where your therapy has no power' (12). What follows is the 'theatrical exploration' of these ideas. Lisa starts by explaining that she comes from a family where illness is the norm; as she characteristically says, 'it's the way we keep time' (13), suggesting that it has become inseparable from life history. She lists a number of what she calls 'recognizable' or 'identifiable' illnesses, like cancer, heart disease and diabetes, that some of her family members have, and then turns to 'the family mystery illness – the general inability to move, to physically cope, to stay awake' (13). Unlike the aforementioned illnesses, which have been medicalised and have stable labels, her mother's condition is described as a 'malady', which dictionaries associate with a chronic or 'morbid and desperate condition'.[13] The word choice indicates disbelief on the part of the daughter, and a sense of frustration at her mother's exaggerated lament or refusal to give up her belief in this condition. This is also conveyed in the ironic tone of the following words: 'My mother attributes her condition to "allergies." To my mother allergies are a highly underrated, sinister, life-destroying force that is kept secret from us by the evil AMA-controlled medical establishment' (13). Once more the daughter affirms her superior knowledge by discrediting the mother's diagnosis, explaining that her condition today 'would probably be labelled chronic fatigue syndrome or fibromyalgia' (13). Lisa seems to repeat here the kind of delegitimisation of their illness experience that both CFS patients and patients of multiple chemical sensitivity (MCS) have suffered, and in many ways continue to suffer.

Both CFS and MCS are contested illnesses; they are difficult to diagnose and treat, as they are largely based on symptoms reported by patients rather than clinical signs and markers. CFS has remained a syndrome rather than a disease (it was named and defined in 1988), but MCS has not been given legitimacy as a diagnosis by the American Medical Association, and many doctors consider those who validate their patients' views by providing organic causes to be mere charlatans. Chronic fatigue, also known as ME (myalgic encephalomyelitis), often shakes medical practitioners' claims to competence and authority, and because of the uncertainty surrounding its diagnosis and treatment, which equally characterises MCS, some doctors resort to outright dismissal of their patients' symptoms or deploy more subtle avoidance strategies.[14] As Alison Reiheld (2010) explains about the history of CFS, typically the patients who complained about it were female and before the nineties the majority of them encountered responses by physicians that dismissed their symptoms or attributed them to psychosomatic causes. Ann confirms this in the play when she mentions that one of the doctors told her she had 'Tired Housewives Syndrome' (37); a label that refutes the idea of an organic cause for her condition. CFS patients have been treated as hypochondriacs or present-day neurasthenics by many social historians; in their view, CFS sufferers are 'somatizers' who shape their symptoms from cultural and media narratives that have contributed to the proliferation of 'modern psychological epidemics' and fashionable disease theories (Shorter 1992; Showalter 1997: 131). Similarly, because MCS affects some people but not others and is caused by toxins and chemical substances that are part of everyday life, it is dismissed as another contemporary form of hysteria[15] even as there is increasing interest in the environmental sources of contemporary illness as well as in environmental medicine.[16] Despite the increase of medical studies about potential organic causes for these conditions, the majority of doctors and researchers today view them as psychological syndromes.

Ann's belief in the Allergy Unit, the place 'where they took allergies seriously' (18) – this was the Ecology Unit of Henrotin Hospital in Chicago, operated between 1983 and 1986 by Dr Theron G. Randolph, who pioneered an alternative approach to allergies[17] – is a welcome alternative to orthodox medical thinking. Conventional medicine has often dismissed the fatigue and debilitating pain of chronically ill people as being 'all in their heads'. But Lisa disputes her mother's interpretation that her daughter got well because she spent time in the Allergy Unit. Lisa believes that she recovered through a different mixture of treatments after she left home. Ann's wish to medicalise her chronic fatigue, in the sense of attributing an organic cause to it, is not necessarily a conservative gesture. Considering the history of CFS as well as other conditions, I would agree with Reiheld (2010) that medicalisation is a complex process which does not simply reinforce unjust social structures in a straightforward way, but can also contribute to destigmatisation and demarginalisation by legitimising ill people's experiences of their own bodies. Of course it also raises important questions about how physical and psychological conditions are perceived in the wider cultural imagination and why there is a tendency to consider the former more 'real' or legitimate than the other, thus perpetuating the stigma attached to psychiatric and even social explanations of illness. A scene that opens these questions for further reflection is when the actor named A tells Ann of her feeling of sickness when she goes to a mall, which annoys her friends. Ann explains that it is an allergic reaction to the 'formaldehyde fumes in all the merchandise' and gives her a copy of a document that confirms this, imparting her knowledge about allergies. A responds, 'I just thought it was some spiritual response to consumerist culture' (43), and is relieved to discover that she is not to blame. The incident concludes with Ann's point, via Sontag's work, about the psychological and moralistic assumptions surrounding mysterious illnesses that disappear once the 'medical root of the illness' is discovered by scientific medicine (44). According to this view, the only 'proper' illness is organic, while everything else is reduced to a form of moral weakness.

If Ann's words are indicative of her faith in the biomedical model (albeit a non-conventional one) as the only one that does not trivialise her experience, Lisa exposes the disciplining of individual bodies that takes place in the name of health. The Allergy Unit scenes, as rehearsed by Lisa and the actors she has hired, combine humour and irony. But they also have strong links with Foucault's discussion of 'docile bodies' in *Discipline and Punish* (1977), where he talks about the training of soldiers, and with his notion of 'technologies of the self' (Foucault 1998: 16); those techniques and practices that discipline and regulate bodies and are enforced by systems of power as well as by individuals themselves. Lisa jokes that withdrawing from college to enter the Allergy Unit when she was nineteen 'was going to be a milestone like a bat mitzvah' (19). She quickly tries to differentiate herself from the other sick people in the hospital (mostly middle-aged women) and the younger patients who attribute everything to allergies and have happily subjected themselves to thorough surveillance: fasting to clear the body of toxins, inspecting bowel movements and taking their pulse after they have been exposed to various inhalants and food in order to check whether they are having an allergic reaction. In the Allergy Unit, control, responsibility and co-operation are presented as essential to getting better. Having a reaction is portrayed as an event worth celebrating, despite the distress it brings, because it confirms the legitimacy of the condition. In one of the scenes, Kay, a patient who has had a strong reaction, 'filled with joy and amazement', tells the head nurse, 'I know what it is now. I'm not crazy' (20). Irrespective of whether we agree with Edward Shorter's 'somatization' thesis (1997), by presenting the Allergy Unit nurses as eager to propel symptoms in their suggestible patients, Kron seems here to probe into the ways medical propaganda (even coming from the fringes of orthodox medicine) can 'shape' the pattern and choices of particular symptoms. Lisa mocks the rituals that take place in the unit – she calls the 'safe water' she tastes 'delicious' (26) and asks whether the corn is so good 'because it is organic or because I haven't eaten anything in six days' (41). The other patients respond without a hint of irony: 'If you love food, chances are you're allergic to it' (42). Even though such routine is less familiar than the tuberculosis routine we find in sanatorium narratives, the Allergy Unit scenes emphasise what many sanatorium narratives expose – namely that the cure of allergies is 'not medicine but a new regime of living' that continues for a lifetime (Diedrich 2007: 13).

Lisa's portrayal of her mother's belief in racial integration is treated differently. Even though Lisa is sceptical of Ann's strong belief in allergies, her statement 'the two main things we believe in as a family are allergies and racial integration' (22), which introduces the Neighbourhood meeting scenes, is not ironic. Through this description Lisa conveys her mother's political beliefs, her strong conviction in the power of difference (whether this refers to health or racial difference) and Lisa's own admiration for Ann's tireless struggle to create an integrated community. Compensating for the previous portrayal of her mother as unable to move or cope, she makes it clear that energy does not have a single meaning and describes her mother as a 'fantastically energetic person trapped in an utterly exhausted body' (15). By linking her mother's view that her symptoms are real rather than psychosomatic to her belief in the positive effects of racial integration, Kron suggests that Ann had to fight hard to have both her allergies *and* racial integration taken seriously at the time; in both cases, believing in them would have been seen as crazy. In the Neighbourhood scenes, Ann first shows that sickness is more than an individual phenomenon. Drawing on the example of her community, she explains that a slum is created not because 'the people who live in the neighborhood aren't taking care of themselves', but when 'the city withdraws all the resources' (24). Here she is not referring to medical care, but care for the community more broadly. The aim of the Association she starts is to create an integrated and thus 'healthier' neighbourhood, in order to fight off the assumption that the neighbourhood is unstable or sick. Ann thinks that 'social activities', as opposed to strictly 'political work', have more potential to promote racial integration, as they will make people feel needed. She therefore works hard to organise volunteers to make Christmas carolling and baseball games and Fourth of July parades happen (25). As she notes, 'Everybody thought that I was kooky about that, just like they think I'm kooky about the allergies now.' But Lisa, contrary to her earlier dismissal of her mother's ignorance when it comes to the rules of theatre, calls her a 'housewife savant' (33), confirming the importance of non-expert or local knowledge as political methodology. After the organisation she helped set up gains power, Ann is condescendingly told that 'it was time for a man to take over'. She steps down, only to be overwhelmingly re-elected the following year (50).

As the Neighbourhood scene rehearsals continue, the actors find some of Ann's stories more interesting and Lisa becomes frustrated with her mother's interruptions, even though for the first time there is a moment of bonding when they are both delighted by sharing the same idea of telling a particular story (35). The opportunity this story opens for a joint narrative does not last, though; once again,

Ann draws attention to her daughter's attempt to compress and simplify complicated political work (51). One of the scenes that keeps erupting in the play without Lisa having planned it is her experience of being tormented by a black girl from her childhood named Lori, which she tries to edit out as it does not fit the integration story she is trying to tell. As her mother reminds her, the good thing about 'growing up in an integrated neighborhood was that you didn't have to extrapolate from abstract impressions of black people, because you knew actual people' (57). This is a lesson that also applies to the stories of illness and wellness in the individual and the community explored in the play; Lisa's mantra, 'I was sick and then I got well, the neighborhood was sick and it got well' (33) is problematic as it does not make room for those representations that do not fit such triumphant stories, such as her mother or Lori. This is the message conveyed at the end of the play when Lisa – not unlike Wenders, whose film ends with Ray's words from his diary superimposed onto the image – reads what her mother has written about the Association and its fight for integration: 'Integration means weaving into the whole even the parts that are uncomfortable or don't seem to fit. Even those which are complicated and painful. What is more worthy of our time and our love than this?' (76). This lesson is equally applicable to the aesthetically incoherent or 'messy' play *Well*.

'Why can't you make yourself well?': coherence and messiness

One of the turning points in *Well* that compels the actors to abandon what they call 'a manipulative and wrong setup' (66) is when Ann confronts Lisa by asking her when she is going to do the scene when she had a strong wheat reaction. Prior to that, the actors impersonating the patients interrupt an Allergy Unit scene to clarify whether they are supposed to play these characters as 'whacked' or whether the purpose of the scenes is to convey that people in the hospital 'actually got better' (37). Ann rushes to provide an affirmative answer, and her subsequent facts about allergies attract the actors' interest as they gradually move into her space on the stage. Lisa, frustrated as ever with yet another interruption by Ann, recedes into the background, and Ann is given for the first time a long monologue. She talks about her life in segregated Baltimore in the fifties, her misguided belief that 'being black was just like being white only you were also black' (62), and her first 'real' or 'practical' encounter with difference (when she was refused employment because she lived in a black neighbourhood), which changed her life. Earlier, Kay, a sick patient in the Allergy Unit, mentions that when people imagine what her life is like, they erroneously 'imagine having your sickness on top of their health' (59); in both cases, the assumption is that oppressed groups such as disabled/ill people, people of colour and immigrants could triumph over adversity by changing their attitudes, if they would only try hard enough. Through this connection the play interrogates the myth of individual achievement over adversity and exposes the structural and societal aspects (discrimination, economic injustice and lack of access) occluded by such dominant interpretations.

At the same time, *Well* refuses simplistic models of empathy or identification. Ann's monologue ends with a simultaneous affirmation of her connection to, and difference from, her daughter: 'To see her branch off and to have a life so different, and to have all that energy that I couldn't even imagine. But I guess I never questioned that we were starting from the same place. But I think maybe she doesn't feel that' (63). Ann waits for a response from Lisa, but there is none. Instead, Lisa expresses her anger at her mother's 'comatose state' and her constant 'moaning' (66) to the actors, who by this point are very uncomfortable, and abandon the production. Lisa then steps into the special light for the last time. What follows is her theory as to why, unlike her mother, she got well. She starts by expressing the strange feeling of embarrassment when she had to tell an extremely chemically sensitive person who lived in a specially fitted RV that she got better. She could not forget the look on his face as he said 'How did you get better? No one gets better' (69). While she responded with 'I don't know' during that particular incident, she now shares with the audience that what actually got her better was leaving home, doing therapy, studying theatre and having sex:

> I was thinking – it's sex. I've got this girlfriend who's cured me with sex. It's therapy. I moved to New York and got into therapy. I left Lansing and started to eat better food. I studied theater so I learned how to breathe and stretch. I learned, finally, what I never learned at home, that there is a correlation between not sleeping at night and feeling tired during the day, something I truly did not know before. I started to learn how to inhabit my body – that there is an alternative to dragging your body around like a stone and wishing it would disappear. That it is possible to integrate your physical self with the rest of you ... I escaped to the land of the healthy people. (69)

Marta Fernández-Morales has read this scene, and Lisa's subsequent revelation to her mother that it was not the Allergy Unit that helped her recover but rather these different choices, in wholly positive terms. In rejecting the medical label of allergies ('it doesn't work for me', she says during the above scene) and the passive sick role, Lisa questions traditional conceptualisations of sickness and views healing as 'a consciousness-raising process built on relationships ... and, more importantly, her insertion into a new community as a free, sexual, and active professional woman' (2012: 54). This connection between the personal and the political is prominent in feminist and lesbian illness narratives – Lorde's *The Cancer Journals* comes to mind once again – but Fernández-Morales also points to the ways it resonates with other personal plays about health and illness, such as Susan Miller's *My Left Breast* (1994) and Eve Ensler's *The Vagina Monologues* (1996). Even though promoting well-being through alternative treatments and endorsing a broader healthcare context is an important legacy of the women's health movement from which the critical medical humanities can benefit, painful divisions can be created if this leads to judgement of those 'sick' people who are unable to get better or 'perform' their illness following a particular 'feminist' narrative, as discussed in Chapter 1.

In her monologue, Lisa presents sick people as always 'trying to pull me down and make me like them'. Her mention of the word 'choice' when she says, 'I escaped to the land of the healthy people – people who have chosen strength and health and sex and attractive clothes and organic foods' (69–70) is especially problematic. It reinforces the myth that some sick people have the resources to get better, but do not try hard enough (for example, they deny that their suffering might have a psychological cause), affirms the neoliberal discourse of personal responsibility for one's health and sustains the binary opposition between tradition and modernity – the latter associated here with professional status and sexual liberation (more specifically lesbianism). Like the modernised daughters who escape the passive fate of their mothers in many mother–daughter narratives,[18] Lisa, albeit with more ambivalence, says that she thought she was going to grow up to become like her mother: 'I thought I was going to be a housewife and I thought I'd have kids and I'd have a house to organize and I'd have a husband ... But in order to get better, I had to grow in a different direction' (72). Lisa pathologises her mother's life choices and attributes her chronic ill health to them. 'Did you really bring me out here to make people think that I'm crazy and ... whiney ... and a hypochondriac?' (70), asks Ann in the play. When Lisa finally asks her the question, 'WHY CAN'T YOU MAKE YOURSELF WELL?!' Ann responds that it is a 'horrible question', and simply reminds her daughter that they 'are not the same person' (72). The real Ann Kron notes in an interview 'It was very hard reading the script ... I still feel frustrated that Lisa simplifies it so much. There's no explaining what this overwhelming exhaustion is like to anyone who hasn't experienced it. Even to myself ... Is she saying that because she's not sick, I'm not either?' (quoted in Green 2004).

Commenting on her 1991 show about 'the crisis' of turning thirty, called *Facing Life's Problems,* Kron notes, 'I looked at a video afterward and was so humiliated ... I'd thought I was so frank and funny, but really I was totally protective' (quoted in Green 2004). We have encountered a similar confession in Chapter 4, when Wenders admits that because of his fear he made images that were pretty or 'licked off' and, as he further reflects during the shooting of *Lightning over Water,* 'knowing the end of the lines' made him a bad actor in the film (Ray et al. 1993: 212). As Kron continues, 'You're supposed to think [in the theatre] you're going from A to B and then get sideswiped from A to P. But how do you do that: give it coherence while still acknowledging the messiness of life?' (quoted in Green 2004). *Well* draws attention to the same dilemma. As Lisa acknowledges at the end of the play: 'The purpose of this entire endeavor was to give coherence to things that are really confusing. Because otherwise it's just too messy' (75). In her experimentation with a structure that challenges her solo practice, Kron affirms her belief in the need to be inventive – which, as she writes in the preface of *Well,* leads to 'authentic, unplanned encounters' and 'vulnerable revelation', 'the moment of not knowing the outcome or effect' when 'something is told for the first time' (x). In the play this pertains not only to her confrontation with, and renewed understanding of, her mother's perspective, but also to the broader questions around illness (why do some people get well and others stay sick?) which, as Jayne tells her, are 'very seductive because it would be so much easier if we could answer them. But we can't. You can't answer them' (74). Lisa is forced to renegotiate or rewrite her ending, as many illness narratives do,[19] as a way of recognising the difficulty of answering these questions or providing narrative closure. Erasing the line that her play has been drawing, 'putting the sick people over here and the healthy people over there' (75), just like some of the early shots of Wenders' film, and reading her mother's speech, Lisa comes to understand the true purpose of integration: to weave 'into the whole even the parts that don't seem to fit' (76).

And yet, as much as *Well* breaks down its tight structure to show how art – or a particular agenda and vision – fails to give coherence, this failure is orchestrated. On the one hand, the audience is encouraged to reflect on the tension between coherence and messiness by being presented with a precarious situation unfolding spontaneously on stage. But on the other, the messy confrontation between mother, daughter and the rest of the characters in the play that stimulates these larger reflections has been meticulously worked between Kron, Silverman and the actors over many years. If *Well* has been all along about 'making room enough to allow life to spill over in all its contradictory messiness', this messiness is contained within a consoling 'superstructure', a container 'large enough to hold all the chaos and contradiction' that has emerged in the play (xii). Moreover, given the specific self-reflexive mode of telling the mother's story that has been chosen, Ann is allowed to interrupt and rewrite the script – but she is still a character in a play authored by Kron. Lyn Gardner (2009) suggests that if Kron's real mother 'were on stage, perhaps something unexpected and moving might occur' – as in Ursula Martinez's 1998 autobiographical show *A Family Outing*, when she appeared on stage with her parents. Even though the making of *Well* entailed significant collaboration between mother and daughter, Kron could have opted for an alternative model to facilitate her mother to write or even act her story: 'In spite of Kron's stated desire to question her omniscience as a narrator it is telling that when asked whether she would ever consider having her parents on stage with her ... Kron replies that "What I do on stage is way too tightly controlled for that"' (Heddon 2008: 156). In this sense, and thinking back to the previous chapter, Wenders' collaborative work, despite being poised between document and fiction and largely completed in the cutting room, is more successful in giving us a glimpse of what happens when tight structures of control and consolation break down; and not just because it was filmed against a background noise of mortality. Nevertheless, *Well* manages to fashion a porous performance structure that allows healthy doses of messiness to seep through and, at times, to spill over.

Notes

1. See the Wit Educational Initiative, created in 2000 by UCLA's Doctors Karl Lorenz, Jillisa Steckart, and Kenneth Rosenfeld, which brought performances of *Wit* to medical schools across North America (2004).
2. For an alternative reading of the play that is attentive to its metafictional qualities, see Rossiter 2012.
3. Subsequent quotations from *Well*, including Kron's preface, are taken from this edition. Only page numbers are given in brackets.
4. In this sense, it is not unlike Wenders' compulsive doubting about whether he should continue shooting Ray in *Lightning over Water*.
5. Kron (2006b) specifically celebrates the fact that *Well* 'draws the audience deep into the inner life of a woman most people wouldn't even see if they passed her on the street ... The thought that this could be seen on Broadway is incredible to me.'
6. The playful 'warnings' on the cover of the published script of *Well* (**CAUTION**: On-stage presence of **ACTUAL FAMILY MEMBER** may alter your ability to control play's outcome) give the same impression.
7. See Luigi Pirandello's play *Six Characters in Search of an Author* (1921).
8. For a good example of a narrative in the clinical context that raises similar questions about the shared experience and multiple perspectives of illness, see Kirmayer 2000.
9. See Brodzinski 2014 for the relationship between 'social' and 'aesthetic drama'.
10. Lisa Kron, <http://www.lisakron.com/artstmt.html> (this link refers to an old version of her official website that is no longer available).
11. Bailes (2011) focuses on the work of the performance groups Forced Entertainment, Goat Island and Elevator Repair Service.
12. Reviews of *Well* still debate the extent to which this performance is 'successful'; one favourable review by Matty Hughley (2010) puts it thus: 'It's kind of a mess, frankly, but that's OK, because it's clearly set out to become just that. All the ideas don't cohere, but the point is more about the value of complexity and multiple perspectives and the varying ways in which we can (perhaps should) think about the stories we tell to each other and to ourselves.'
13. See for example the following definition: <http://dictionary.reference.com/browse/malady> (last accessed 27 July 2015).
14. On MCS, see Radetsky 1997, McCormick 2001 and the website <http://www.ourlittleplace.com/mcs.html> (last accessed 27 July 2015).
15. See some of the negative responses from within the CFS/ME community to Elaine Showalter's study *Hystories: Hysterical Epidemics and Modern Culture* (1997), which seems to disregard biomedical perspectives on this condition's causes. Indicative of this is Mary Schweitzer's review (1997).

16. See Morris 1998, Chapter 3, and his 'bio-cultural model', which underlines the convergence of biology with culture in the production of illness.
17. Randolph, associated with the field of clinical ecology, expanded the definition of allergy concentrating on foods and seemingly harmless chemicals used in homes and workplaces (rather than obviously high toxic chemicals). Instead of using drugs for the treatment of his patients, he relied on individualised and time-consuming food ingestion tests carried out in hospitals and physical environments which were scientifically controlled and managed. See Randolph and Moss 1980.
18. This criticism is frequent in cross-cultural narratives – see Bow 2001 and Bolaki 2011b.
19. See Conway 2007, Chapter VI, 'Endings'.

Chapter 6

Animated Documentary and Mental Health

The ethical responsibilities of collaborative narrative for both those who create the work and the audiences who receive it, as well as the importance of keeping open the possibility of witnessing for others through particular formal strategies, are evident from the discussion in Chapters 4 and 5. A form that returns to these questions but also sheds new light on the intersubjective relations that connect filmmakers, subjects and viewers is the animated documentary. In exploring animated documentaries that treat mental illness this chapter also returns to, and develops further, several previous threads: the politics of visibility/concealment and the need to expand narratives about health, allowing multiple perspectives and open-endedness, with which this book opened; the distinct ways the animated documentary negotiates the attempt (and failure) to apprehend the experience of illness that many of the chapters have examined in relation to various forms and collaborations; the medium's political and broadly pedagogical significance for fighting stigma and intervening in debates within medicine and broader culture; and finally, the need to challenge instrumentalising approaches towards animation coming from either the sciences or the arts through creative dialogue and critical interloping.

Since the twentieth century, animation has been used for clarification and illustration as well as for educational, training and propaganda purposes. Even when it deals with complex social issues, the visual language it uses, like that of comics, allows it to communicate information in a more accessible manner than the written word, especially for an increasingly visual-literate population. This accessibility means that, while still widely associated with entertainment because of Disney's central role in the industry, animation is used in several cultural fields including science, education, politics, film, art and occupational therapy.[1] In recent years it has increasingly been given serious attention by animation and documentary critics and has entered a range of non-fiction media practices.[2] The recent production of animated documentaries on topics such as blood donation, plastic surgery, autism, blindness and synaesthesia is an indication of the ways this genre is used to engage with concerns of contemporary life, including with public health.[3] The histories of comics and animation – forms traditionally associated with children, fantasy or marginalised tastes – have only begun to be written and documented in the medical/health humanities, and their full potential for communicating illness experience is still to be examined.

One key example in relation to health and illness explored in this chapter is *Animated Minds* (2003). This series of short films could be grouped under what has been called 'alternative psychiatric narratives' both in terms of pioneering the use of animated documentary in the UK, an unconventional form to address mental health issues, and moving away from an earlier focus on formal psychiatric spaces and doctor-patient relationships.[4] The idea was conceived in 2003 as an attempt to raise public awareness by communicating the subjective experience of a variety of 'conditions' to a wider audience. The producer and director of *Animated Minds*, documentary filmmaker Andy Glynne, originally trained as a clinical psychologist, and his idea for the series was to record the testimony of a variety of people with experience of mental distress and then animate it with the help of different animators. As we read on the *Animated Minds* website (2014), ' "mental illness" is still ... shrouded in misconceptions and prejudice' – and not talked about, despite the large number of people who experience mental health problems at some point during their lives.[5]

The first series, commissioned by British public-service television broadcaster Channel 4, is aimed at adults. As part of this series, in *Dimensions* Chas talks about his experience with psychosis; Steve reveals the repetitive behaviour induced by obsessive compulsive disorder in *Obsessively Compulsive*; *Fish on a Hook* features Mike, who suffers from agoraphobia and panic attacks; and *The Light Bulb Thing* communicates the highs and lows Hannah endured with manic depression, or what is now described as bipolar disorder. The second series, originally called *Troubled Minds* (2009), focuses on young people and was made for the UK cable channel Teachers TV and funded by the Wellcome Trust. In *An Alien in the Playground* Josh offers an insight into the world of Asperger's syndrome and the emotional distress he suffered while at school;⁶ in *Over and Over (and Over) Again*, Danny talks about his struggle with everyday routines like leaving the house for school and his obsession with specific numbers caused by obsessive compulsive disorder; *My Blood is My Tears* includes the testimonies of Abbie, Lois and Nicole on the impulses that cause young people like them to self-harm; and finally, in *Becoming Invisible* Nicole suggests that people can develop eating disorders for reasons that go beyond the peer and cultural pressure to fit smaller clothes. The reception of the films was far greater than expected. Not only did they reach a large audience through various broadcast partners and receive awards, but they have also been used by teaching hospitals, schools, universities, mental health community centres and charities, and by service users themselves to show others what their experience is like.⁷

The animated documentary has not received the same degree of recognition in the medical humanities as graphic pathographies. Despite not yet being as widely integrated in the field as literary narrative, Harvey Pekar's *Our Cancer Year* (1994), Brian Fies' *Mom's Cancer* (2006), David B.'s *Epileptic* (2006), and Marisa Marchetto's *Cancer Vixen* (2007) have all attracted critical attention and feature in the 'Graphic Medicine' website that explores the interaction between the medium of comics and the discourse of healthcare.⁸ In contrast, the discussion within animation and documentary communities has until very recently been more insular. It has revolved around defining the paradoxical genre 'animated documentary' and devising typologies, either attempting to fit the genre under existing categories of the documentary⁹ or creating new ones to do more justice to the distinctiveness of the form. The emphasis on categorisation, however important it was in the early years for identifying a discrete form, meant that other aspects of the genre such as its usefulness and functionality were neglected. In the 1990s the debate revolved around the 'so-called crisis of postmodernism in documentary' and the use of animation was seen as a form of critique of documentary's attempts to objectively represent reality (Roe 2013: 21–2).

Current scholarship is drawing more attention to what aspects of reality animation can represent (as opposed to whether it can represent reality) and to the work that it does. This is how we can interpret Samantha Moore's call to her fellow animators, on the occasion of three conferences on animation and documentary studies in 2010, to stop paying so much attention to methodological and craft-based concerns and take a closer look at content and purpose. Similarly, in his 2011 address at the Animated Realities conference,

Paul Wells stressed how important it is for animation and animated non-fiction studies scholars to overcome a tendency to remain inward-looking by drawing on other fields such as autobiographical studies; he also spoke of the importance of carefully examining within animation practice the kind of responsibility that animators have towards their interview subjects. Referring to scientific and medical uses of animation, Moore (2010) observes with regard to a conference about neuropsychology and synaesthesia (organised by the American Synesthesia Association), that neither animation nor documentary was given careful attention: 'The response and discussion, from an audience of neuro-psychologists and synaesthetes, was entirely based on the content of the [animated] work and its "correctness" in conveying synaesthesia, with no interest in form and little in methodology.' This is also true of medical animation, short films rendered through 3D computer graphics, usually based around a physiological or surgical topic and most commonly used as an instructional tool for medical professionals or their patients.[10]

As with the preceding chapters, which speak for the need to include a diversity of forms and methods in our conceptualisation of the medical humanities so that the field remains inclusive and experimental rather than narrow and instrumental, this chapter seeks to bridge the gap between the study of animation in the arts and sciences and to establish conversations between researchers and practitioners working in animation, documentary and the medical humanities. My analysis moves beyond an empty formalism that approaches animation as a cosmetic addition and explores its functions, ethical questions and larger messages when it deals with topics that are of a broader interest, such as health and illness. At the same time, I am equally critical of approaches that see animation merely as a tool or strictly in terms of its content, which reflects a broader utilitarian sensibility to the ways illness narratives are employed. Animation does not simply provide information or data, and its function cannot be reduced to accurate representations of symptoms. Animated illness narratives are expressive vehicles and the ways they are put together – in other words, their aesthetic aspects – matter for their ability to function as testimonies and to draw their viewers as witnesses to the experiences they animate. *Animated Minds* offers a rich example of the evocative function of animation when it comes to communicating embodied perceptions and mental states that are hard to describe, as well as of the ethical and political role animated documentary can play in fighting stigma and raising broader public awareness about mental health difficulties.

Animated documentary's evocative function: absence and excess

Recent work on the animated documentary as a genre suggests that animation functions in three key, though not mutually exclusive, ways in animated documentaries: 'mimetic substitution' (when real-life footage is missing), 'non-mimetic substitution' (when animation has its own intrinsic value and is used to creatively interpret a person's testimony) and 'evocation' of subjective states of mind, as they are difficult to visualise (Roe 2013: 23). In *Beyond Words* Kathlyn Conway contends that emotional suffering and particular experiences such as depression can be better captured through non-narrative means. Film, drama, painting and music offer an 'expressive language' (2007: 79) missing from diagnostic and statistical manuals used by mental health professionals as well as from literary writing, which is often 'devoid of evocative images' (91). Like other generically mixed work considered so far, *Animated Minds* combines the narrative potential of oral testimony with the ability of animation to evoke feelings and experiences that cannot be easily put into words and, as a result, add to people's isolation and stigma. Rather than advocating the animated documentary for its own sake, Glynne insists that animation should be used only when it can help to tell a story more effectively (2013: 73). His challenge with the *Animated Minds* project was to see if there was a way animation, with its 'power of penetration' (Wells 1998: 122), could capture various experiences of mental and emotional distress in a more effective way than live-action film or just verbal narrative. Protecting the anonymity of his participants was important, but so was the attempt to capture a sense of what the world looks like from within for these people – a central concern of phenomenological approaches to illness[11] – and to communicate it to others.

The process of making the *Animated Minds* films was as collaborative as possible, as we find out on the project's official website. Glynne recorded interviews with individuals who wanted to take part in the project. The majority of them were in advocacy and support groups and were strongly motivated to talk about their daily difficulties (Glynne in Bolaki 2014). He then edited the interviews down to create short first-person narratives 'rich in visual metaphors' and assigned these to different animators, who were asked to creatively interpret the soundtrack. The films have distinct animation styles, and the choice of animators was made on the basis of the fit between the audio interview, or the aesthetics of the story, and the animators' own animation style/creative approach.

There is of course an ethical dimension to the collaborative character of the process. As Glynne explains, 'you're taking someone's heartfelt story and you're going to put it into pictures that in some ways aren't representative of what they look like or what their world is like'. He advises those who contemplate using animation to 'spend a lot of time with the people you're making the animation around and make sure you're getting your research right' (in Hamilton 2012). Moreover, editing an interview down to three minutes (often dictated by budget constraints) is another example of a potentially problematic intervention. As with other collaborative projects across media, and considering the treatment of this theme in Kron's play *Well*, it requires 'trust' that the director can convey the most important aspects of the experience in that time (Glynne in Bolaki 2014). When everyone felt happy with the final product, composers were brought in to add a soundscape and music to the finished piece.

While the process of creating the films was collaborative, the interaction between animators and participants was mediated; they did not meet in person and the animators only had access to the edited narrative, even though the participants were consulted at various stages throughout the process. Other animators who work with interview subjects are interested in developing a more explicit methodology for collaboration. For example, in a presentation drawing on her own practice as she was making *An Eyeful of Sound*, Moore (2011) explores the extent to which 'the frame within an animated documentary can become a collaborative space, working with the interviewees to create the image, and how a filmmaker might go about creating and sustaining that collaboration'. In the case of *Animated Minds*, the collaborative space can be glimpsed through the interaction between soundtrack and image and the creative interventions by the animators, who sometimes do not mirror closely the words heard (an aspect I return to later).

With and especially without collaboration, rather than empowering people, animated documentaries more generally could be criticised for objectifying already marginalised individuals and trivialising their complex lived experiences through the aestheticisation of their bodies and stories. Even though, as shown in Chapter 4, not all documentary film gazes are ethical, visibility and politics are often bound up together in different media; writing about the documentary as a genre, Bill Nichols notes that 'it is not simply the knowledge possessed by witnesses and experts that needs to be conveyed through their speech, but also the unspoken knowledge that needs to be conveyed by the body itself' (1993: 175). I have discussed the politics of visibility by examining scarred bodies in Chapter 1 and their relation to a feminist tradition of breast cancer narratives. However, visibility has a complicated history if we consider representations of illness – not just of breast cancer but also of madness, homosexuality and AIDS – across the history of Western medicine that have sustained a medical gaze categorising and pathologising various groups of people. Sander L. Gilman has provided an overview of the history of psychiatric illustration – from drawings of the physiognomy of certain forms of insanity (for example, melancholia) in the eighteenth century to the more 'scientific' late-nineteenth-century photographs of the manifestations of hysteria by the head of Salpêtrière Hospital, Charcot – which 'dominated the visualisation of the insane well into the twentieth century' (1988: 43). Behind those visual iconographies was the conviction that the mad are recognisable by their external appearance, and the illustrations and photographs were used as an aid in diagnosis. As Gilman notes, even though psychoanalysis challenged such a focus on the visual aspect of diagnosis, the kinds of photographs that stress expression and position in standard clinical psychiatry books used today are the direct descendants of nineteenth-century psychiatric atlases. The visual stereotyping of mentally ill people continues, not only in the mainstream media but also by clinicians, who are often reported to have difficulty identifying debilitating side-effects (the result of medication) in patients who are supposed 'to look crazy' (Gilman 1988: 49). The invisibility or 'masking'[12] on which animated documentaries rely may, similar to 'the mask of prosthesis' (Herndl 2002: 154), be considered to exacerbate ill people's lack of voice or representation in the public sphere. But, in light of the above history, it can be also linked to a kind of alternative portraiture that, like the breast cancer narratives of re-covery discussed in Chapter 1, can give 'new face' by avoiding exposure and other conventional ways of looking at mental illness.[13]

While assessing the place of the animated documentary in discourses about visibility, it is also important to return to another point made in Chapter 1: visibility does not take a single form, as there are many ways something can be made visible even if the impression is that of covering or masking reality. The first chapter of this book considered the relation between image/caption and visible self/voice in textual and photographic illness narratives; in the case of animated documentary, we can turn to the relation between animated images and audio recording. The latter retains the link to a real person, as in conventional documentary, and the voice – both the words and the medium of the voice itself – in the verbal testimony communicate a whole range of meanings despite the absence of conventional visually indexical material such as the body. In addition to sound/language, animation's ability to 'reveal conditions or principles' that are 'hidden or beyond the comprehension of the viewer' (Wells 1998: 122) can be attributed to the interplay of several aspects. As with comics and artists' books, design, movement, shape, colour, and texture all contribute to the production of meaning and knowledge. Annabelle Honess Roe summarises the animated documentary's distinctive strength by referring to the dialectical relationship or tension between 'absence and excess' (2013: 39). The animated documentary's evocative power, and the multiple ways it visualises and penetrates embodied experiences in spite of the body's absence, can be illustrated by looking more closely at the *Animated Minds* films.

Dimensions consists of fragmentary and shifting animation mixed with live-action images that capture the way Chas perceives the world. One of animation's unique devices is 'metamorphosis', when an image literally changes or morphs into another through the evolution of the line or the manipulation of objects. This creates a much more fluid linking of images (however unrelated they may be) than film editing. Wells calls metamorphosis 'the constituent core of animation itself' (1998: 69) and describes its effect in the following way: 'in enabling the collapse of the illusion of physical space, metamorphosis destabilises the image, conflating horror and humour, dream and reality, certainty and speculation' (69). While metamorphosis is a central ingredient of fairy tales, in *Dimensions* the destabilisation of the image is apt for a film that tries to describe hallucinations and delusions, experiences that are difficult to capture visually. We see the words on a newspaper headline change so that the headline seems to refer to the film's subject. The use of sound further helps the representation of his sense of 'being-in-the-world'; the quick and disorienting images at the start are accompanied by sounds of tuning a radio or another device, and subliminal messages that flash too quickly for the eye to register their presence are complemented with what is difficult to decipher at first: whispers from various persecutory voices. These devices enhance our understanding of the accompanying verbal testimony in a distinctly embodied way: 'I do find it amazing the power of the human brain that it can recreate you know ten, twenty voices perfectly. I mean the voices were very distressing the, the, the impression is they were encouraging me to self-harm or commit suicide.' As we watch the film and hear the person speaking, we also begin to hear these voices.

Similarly, in *An Alien in the Playground*, the background sounds used in the film capture Josh's difficulty with receiving a range of stimuli from his environment: 'I'll be hearing every single pen or pencil scribbling at different times, at different speeds, at different pressures. I'll be hearing the cars and the buses outside, noticing aeroplanes going past, trains going past, people in the streets.' In *Becoming Invisible*, the alienation Nicole experiences from her own body is accentuated in the opening scene through the contrasting use of colour as the speaker reveals that she feels as if she is the only one who lives 'in black and white while others live in colour'. All of these techniques and devices that complement the audio narrative and engage several senses offer viewers 'an intensified route' into an individual's complex experiences (Ward 2005: 91).

On some occasions the animation style seems to clash with the soundtrack, as in the case of *An Alien in the Playground*, where the innocent animation and drawing style collide with the narrative, which documents experiences of bullying and discrimination. In other films a particular animation production technique is chosen to capture the specific nature of the difficulties described. For example, *Obsessively Compulsive* uses a stop-motion, looped animation of an actor to register the repetitive and cyclical nature of the experience described by the actual voice of the interviewee:

> A big problem I did have was walking from one side of the room to another in the absence of an intrusive thought. If an intrusive thought came through I would have to retrace my steps back a bit like someone who walks through the mine field really ... From half way through reading to cut sentences and paragraphs and an intrusive thought came through I'd have to return to the section again and read it again and make sure that I had blanked the intrusive thought out. If I breathed in while an intrusive thought came through I thought well I am polluting my lungs I'd have to breathe out very sharply and breathe in again.

Steve's intrusive thoughts are related to Saddam Hussein, and live-action footage is used to represent the appearance of such thoughts while attempting to do the above activities. We see images of the Gulf War physically invading his body, playing inside his head, onto a cup of coffee or onto a book. Repetition is one of the fundamental structures of comedy, and many cartoons (animated or not) rely on it for their humorous effect: 'Recognising formulaic patterns and knowing what to expect gives viewers pleasure' (Wells 1998: 169).

Figure 6.1 Still from *Obsessively Compulsive*, dir. Andy Glynne, animation dir. Gemma Carrington, Mosaic Films, 2003, © Mosaic Films.

Here this central aspect of animation is turned on its feet and captures the ways the 'normal' intentionality of mental acts is disturbed in the case of the obsessionality experienced by the subject. The film finishes with a split screen, an image compartmentalised into smaller images in which the figure of the actor is repeating a different action in every individual panel, suggesting that the painful experiences continue day after day. In *Over and Over (and Over) Again*, also about OCD, the obsessive compulsion of checking that doors are closed before leaving the house is visualised through a sequence of doors falling like dominoes on the animated character. Here the animation does not closely mirror the words on the soundtrack, but creatively interprets them: 'it's not like there's a little voice in your head saying, "you've gotta do this," it's just like there's someone there and they're pushing you, and they're pushing you and pushing you'.

Like the comics medium, animated documentaries can explore both the somatic and social aspects of disability and illness through aspects of character design and attention to gesture and facial expression. Because cartoon or animated bodies are more foreign and unfamiliar than a filmed body (the latter retains its connection to a real body), comics and animation can capture some of the changes that happen to the body in a more powerful manner than conventional documentary.

The body becomes conspicuous in illness; there is loss of control and a new understanding of the world as unpredictable – or, as Fredrik Svenaeus describes it, illness becomes 'a threat to the homelike being-in-the-world' in its otherness (2011: 335). Animation can visualise bodily sensations for which no adequate language exists, not to mention its freedom to create malleable, elastic and even non-human bodies, and can in this way penetrate the kind of unhomelikeness attached to illness, which is not merely a metaphor. *Fish on a Hook* employs drawn animation and uses a faceless white figure, distinguished from other characters in the film who are drawn with more precision and in black; the fact that this character is not realistic means that it can describe many people (McCloud 1993: 31), but in addition to universality the choice of cartoon imagery also emphasises aspects of his social invisibility. *An Alien in the Playground* also opts for a simple cartoon-like character that suits the subject matter and expresses the child's vulnerability as he becomes exposed to bullying at school. Svenaeus writes that 'the unhomelikeness of illness always involves a primary alienation within the domains of our embodiment. … There is nowhere else to go, because the body cannot be left behind: the uncanny unhomelikeness strikes at the *heart* of existence' (2011: 341). The film *My Blood is My Tears* captures this complex idea visually through the image of tearing off the skin in order to escape, which closely mirrors the soundtrack viewers hear: 'Literally sometimes I would feel this desperate need to tear off my skin because I cannot stand to sit in it, and it's the most tortuous feeling of being trapped in yourself because there is absolutely no escape.'

Animation scholars have argued that, despite the lack of verisimilitude between animated and 'real' bodies, there still exists an essential link between the two, and in the case of *Animated Minds*, as further discussed below, the use of the people's actual voices sutures this link by adding corporeality to the animated characters. Animated bodies more generally can offer viewers radical embodied experiences; certain animation techniques, as we have seen, allow us to participate, however briefly, 'in the intense physicality' (Bouldin 2000: 65) of other people who may for one reason or another experience their bodies differently. One such device is rotoscoping.[14] Because this technique retains a trace of the original filmed body, 'bodies acquire a certain thickness and density' (Bouldin 2004: 7) that in turn creates a strange viewing experience, as we are aware of both the realness and unrealness of the animated character. This ambiguity can be understood through Freud's notion of the uncanny (*unheimlich*): an instance when something that was 'once very familiar' becomes 'frightening' (2003: 124). Puppet animation is another technique that can cause a similar uncanny presence of the body, and is used in *Becoming Invisible*. The puppet functions as an automaton; it is both like a human, and non-human: 'It is the embodiment of some degree of living spirit and energy but also inhuman and remote' (Wells 1998: 61).[15] As the film opens, Nicole speaks of her 'vivid awareness' that there is something wrong with her body. She describes it as 'something intangible', while we see a puppet figure moving in a human but also mechanical way. It is this animation practice that aids in our temporary experience of what it is like not to feel at home in one's body, as expressed by Nicole in the soundtrack.

Animated documentaries often reject a plot with a beginning, middle and end in favour of symbols or metaphors. In gesturing towards a story, metaphor 'occupies an intermediate ground between embodied experience and the overarching narrative structures of plots, myths, and ideologies' (Woods 2011a: 76). As such it is able to open a direction beyond narrative without sacrificing the power of stories. Glynne has explained that the interviewees were encouraged to use metaphors to describe their experiences (2013: 74), and many of the *Animated Minds* films are structured around a central linguistic metaphor that is enhanced and sustained through the animation. For example, in *The Light Bulb Thing* a literal light bulb is visible at different moments in the film. At the end we see the animated character seated in an empty space and the words 'it's like the thing that turns you on, the light bulb thing, that's not there anymore' are animated through the disappearance of the light bulb from the image. The metaphor captures the idea that when one experiences the mood swings from euphoria to depression that the speaker does, 'the brightness within' 'has gone out'.[16] The washed-out quality and pale colours of the whole film further enhance this metaphor.

Fish on a Hook uses a number of similes and metaphors to describe the fear of public/open spaces and the subject's panic attacks. Mike compares the experience of going to the supermarket Sainsbury's for his shopping to 'hell' and to being 'a prisoner who has moved out into a very hostile area'. The contrast between the small flat he lives in and the boundlessness of the outside world is emphasised through the animation and evokes his fear of open spaces much better than any verbal explanation. His feeling of being strangled when his chest tightens with anxiety is visually conveyed with an image of an animated character being pulled down into water by a hook around his neck. This image becomes extended at the film's conclusion through the use of metamorphosis and another simile: 'It's rather like a fish wriggling on the end of a hook. So initially one might think Mike is wriggling and it makes no sense at all. He is doing the crazy dance

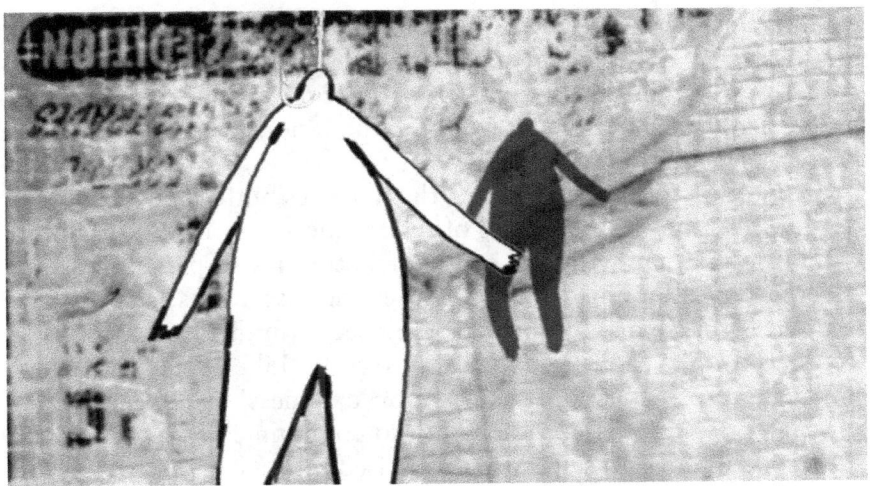

Figure 6.2 Still from *Fish on a Hook*, dir. Andy Glynne, animation dir. Jim Field, Mosaic Films, 2003, © Mosaic Films.

until you see the hook in my gullet then it starts making sense.' His condition is compared to the hook, which remains invisible to the majority of people who cannot understand his strange behaviour. It is a kind of image that requires both an empathic and an intellectual response, as Mike tells us that his 'crazy dance' needs to be viewed in context. Here the unique narrative feature of metamorphosis (the fish transforms into Mike's body and the hook becomes visible) makes the image, and the message that he should not be judged for his behaviour, even more poignant for viewers.

Metaphor is also important in *My Blood is My Tears*, which uses 'paper as a metaphor for the skin'. The cultural, material and metaphorical associations between the book and the body were discussed in Chapter 2 in relation to Hall's artists' books. Here paper is chosen by the animator because 'it gets ripped and it tears and bears marks' and in this way allows her and the interviewees to talk about the subject of self-harm 'without being too graphic or distressing'.[17] As we hear the opening of the audio recording – 'I think the first time I self-harmed, I found a needle in my room ... and, I just drew it across my skin. And I remember the sight of blood, and feeling like I had discovered something' – the animation shows a sewing needle tracing the paper, leaving behind a trail of red ink to mark blood. Other instances describe bruises and scratches, once again represented through patches of colour, marks and lines on paper that convey a tactile feeling. The body is also compared to a sketchbook when we hear one of the speakers saying that 'every scar has a meaning, and it's like a sketchbook when I look at them – 'cause it's so much on the same arm, and they cross over so many times, and it is like they tell a story'. Even though the film is a hybrid of live images (of body parts such as a hand or an eye) and animation, it avoids depicting any violence on the actual body.

In addition to the use of paper, the film uses butterflies to allude to self-harming and to the bodies of the female speakers. Most viewers would be familiar with the image of butterflies displayed in glass-covered boxes mounted on specially made insect pins, and the film references this image by showing the needle (in this case a common household one) entering a butterfly's body. Like metaphor, which 'invites interpretation but insists upon openness' (Wells 1998: 84), this potent symbol is used not only to communicate harm but also the strong impulse to self-harm (visualised through a butterfly drawn to a light bulb despite physical pain) and the peculiar kind of release felt by the girls after they engage in self-harming. The butterfly is thought to symbolise the soul's spiritual journey in different mythologies and is also connected to metamorphosis and transformation (Kritsky and Cherry 2000: 8). These associations perhaps explain the choice to animate the following lines with butterflies coming out of an animated figure's exposed skin: 'And, yeah, sometimes self-harming gives that illusion of breaking out, almost.' The central metaphor of the film is summed up in the title, *My Blood is My Tears*. This is animated through the same needle of the opening of the film, drawing a pair of eyes on paper that shed tears in the form of red ink/blood as we hear the last lines of the soundtrack: 'People cry, I can't cry. My blood is my tears because I can't cry – there's no way for me to show emotion that isn't self-harm.'

Animation's paradoxical capacity to conceal and expose is suggested through the recurring of masks in several of the *Animated Minds* films. Many of the individuals who speak in the films explain that their conditions very often force them to adopt a mask in order to communicate with other people. Josh says in *An Alien in the Playground*: 'What I had to do when I met someone was to build up what I like to call an equation for their personality, so I used this equation to build a mask if you like, in which to speak through so that I can interact with this person well.' In *Becoming Invisible*, we equally see the happy mask that Nicole wears to maintain the invisibility of her suffering. Yet in the process of the films, the mask – both literal and figurative – is momentarily peeled off to reveal what lies beneath. The voice of the speaker tells us that if you had been in her head or skin, what you would have seen or heard is 'I'm terrified, alone,

Figure 6.3 Still from *An Alien in the Playground*, dir. Andy Glynne, animation dir. Matthew Morgan, Mosaic Films, 2003, © Mosaic Films.

don't know how to voice this, and yet no one can see it.' At this point the mask closes on the animated figure, and us as viewers, once more. There is a self-reflexive aspect in such use of masks as central metaphors in the documentaries, because animation itself relies on a type of masking for its formal language. But even as the interviewees remain masked or hidden under their animated personas, films like *Becoming Invisible* manage to define and illustrate the invisibility they are concerned with – both through their public existence as documentaries that seek to give voice to certain non-normative experiences, and through the particular visual metaphors they employ.

The voice in animated documentary

While an excess of meaning is conveyed through the animation style and techniques in *Animated Minds* that helps capture the speakers' lived experience, voice can also have a similar evocative and expressive function. In *The Voice in Cinema* Michel Chion draws attention to the often overlooked distinction between voice and speech: 'From the speech act we usually retain only the significations it bears, forgetting the medium of the voice itself' (1999: 1). Paying attention to the materiality of the voice through aspects such as intonation, delivery and breathing can communicate embodied information even if the actual body is missing. It can enhance the meaning of the images, and impact viewers cognitively and affectively. In the *Animated Minds* documentaries, there are many hesitations and pauses with such a function as when in *The Light Bulb Thing* Hannah says 'So you feel that you don't have a place and you don't have a [*pause*] meaning anymore.' Similarly, in *Becoming Invisible* Nicole's voice wavers when she notes at the end that it is the decision to continue living that is the most difficult. In *Over and Over (and Over) Again* the reported dialogue captures the feeling of being compelled to repeat an action beyond any rational justification: 'Called my mum and was like, "mum, I think I've left the door open". She was like, "you haven't, you know you haven't". I was like, "But ... I have to check."' What strengthens the psychological hold these words have on us as viewers is the urgency with which the phrase 'but ... I have to check' is uttered by Danny. The fact that these voices are closely miked creates a sense of intimacy that is similar to listening to the radio, and this enhances the testimonial address to the viewer.[18]

At the same time, what gives these voices more power is the fact that they come from absent bodies. Chion has coined the term 'acousmêtre' (1999: 9), referring to the character of the disembodied voice in cinema, whose presence is not entirely inside or out of the narrative frame. The term acousmatic refers to a sound that is 'heard without its source or cause being seen' (18), and Chion cites the voice of God and the maternal voice as the precedents of the acousmêtre in the cinema (17, 19). In narrative film and in particular genres, for example the horror film, acousmatic sound is important as it can cause tension and uncertainty, but the term has been used in other contexts too, including documentary (both live-action and animated). In his exploration of Derek Jarman's film *Blue* (1993), described as 'the most bodyless film ever produced', Roger Hallas draws on the idea of the 'acousmatic witness' (2007: 41). Made at the time Jarman was struggling with the onset of AIDS-related blindness, the film consists of a single shot of saturated blue colour filling the screen, as background to a soundtrack with Jarman's and three other voices. Hallas suggests that the 'visual iconoclasm' of the film and the prioritisation of sound over image challenge 'the dominant regime of AIDS representation that has historically pathologised HIV-infected people through the visual discourses of techno science and social documentary' (42). The acousmêtre is 'off screen, outside the image and at the same time in the image; it is as if the voice were wandering along the surface, at once inside and outside, seeking a place to settle' (Chion 1999: 23). Its power, however, is neutralised when it becomes embodied, visualised or de-acousmatised. Drawing on these insights, Hallas notes that *Blue* never offers a place where the voice can be located on screen. Anyone who has watched this film will no doubt have felt that strange anticipation of the imminent arrival of a body that never takes place. Instead, 'the spectator's vision is denied an external body on the screen to either misrecognise in the phantasmatic process of identification or to repudiate through a disidentification with it as an abject other' (Hallas 2007: 46). In this way *Blue* offers a bold reconsideration of the intersubjective relation between spectator and filmmaker, and of the process of bearing witness to another person's experience.

Hallas' insights about the visual experimentation and use of voice in Jarman's *Blue* are useful when examining the *Animated Minds* series. Like *Blue*'s challenge of dominant representations of AIDS within social documentary, the *Animated Minds* films escape common media representations of mental illness through their alternative visuality. If the documentaries manage to prevent responses that pathologise and repudiate people who experience mental distress, what kind of identification do they encourage viewers to adopt through the non-realist or cartoon-like images of bodies deployed? Scott McCloud claims that the reason why many people identify with comic-book characters is because everyone can see themselves in a simplified cartoon face, whereas only a few can identify with a photograph. As he elaborates, when we interact with people, our mental picture of their faces is 'just a sketchy arrangement ... something as simple and basic as a cartoon'. As a result, when we look at a face in a photograph, we see it as the face of another, whereas when we look at a cartoon we see ourselves: 'the cartoon is a vacuum into which our identity and awareness are pulled ... we don't just observe the cartoon, we become it!' (1993: 36). Erasing the distance between a 'healthy' and a mentally distressed person, following McCloud's interpretation, is certainly an achievement, given the stigma that surrounds mental illness. It remains to be established, though, whether such identification is merely a fantasy – that is, a way of getting close to these experiences and people, but not *too* close (this is the problem with the fictional sequences of *Lightning over Water*, as discussed in Chapter 4). If this is the case, animation becomes a vehicle that enables us to 'travel in another realm' (1999: 36) but only temporarily. At the same time, it could be argued that what is problematic about approaching cartoon-like images in the way McCloud indicates is that by imagining being in the place of the other ('we don't just observe the cartoon or animation, we become it!'), we only eradicate rather than inhabit the space between self and other that keeps open the possibility of encountering and witnessing difference.

Unlike *Blue*, in which the voice remains disembodied, animation functions in *Animated Minds* as a bridge between the voice and the spectator. And yet, the bodies that these films show to locate the voice somewhere do not belong to the people whose testimony we hear. Even in *Obsessively Compulsive*, where we see a realistic body, it is that of an actor, and further removed through the process of being animated. Describing the kind of identification that animated documentaries encourage, Roe writes that the unique 'push-and-pull between presence and non-presence, excess and absence' creates 'a space in which our imagination positions us in someone else's subjectivity' (2009: 223). Such a space is significant in ethical terms even as it does not strictly operate in the context of the face-to-face relation;[19] in being characterised by suspension (the push and pull), we could clarify, following Hallas, that this relation in *Animated Minds* corresponds to an encounter with an other that is different to either full identification, which would reduce an other to the same,[20] or disidentification, which would reduce an other to *the* other. In escaping the limitations of these two options, such an encounter redefines viewers' ethical response-ability by keeping it open. Moreover, while it may not stimulate the radical form of 'corporeal implication' we find in *Blue*,[21] it does not cease to implicate its viewers on various levels. As Paul Ward writes about the animated documentary more generally, the gap in the relation between constructed images and real aural testimony encourages viewers to ask themselves the following:

> If someone is speaking about something, should we be watching *them*; or perhaps we should be watching *a re-enacted version of what they are talking about*;[22] or watching *an animated version* of what they are talking about; or perhaps we should simply leave the room and wander outside, taking in the view? (2005: 99)

These questions do not merely attest to the self-reflexive nature of the animated documentary as a genre but, as was the case with interactive media such as artists' books and performance art discussed in earlier chapters, they are crucially concerned with the viewers currently engaging the films and the ethical and political commitments that distinct kinds of engagement can generate.

Excess and bearing witness

If one of the most characteristic aspects of the animated documentary is its 'excess', we can read this excess and the animated documentary's evocative function beyond the question of what animation can do better than its live-action alternative while not losing sight of the medium's distinctive characteristics. The excess characterising *Animated Minds* is not simply a stylistic aspect to be fetishised, as is the case with the dominant reception of animation in the entertainment industry or even with those documentary filmmakers who embrace the form because of its popularity. Even when excess is taken seriously by animation scholars and approached in terms of the evocative functionality of the animated documentary, there is a risk that such functionality becomes instrumentalised, in the sense of being turned into a tool of measuring what the animated documentary can do better than the conventional documentary. Roe points that 'when something has no visual equivalent, it is impossible to mimetically represent it. Neither depression nor autism "look" like anything, and, as such, cannot be re-presented' (2013: 109). This comment betrays a greater interest in the ways animated documentary can broaden the epistemological parameters of conventional documentary. Instead, in this section, I want to consider how the excess characterising animation speaks to current understandings of the aesthetic and ethical work of illness narratives. This entails an interloping of critical practices and methodologies so that they encroach upon one another to enlarge the respective work of animation studies and the medical humanities.

Though not concerned with animation, Radley stresses the evocative and expressive qualities of a range of illness representations. Works of illness do not 'denote' but 'exemplify' or 'show forth', and this is where he locates their excess (2009: 187), which differentiates the work they do from that of designating with accuracy, the primary mode of scientific endeavour and the dominant way animation is used in science and medicine: 'To simply say this happened to me is not enough … something *in excess of* the story as a series of events, or even as a plot, must be expressed' (88, emphasis added).[23] This is reflected in how the story is put together, so as to convey 'a semblance of a world in which the writer bears his/her pain' (91). The idea of semblance distinguishes this way of showing from 'the documentary, be it in narrative or photographic form'. As Radley further explains, 'It is not a more distinct and public confirmation of the real that is proposed in such works, but something nearer to the sublime in the sense of conveying what, even if it cannot be seen, might yet be touched' (81). Like Hall's artists' books, *Animated Minds* gesture towards a practice of witnessing that exceeds the boundaries of vision and recognition that we find in more conventional documentary.

Works of illness, as mentioned in previous chapters, involve 'worldmaking', and here animated documentary can crystallise this idea in that, while real-action documentaries and other works of art are also 'made up', animated works are more explicitly so. For example, while we can conflate the person denoted by *Lightning over Water* (Nicholas Ray) with the figure presented in the film (despite the blurring of boundaries between fiction and documentary), or mistake Hall's appointment cards in *The Rest of My Life* for real ones – though they are the actual cards used by her, they stand for something else in this work[24] – it is unlikely that we will confuse animated worlds for real. We know that the final product was the result of a series of interactions, and that what we see has been constructed frame by frame. This focus on their fabrication is a reminder to those working in the medical humanities and viewers more generally that, while offering phenomenologically 'thicker' accounts of illness than medical interpretations, first-person narratives do not provide 'direct' access to people's lived experience. And yet, as Radley reminds us about works of illness in a broader context (2009: 190–1), films like *Animated Minds* may be configuring a made-up world, but this is not separate from notions of a real world, nor is it an escapist tool (as animation is commonly seen). Indeed, many of the speakers reveal a sense of disconnection from ordinary social experience, and of inhabiting a different world. Each of the *Animated Minds* films stands then as a 'fragment' of an alternative world and invites the viewer to bear witness; to see as a participant in that figured world, rather than necessarily see with the ill person's own eyes.

Central to the configuration of such a world, and to bearing witness, is a kind of 'internal framing', which in turn involves 'replication' and 'de-positioning' (Radley 2009: 200). What we see when we watch the *Animated Minds* films is de-positioned from its original niche or sphere – whether this is the hospital, or the space where the person has his or her distressing experiences – through the work of animation. Even though the actual voice of the ill person arguably interrupts such refiguring, in that it does not change (it even retains such authentic markers such as pauses), it is now the soundtrack of an animated world – that is, a 'replica' in Radley's sense. Similarly, de-positioning problematises the trace understood as a sign/symptom, literal or metaphorical scar, but also a conventional or expected way of viewing that signifies illness. In the previous chapters this is true, for example, of the mastectomy scar featured in some of the breast cancer photographs of Chapter 1, the appointment cards in Hall's book *The Rest of My Life* in Chapter 2, and, in the case of *Animated Minds*, the blood and scars from self-harming that we see in *My Blood is My Tears* or in *Obsessively Compulsive*. It is this aspect of framing that allows us to confront these images and even appreciate them aesthetically, even though our response cannot be contained exclusively in such appreciation. If we do not recognise/witness the work of framing, we simply see the film as denoting something; we see things that should be abjected, kept private or removed. And yet, despite such transmutation – which animation can effect very powerfully due to its production techniques and unique features such as metamorphosis and associative linking – such works remain exemplars of pain and suffering, both demanding and at times defying witnessing. As Glynne writes, 'It's all metaphor and the team behind the *Animated Minds* films knows that it can never be fully understood what it feels like to actually experience some of the difficulties covered in these films' (*Animated Minds* 2014).

An important difference between *Animated Minds* and the works of illness that Radley explores in his study is that the former are not exclusively made by the people whose voices we hear. As we know, the animation was made by professional animators who never met the interviewees but only had access to an edited soundtrack, and further elements such as sound effects were added afterwards. The judgement about works made by others is that they are works *about* rather than *of* illness, to use Radley's distinction (2009: 93–4): even though this does not necessarily foreclose their capacity to evoke compassion, there are objections that draw attention to the asymmetrical relationship between artist and subject, with all the surrounding risks of objectification and victimisation. Collaborative projects like *Animated Minds* and the examples discussed in the previous chapters complicate easy divisions between self-authored and third-party narratives. The soundtrack of *Animated Minds* consists of first-person testimonies and, unlike verbatim theatre as examined in Chapter 5, the voice corresponds to the people who were interviewed rather than to an actor. Moreover, what is central to the distinction between works *of* illness and works *about* illness is that through aesthetic practice the former re-present, in the sense of bringing into the presence of the viewer, the experience that the ill person witnessed. Making present is much more than remembering the past or something which is distant; thus the choice to use present tense in the testimony of *Fish on a Hook* is significant: 'I'm overwhelmed, I mean to be surrounded by cacophony ... I'm now stuck behind someone and I'm trying to get how long is it going to be before I get to the counter because I'm frozen with ... with ... with an anxiety, this is just a bloody nightmare!' Even though the animated images of *Animated Minds* were created by others, and thus the *animated* films can be paralleled to third person-accounts, such accounts can function as works *of* illness provided that they 'preserve and show again those features of the sufferer's story that struck them when they first heard it' (Radley 2009: 98). This is what many of the animators do in their visualisation, as well as creative interpretation of the words of the testimony they have in front of them.

Consider the example of an episode narrated in Hannah's testimony in *The Light Bulb Thing*, that of cutting her fingernails – not a depiction of suffering per se, but one that evokes it by alluding to the slowing down of time that characterises her experience: 'I remember looking at my fingernails and fingernails had grown, and I'm thinking because it seems it's like all the same day and I used to think oh God I got to cut my fingernails. They think, my fingernails think the time has passed but it hasn't.' This episode is visualised faithfully but the animator, Paul Rains, has also chosen to transform the cut fingernails into falling tree leaves through the device of metamorphosis. I see this intervention as much more than a means of ensuring narrative economy or a clever manipulation of the visual similarity of cut fingernails with tree leaves; it is all these things, of course, but it can be also approached as an example of something that struck that animator in the speaker's testimony and made him preserve and show it again in the film, enhancing its potential to conjure that particular 'world of illness'. In this sense, the kind of 'freedom' that Radley suggests is realised through aesthetic work (2009: 38) is here the outcome of the collaboration between animator and speaker, even when the two have not met in person.

The ultimate test of whether something is a work of illness is its capacity to evoke in the reader or viewer experiences that were formerly difficult to communicate, and to be recognised and received in this way again and again. Recognition does not have to necessarily relate to shared experiences, but a response by someone who has experienced similar feelings confirms the capacity of the work to touch others. For example, Glynne mentions that the best feedback of all he got was when a patient wrote to him and said, 'At last. I've been trying to explain to my consultant [psychiatrist] for years what it feels like to live with and experience this disorder. Now I can show him' (2013: 75). I read in this comment that the meaning of the film goes beyond its instrumental value (even though the ways animation can inform empirical science should not be dismissed) as it confirms something given to him or her that can now be passed on. At the same time, this dimension of allowing something to be seen anew by others is what enables illness representations to be in dialogue with the sphere of medicine and broader cultural attitudes to illness, to which the next section turns.

Testimonies of mental distress

While animation, through its excess, generates a kind of 'thickening', allowing the animated documentary to reveal more of the reality of a situation than conventional narrative, there is a danger that on another level it is associated with a 'thinning' out (Skoller 2011: 211). It is important at this point to consider what kind of alternative knowledges documentaries like the *Animated Minds* series are able to offer about the experiences they animate. To what extent do they intervene in medical or psychiatric understandings of various 'mental conditions'? How do they redress popular misconceptions and myths that inform representations of specific 'disorders' in the media? Do they manage to transform broader social attitudes about mental illness that end up stigmatising people? Ultimately, how should these animated documentaries be viewed?

Part of the aim in making these animated films was to shift attention away from individuals to particular conditions or experiences (Glynne 2013: 75). A live-action documentary would not have served this purpose as well as animation, which, like cartooning, has the ability to 'simplify images towards a purpose', thus paradoxically amplifying the experiences and details it focuses on.[25] An opportunity to resist the pressures of the individual and autobiographical self while at the same time avoiding demographic generalisations (through the audio testimony that prioritises subjective/lived experience), appears to be a good compromise between the particular and the general. Such difference is arguably subtle, given that *Animated Minds*, even though they do not disclose the identity of participants and are not characterised by the narrative anxiety typical of linear stories with a fixed closure, still revolve on an individualised view of the self. For example, we do not have any information that could place these testimonies in a broader social context. At the same time – and this is reflected in some of the titles of the documentaries and the section 'resources' on the films' website – by giving priority to representing what it is like to suffer from 'a specific mental health condition' (Glynne 2013: 75) they remain confined within diagnostic categories, some of which are contested or rejected by psychiatric survivors. Even when these categories or the medical model they abide by are not questioned, there is still the risk that the documentaries might be seen as representative of the condition in question. Different disorders become associated with particular symptoms, but not everybody will experience them in the same way (for example, schizophrenia is not always accompanied by hallucinations, as in *Dimensions*), and this may create inaccuracies or even undermine the goal of using these films as tools for communicating with others. The *Animated Minds* films manage to defuse some of these dangers by avoiding, for the most part, attaching clinical labels; by making certain distinctions (*Dimensions* chooses to describe the experience animated through the term 'psychosis' rather than schizophrenia in the audio track); and by including a variety of resources on the *Animated Minds* website that do not endorse one theory, model or treatment of mental illness. More importantly, focusing on a specific condition, however contested and complex, allows them to tackle particular assumptions and myths surrounding a range of non-normative experiences, and as such, to challenge the stigma attached to them.

While the mixture of animation and live-action shots and the use of distinct production techniques were largely successful in conveying illness experiences in *Animated Minds*, there is a broader concern about a medium like animation, which often relies on spectacular visuals (especially when it is computer-generated). In other words, stylised images and special effects could become implicated in sensationalising certain conditions or investing them with glamour.[26] This problem can have more serious consequences with an audience of young adult viewers. Echoing criticisms directed at the rise of what is disparagingly called 'sick lit' – namely books that deal with experiences such as terminal illness, self-harming, depression and death – Meghan Cox Gurdon (2011) cautions against representations that may inadvertently 'normalize [pathologies] and, in the case of self-harm, may even spread their plausibility and likelihood to young people who might otherwise never have imagined such extreme measures'. As she adds, 'Self-destructive adolescent behaviors are observably infectious and have periods of vogue. That is not to discount the real suffering that some young people endure; it is an argument for taking care.' It is likely that this critic would have found films such as *My Blood is My Tears* or *Becoming Invisible* caught up in such dilemmas. These two films, through their visceral and at times beautiful images (and, in the case of the former, the truthful account of the release accompanying self-harm, which could be mistaken for pleasure) may be approached as brushing the temptations of the glamour of self-slaughter that circulates across a number of media in contemporary society. However, *My Blood is My Tears* resists investing this suffering with a romantic aura, and here it is worth underlining the important role played by the audio narrative as well as the external framing of these films as animated documentaries (the importance of the non-fiction context) and the accompanying online resources that contextualise the documentaries. This contextualisation is important when showing these films in schools and other educational settings, or for anyone accessing them through the Internet.

While I have devoted much space to animation as a medium and to its distinct characteristics in this chapter, it is important to stress the equally important role of the spoken testimony. As Glynne tells us of the production process, the story was the building block on which the animation was based (in Hamilton 2012). There is a wider claim to make about mental illness testimony and its place within illness narrative scholarship: mentally ill people have been excluded from Frank's conception of the 'wounded storyteller'; many conditions, most notably schizophrenia, are considered to be anti-narrative,[27] and there is an absence of a range of different stories from public discourse. As discussed earlier, animation in *Animated Minds* serves to visualise feelings and sensations that are 'invisible' or difficult to put into words, and its simplicity makes it a medium that has broader appeal. But these documentaries also invite us to listen to the testimonies they include – first-person perspectives of health and illness speaking against the kind of stigma that renders distressed people mute and invisible in the first place. This is no easy task, of course, but is significant when put against the history of 'visualising madness' through medical illustration and photography, as well as mainstream visual representations that rely on spectacle and sensationalism, from which animation as a genre is not excluded. Moreover, it is this aspect of putting these voices at the centre that serves the ethical and political objectives of these documentaries.

Given their brevity and use of metaphor, *Animated Minds* lack the larger temporal structure that we find in many illness narratives (a beginning, middle and end, usually covering diagnosis, treatment and recovery).[28] Neither do they reproduce hegemonic accounts of mental health such as 'recovery narratives which tend to be highly formulaic stories of an individual's journey through and triumph over particular difficulties' (Woods 2013: 49). Common themes in these stories that are produced and consumed in certain clinical and advocacy settings include: 'How this or that service saved my life; how this or that medication saved my life; and how this or that pursuit of a normal existence saved my life. The ubiquitous message is that mental illness is a biological problem and treatment (i.e. pharmaceuticals) the solution' (Costa et al. 2012: 89). The absence of psychiatrists and other experts is a notable characteristic shared by the documentaries. Insofar as *Animated Minds* place the voices of the interviewees centre stage and capture the distress they experience without connecting it to any larger explanatory framework, whether medical or social, they could be described as products of what Patrick Bracken and Philip Thomas (2005) have named an era of 'postpsychiatry'. Despite their differences, psychiatry and antipsychiatry approach mentally ill people as victims (either of disease or environment) and try to save them by resorting to distinct forms of authority and expertise. What differentiates postpsychiatry is that it moves beyond this conflict, which ignores people's suffering.

There is nothing sentimental or sanitised about the stories the *Animated Minds* films tell. They make no claims regarding the causes of the conditions they describe, and there is no closure in the sense of a happy outcome. We assume that the speakers are narrating their experiences from a certain distance; while some of the documentaries suggest that they have found ways to cope without specifying what kind of treatment made that possible (for example, in *Fish on a Hook* the voice says that 'Now because I have been feeling these things for decades I realised that there is a way through this'), other narratives do not imply recovery but end in the kind of uncertainty, or rather honesty, characterising chronic illness. The concluding words of *My Blood is My Tears*, 'People cry, I can't cry …' are significantly put in the present tense. Stories can be unfinished, and I agree with Unni Wikan that what marks 'the true turning point' and gives narrative its power is the beginning (2000: 225); when silence is transformed into language and action, as Audre Lorde has described it in *The Cancer Journals*.

Contrary to the way mental illness is treated in mainstream cinema or the mass media, *Animated Minds* are about ordinary people speaking about their struggles to live an ordinary life through the description and animation of activities that are largely taken for granted, such as leaving the house to go to school or venturing out from one's flat to go shopping. Referring specifically to schizophrenia, Catherine Prendergast writes about the need to give up 'the stable schizophrenic, easy to incarcerate, or easy to celebrate as the occasion requires' (2008: 61). Instead she points to those narratives produced by people who mark themselves 'as non-exceptional [ordinary] schizophrenics' (55) and claim the right to own their experiences by speaking publicly on those issues that affect their lives. The *Animated Minds* films, though relying on collaboration, make precisely such claims. The focus on the lived experience of mental distress also challenges the ways many conditions become invested with metaphorical associations or referenced superficially and casually in public discourse. Research on the uses of the term schizophrenia in UK and US newspapers attests to such metaphorical use (when the disease becomes 'adjectival' and becomes attached to things that inspire horror), which furthers the stigmatisation of mental distress.[29] The language used to describe mental difficulties has made its way into our everyday conversations (when someone behaves in a bizarre manner, they are likely to be labelled as having Asperger's, or an extremely organised person *must be* OCD), yet somehow, mental illness remains taboo.

Even though the testimonies of the individual films are short, they manage to gesture towards some of the complexities that are lost by trivialising the kinds of anxiety and feelings reported by those who experience them. The two documentaries about OCD make it clear that this condition is not all about cleanliness and avoiding cracks in pavements. It can mean spending hours a day obsessing over whether one's home and family are safe from harm or over whether thinking about Saddam Hussein, as in the case of Steve, 'could cause the conflict in the Gulf to increase'. In *My Blood is My Tears*, self-harm becomes linked to a struggle with 'feeling like I wasn't human or like I wasn't part of the world' rather than a form of attention-seeking. Similarly, eating disorders are not just about food or a superficial fashion phenomenon; as Nicole explains in her testimony, giving her experience a more existential dimension, she did not stop eating 'to fit her clothes but to take less space in the world, to disappear'. These words hardly scratch the surface of the debate that has been raging for decades over proponents of the feminist cultural model of eating disorders, which pays attention to the disproportionate rate of the disorder among women/girls and draws on historical lessons such as understandings of hysteria, and supporters of the traditional medical model who see the condition as a purely biological dysfunction.[30] Nonetheless, Nicole's words, despite the universality of animation, draw attention to the need to attend to the suffering of *individual women*, which risks being effaced by both the medical model's appeal to a Cartesian disembodied self and its replacement by feminism's 'cultural body' (Lester 1997: 481).

In terms of diagnosis, an extremely powerful aspect of shaping people's experience of mental health problems as well as wider perceptions, most of the speakers do not name the conditions they describe, even though the blurbs and further resources that accompany them on the website use the names of disorders covered in the American Psychiatric Association's *Diagnostic and Statistical Manual of Mental Disorders* such as schizophrenia, Asperger's, OCD and others. Even when the interviewees explicitly allude to the medical model, there is room for alternative interpretations of the experiences they describe – as when we hear in *Dimensions* the words, 'I suppose [*hesitant voice*] taking on some of the medical interpretation that this is psychosis gave me some more options.' Very few people would contest the extraordinary diversity of schizophrenia, and with the publication of the fifth edition of the *DSM* in May 2013 and the eleventh revision of the World Health Organisation's *International Classification of Diseases* under way, these debates are likely to continue. However, the words above suggest that labelling one condition might give some people a sense of relief in that, as with CFS and MCS (discussed in Chapter 5), it provides one context through which they can understand their behaviour and feelings. Looking at the further resources on the website that accompany *Dimensions*, we see among the sources listed the Hearing Voices Network, established in the UK in 1990 and operating nationally and internationally in alliance with sympathetic professionals. This network, like other organisations and smaller groups, validates voice-hearers' own accounts of their experiences and makes it possible for these experiences to become meaningful, rather than subscribing to a medical model that views them as simply symptoms of a disorder.[31] In this way, the films, and range of accompanying resources, raise public awareness of particularly stigmatised conditions but do not endorse specific models or theories about mental ill health.

In their research on the impact of OCD on constructions of identity, sociologists Dana Fennell and Ana S. Q. Libera note that one way of reducing self-stigma is through personification and analogies which, in positing OCD as an outside influence attacking the healthy self, redefine these individuals as deserving of respect. For example, many of their interview respondents compared OCD to a 'nightmare', 'hell' or something 'that has an identity and substance of its own' (2007: 322–3). In *Over and Over (and Over) Again* we hear the voice of Danny gesturing towards a similar attempt at redefinition, enhanced through the intimate link of the words with the animation: 'And it's like someone's injecting these thoughts into your head – saying, "you've gotta do it again, or this'll happen, or that'll blow up, or that's gonna catch on fire".' While both acts of passing as 'normal' and disclosing OCD can reinforce a conflicting sense of self (the former because it is expected by society), the documentary ends by stressing the importance of sharing one's experience and seeking help, but once again this injunction leaves room for someone to choose different kinds of interpretations or treatments: 'There's people out there that don't want to admit they've got it, and don't know they've got it, and they think they're weird. But they're not ... they need someone to help them.' The words are effectively animated with an image of a city in the night-time, tall buildings with tiny windows lighting up in the darkness as the shot recedes in the distance.

Testimonies of self-harm are even more difficult to bear witness to given prevailing assumptions that self-harm is a form of 'attention-seeking' or a failed act of suicide. Most self-harmers are perceived as 'time-wasters', wasting the time of medical staff as well as their own futures. Such myths are immediately debunked by the testimony of the three girls in *My Blood is My Tears*. While suicide is final, self-harm offers release from emotional pain (as one of the girls says, 'And that pain, even though it hurt, I liked it because almost the physical pain detracted from the emotional pain') and thus can be understood 'as a means of defying death' or a struggle for survival (Kilby 2001: 126). This is confirmed by the testimonies in the film:

> Sometimes I just wanted to see blood and see my skin and know *I was still alive*, because one of the things that I struggled with was feeling unreal, and feeling like I wasn't human or like I wasn't part of the world [...] When I self-harm it's like you're in a scary film, and you finally come to the end where something happy happens, and *you're ok again.* (emphasis added)

Moreover, the comparison of the scars to a sketchbook ('it is like they tell a story') gestures towards the possibility that self-harm is a form of testimony; one, though, that 'represents an exaggerated breaking with language' (Kilby 2001: 125), given that the cutting or self-mutilation becomes a language in itself, communicating what cannot be put into words and re-enacting past trauma with a difference. What is significant about this reading, as opposed to dominant pathological approaches, is that we can envisage and gradually work towards the possibility of moving past the need for self-harm. As Janice McLane describes it, 'this new possibility would not be the hand holding a razor blade which cuts across the skin, but breath being pushed across the larynx, shaped by mouth and tongue into a spoken word' (1996: 117).

The testimonies of *My Blood is My Tears* could be read in this way, even though the words, especially the use of present tense, do not guarantee that the interviewees have permanently passed beyond the need to self-harm. At the same time, we could rephrase McLane's sentence as follows: this new possibility would not be the hand holding a razor blade that cuts across the skin, but the hand drawing a needle on paper or dripping red ink instead of blood. In other words, the animated sequences, though not produced by the self-harmer, could be equally approached as ways of passing beyond self-harm that do not rely on language – animation becomes the language, re-enacting self-harm with a difference. I am intrigued by the choice of the verb 'animate' in Jane Kilby's analysis of self-harm as a form of testimony. To animate (from the Latin verb *animare*) means 'to give life', and Kilby is using it here without thinking of the medium of animation to examine the ways self-harm becomes a way of 'animating the possibilities of life' (2001: 131), offering momentary release and the means of living beyond past trauma. If self-harm animates life, animation re-animates it in *My Blood is My Tears* – and like the oral testimony, or rather together with it, draws attention to the conditions for, or possibility of, passing beyond the need for self-harm.

The question I posed at the start of this section, of how *Animated Minds* should be viewed, cannot be answered without specifying who is viewing these narratives and in what context or purpose. Once this is taken into account, what would it mean to read them critically? The films are characterised by an openness that relates to both the medium of animation and the spoken testimonies. The animated documentary comes with a degree of self-reflexivity that invites viewers to question what we *are* or *should be* watching. As we have seen, the gap between heard voice and animated body, and the push and pull between absence and excess, shapes to a certain extent the way viewers receive the narratives they view and hear. But there is another side to that openness that relates to the testimonies themselves, however artificial a division between soundtrack and images would be. In relation to the question of what we listen for in mental testimony, Lucy Costa et al. observe the following:

> In our research, if we listen only for the 'lived experience' of individuals and only for processes of illness and recovery – we will miss many other vital storylines. We need to complicate what we are listening for: to listen less for stories of healing and recovery and more for stories of resistance and opposition, collective action and social change. (2012: 96)

We have no way of knowing the full story of the people whose voices we hear in *Animated Minds*. While the films focus on their lived experience, their stories are not confined within the clinical framework of patient and illness. If they advocate something, it is coping with distress and the stigma that accompanies it, rather than a biomedical solution or a miraculous recovery. And yet, neither do they speak against inhumane psychiatric care nor explicitly adopt the kinds of views activists in the psychiatric survivor movement would. We could ask, as I have done in Chapter 1 in order to problematise notions of 'feminist' breast cancer narratives, whether this mutes their critical potential – especially when it comes to intervening within dominant biomedical explanations of mental disorders (particularly influential in the United States, but also indicative of a more general shift in recent decades within psychiatry). In the context of the diversity of narratives by people who have experienced mental distress, also reflected in the language adopted – mental health service consumer, psychiatric survivor, ex-patient, and 'mad', by mass movements such as Mad Pride – this openness is not necessarily reactionary or antithetical to the spirit of the critical medical/health humanities. More crucially, it directs attention to each viewer's responsibility for their own position with respect to mental distress as they become witnesses to these testimonies. As Woods has persuasively argued in a different context, 'to be open to the dynamics of testimony is to start to recognise one's own position within the matrix of power-relations in which conflicts over the nature and meaning of mental ill-health, suffering and trauma are articulated' (2013: 49). Whether it relates to practitioners (animators and documentary filmmakers), academic scholars or the wider public, it is this alternative aspect of self-reflexivity, facilitated though not strictly determined by the medium of animation, that adds to the ethical and political force of these documentaries.

Notes

1. For the history of animation see Wells 1998. For the uses of animation in therapy see Mason 2009 and <http://www.animationtherapy.co.uk/public-home.aspx> (last accessed 27 July 2015). For collaborations between artists and scientists that involve animation more generally, see <http://www.silentsignal.org/about/> and <http://animateprojects.org/films/by_date/20141/navigations#hash.bev8vAWb.dpuf> (last accessed 27 July 2015).
2. Despite the craze surrounding the form today, the animated documentary has a long history dating back to *The Sinking of the Lusitania* (1918) by pioneer American animator Winsor McCay (see Roe 2013).
3. See *Blood Matters* (Mosaic Films in association with The National Blood Service, 2004), Ellie Land's *Centrefold* (2012), Tim Webb's *A Is for Autism* (1992), Stephen Palmer's *Blindscape* (1993) and Samantha Moore's *An Eyeful of Sound* (2010). Many of these animated documentaries have been supported by UK public broadcasters and charitable foundations such as Channel 4 and the Wellcome Trust.
4. Alternative Psychiatric Narratives, call for papers, Birkbeck College, London, May 2014, <http://altpsychiatricnarratives.wordpress.com/call-for-papers/> (last accessed 27 July 2015). Two animated documentaries that focus on entering and leaving care which were created by young people in foster and residential care in Cambridgeshire are *My Name is Joe* (2012) and *Finding My Way* (2013). See <http://www.psychiatry.cam.ac.uk/blog/animated-film-made-by-young-care-leavers-wins-best-documentary-prize-at-the-bfi-future-film-awards/> (last accessed 27 July 2015).
5. All references to the soundtrack are taken from the transcripts available on this website.
6. Note that this is a developmental disorder, but the emphasis of the film is on the experience of being bullied and the emotional suffering it brings.
7. Some of the films were presented at Medfest 2012, the UK's only Medical Film Festival, which tours different UK cities every year. Its target audience is medical students, but it usually brings together a range of health professionals, patients as well as members of the public. The topic of that year was HealthScreen: Understanding Illness through Film. See <http://www.medfest-archive.co.uk/medfest2012.htm> (last accessed 27 July 2015).
8. The Graphic Medicine is available at: <http://www.graphicmedicine.org/> (last accessed 27 July 2015). For work in the field of graphic medicine, see Squier 2007, Green and Myers 2010, Vaccarella 2013 and Williams 2014.
9. For example, the modes of 'expository', 'observational', 'participatory' or 'interactive', 'reflexive' and 'performative' (Nichols 2001).

10. Medical animation evolved from the field of realistic medical illustrations before it turned to computer-generated animation in the early 1970s.
11. There is a wealth of phenomenologically-informed medical humanities scholarship. See Toombs 1992, Svenaeus 2000, Carel 2008, Carel and Cooper 2013, Ratcliffe 2014 and Kouba 2014.
12. See Ehrlich 2011.
13. This is not to suggest that comics and animation cannot lead to stereotyping through the development of recognisable symbols. Even a careful study on comics like Scott McCloud's cannot escape reproducing certain types while exemplifying the visual vocabulary of comics (1993: 131, particularly the last panel, which includes a face showing 'dementia').
14. An animated documentary made through this technique is Bob Sabiston's *Snack and Drink* (1999), which explores aspects of the world of autism.
15. Freud discusses the idea of 'a living doll' in his essay (2003: 135).
16. This quotation is taken from the blurb of *The Light Bulb Thing* on the *Animated Minds* website, <http://animatedminds.com/the_films/the_light_bulb_thing/> (last accessed 27 July 2015).
17. See the website of animator Katerina Athanasopoulou: <http://kineticat.co.uk/My-Blood-is-My-Tears> (last accessed 27 July 2015).
18. This effect is heightened when a viewer attempts to listen to the audio testimonies without looking at the animated images.
19. It is important to note that the face in Levinas' philosophy is more than the physical face of a person. For the meanings of face in Levinas see Morgan 2011, specifically Chapter 3.
20. I borrow this term from Levinas, who in turn adapts it from Plato. See Levinas 1998: 48.
21. Since *Blue* forecloses, as Hallas writes of his own viewing experience of this film, 'the ability to imagine the body of the person with AIDS "out there" and thus as wholly other, I come to witness the witness through my very own body' (2007: 45). Discussing *Blue*'s haptic visuality, Hallas concludes that the film offers an encounter that occurs 'within bodies rather than between them, a significant achievement in the context of the widespread stigmatisation and abjection of people with AIDS' (48).
22. As is the case with Wenders' highly stylised documentary.
23. Frank also uses the term 'excess' (1995: 144).
24. See Radley 2009: 204.
25. See McCloud about cartooning as a form of 'amplification through simplification' (1993: 30–1).
26. This is the implicit criticism of one recent animated film, Evan Viera's *Caldera* (2012), which even though it is not described as a documentary, was inspired by Viera's father's experience of schizoaffective disorder. Alex Widdowson (2013) finds the film to be 'a challenging CGI exercise' which left him 'nourished visually but a little under-fed intellectually'.

27. See Woods 2011b and 2012. Frank's new narrative type 'broken narratives' in the second edition of *The Wounded Storyteller* (2013) focuses on cognitive disability (his examples are brain injury and dementia).
28. The interviews were shortened and edited, of course, so we can imagine that they were much more elaborate and definitely 'messier' than the final versions.
29. See Sontag 1991: 59–60 and Chopra and Doody 2007.
30. See Bordo 1993 and Lester 1997 for an exploration of both models.
31. For recent interdisciplinary work on this topic, see 'Hearing the Voice' project at Durham University: <http://hearingthevoice.org/> (last accessed 27 July 2015).

Afterword: #Illness

Critiques about the normativity of the idea of narrative self in illness narratives seem to be recycled in recent debates about the employment of social media. Following his wife's *Guardian* article, American journalist Bill Keller's 2014 column in the *New York Times* about Lisa Bonchek Adams' 'online omnipresence', her 'copious' blogging and tweeting about her metastatic breast cancer, has generated a great deal of negative response by readers who saw it as an attack or at least as a piece lacking in empathy.[1] Bill Keller writes that Adams' 'decision to live her cancer onstage invites us to think about it, debate it, learn from it'. His objection seems to be connected to her 'approach to cancer that honors the warrior' and denigrates those who do not survive or persevere as long as she does, an objection that many of the narratives I have explored in this book share. Hall, as seen in Chapter 2, confronts discourses of survivorhood and failure within medicine, and her artists' books reject the cultural narrative of triumph. Similarly, the breast cancer stories and representations examined in Chapter 1 move beyond the simplistic warrior/victim opposition, and so do the portrayals of mental distress in *Animated Minds* that were discussed in Chapter 6.

Part of the problem with Bill Keller's statement that 'social media have become a kind of self-medication' is that such comments betray a generalised damning attitude that does not consider why some people choose these media or what particular aspects of their stories these media might allow them to express. We could determine, for example, as I have tried to do in the previous chapters, the ways these forms (or the mode of narration they allow) are expressive rather than simply providing too much, or merely graphic, information. If we need to attend to what an account communicates in *excess* of its content – excess read here not as synonymous with exposure that is commonly associated with social media – to respond properly to testimony, should we not respond differently to Adams' act of copious tweeting, irrespective of whether we agree with the narrative it cultivates?[2] Should we not approach it as the means she has chosen to develop her 'own style', to use Broyard's phrase (1992: 63), for her illness? This idea may be too provocative for some but my point is that close attention should be paid to how such narratives do their work, which is often more nuanced than dominant polarised views suggest.

In some ways, online forms of representing illness could be viewed as welcome alternatives to structure, coherence and unity and as promoting the idea of 'illness as many narratives' in all its various meanings. Even online stories that have larger narrative structures and are primarily written from a singular perspective, such as blogs, advance an episodic storytelling[3] that is distinct from the traditional narrative types (for example Frank's typology in the first edition of *The Wounded Storyteller*) long favoured in illness narrative scholarship. In her analysis of blog writing, Bärbel Höttges (2009) argues that 'as the writing process in a blog is fragmented (separate updates covering a very limited amount of time) and directed from a limited point of view (no considerable temporal distance to the events described), narrativization is not – or only in a very limited way – possible in a blog'. It could be suggested that social media, especially micro-blog applications like Twitter, encourage what was described in the Introduction as 'emergent' narratives, since a story unfolds in small chunks.[4] Moreover, the inbuilt interactivity of social network applications challenges the concept of authorship in favour of relational modes of expression; in the case of a webpage's guestbook or in the comments section, other narratives and conversations can be opened up, not always relevant to the main story. Such processes then enable different voices to be heard. Finally, the ability to combine words, images and videos and to link to other sites offers a rare hybridity and can direct readers to new and multiple narratives which may differ every time readers, or even the same reader, have access to online material. And yet, as we have seen in some of the previous chapters, the combination of media forms was possible long before digitisation (in artists' books, for instance), and bringing together many voices may not necessarily foster collaboration or lead to co-authored narratives.

A simple point to make in relation to the ongoing debates about Health 2.0, and the wider phenomenon of media convergence, is that being a patient who uses digital tools to acquire, share and develop knowledge or to raise awareness about certain conditions and the stigma that surrounds them can be empowering and democratising, albeit not inherently so.[5] In the case of Salvatore Iaconesi, an engineer, artist, hacker and advocate of open-source ideology who cracked his medical digital records after being diagnosed with brain cancer in 2012, and shared them with others to allow them to exchange information about any possible cure, digital tools were empowering.[6] The project he created, La Mia Cura Open Source (Open Source Cure), critiques the hierarchies and power structures of medical knowledge, supporting instead a peer-to-peer 'cure' and the right of choice in treatment:

> I have been able to do it [share information] because the data used **open, accessible formats:** [doctors] have been able to open the files using their computers, their tablets. They have been able to reply from home, on Sunday. … **This is a CURE. This is my OPEN SOURCE CURE.**
> *This is an open invitation to take part in the CURE.*
> **CURE, in different cultures, means different things.**
> There are cures for the body, for spirit, for communication.
> **Grab the information about my disease, if you want, and give me a CURE:** create a video, an artwork, a map, a text, a poem, a game, or try to find a solution for my health problem.
> Artists, designers, hackers, scientists, doctors, photographers, videomakers, musicians, writers. **Anyone can give me a CURE.** (Iaconesi 2012)

A visualisation of the 500,000 responses Iaconesi received from 'all over the planet, spanning thousands of years of human history and traditions' can be seen on his website.[7] He received 'cures' including art, music, suggestions for holistic treatments as well as medical options from medical experts, artists and fellow patients. Reflecting on the project, he states that his cures 'were created by people's desire to be a part of a society whose well-being depends on the well-being of all of its members'. Confirming that openness should be put to a particular service rather than embraced for its own sake, he stresses, 'Who cares about all of the openness if it's not matched by radical anthropological and cultural change?' (in Torgovnick 2013). Thus, openness for him also means translating medical language into a more comprehensible idiom and bridging the distance between health practitioners and their patients. In this sense his project is truly situated 'at the crossroad of digital and medical humanities' (Casilli 2012).

Even though Iaconesi used his technical expertise to hack his medical files and open them up for anyone interested in seeing them, most people's daily activities on the Internet do not take the form of Internet activism, and their use of digital tools is more modest, which is not to suggest less important. Personal health blogs, as the quintessential Web 2.0 application, have allowed patients diagnosed with various conditions to transcend geographical contexts, collaborate and share information; this is especially valued with rare or contested diseases, or those that do not have the visibility that cancer has within health culture. But many of them are blogs that place illness in a larger life narrative. Poet Patricia Debney (2011) explains how her blog came about: at her son's diagnosis with type 1 diabetes, she could not locate 'a record of what living with a type 1 child in the family is like. I could not see myself or our family anywhere. I longed for a starting point, a resource and a sense of the future.'

While social media like YouTube and Facebook can provide openings for those who wish to engage public health concerns outside of more traditional media, the freedom they offer is not unconstrained. The information that is posted online or made public becomes automatically subject to several operations that undercut the illusion of ownership. These range from sampling, remixing and annotating to the more ordinary publicisation of individual Facebook activities to a user's 'friends' through the 'news feed function'. Privacy is not the only issue that is at stake when considering how digital data are managed, even as it has received lots of attention. As Hallas is right to argue (more specifically in his case about the database) the whole process of digital management 'threatens to override or conceal the ethical, affective, and political dimensions' (2009: 244–5) of illness testimonies. Chapter 3 examined Gómez-Peña's concern about what happens to his work as a performance artist in the age of the 'mainstream bizarre' when it is decontextualised – that is, emptied of its political and other implications, and disseminated as a spectacle of stylised hybridity and radicalism. This danger becomes exacerbated through social media and the Internet; such media foster a more distracted mode of viewing than, for example, artists' books or performance art, as users are often surrounded by an overwhelming amount of information and images. If we add to this the processes of sampling and mixing to which digital data are often subjected before reaching viewers, we are not far from Hallas' and Gómez-Peña's critiques of the important ethical and political dimensions that may get lost through such operations. In a way, Gómez-Peña's palimpsestuous performances, as much as they mimic these operations, can be read as attempts to restore such losses by re-infusing images with political content.

Social media offer opportunities for new kinds of visibility but also instances of monitoring and surveillance. They encourage making the invisible visible and the private public, but the rules by which they operate are far from straightforward for users. One Facebook user found that some of her mastectomy images, posted on her own Facebook album and on pages for various cancer organisations, had been removed by Facebook under its Nudity and Pornography clause. Her response was to challenge such an act of 'censorship' and to stress that there was nothing pornographic about her images, subsequently reposted by her family and friends, as they were meant to celebrate her survival. The network's response that they 'welcome' mastectomy pictures but some may 'breach regulations' (Arthurs 2012) shows that the boundaries between what is acceptable to be displayed and what is not are very hard to discern. But, more importantly, it betrays an unwillingness and inability on the network's part to attend to this woman's broader illness story, from which the image gathers meaning (captions, text and other framing devices are important, as seen in Chapter 1, for approaching images). Ultimately her experience is suppressed, not in favour of the voice of medicine in this case, but that of law.

Many narratives by women who document their experiences of breast cancer online could be viewed as continuing Lorde's and Spence's projects of breaking silences and connecting with other women, or using photography as a form of therapy. When Emily Helck began chemotherapy after her double mastectomy in 2012, to give one example, she decided to document each day with photos. These are not the distinct head and shoulders crop of a webcam snap (now known as 'selfies'), but full-body images taken from a distance with the use of a camera tripod. At the end of a year, she put the images together in a time-lapse video. Her comments in her blog contextualising the photos resonate with aspects of Spence's work, especially her emphasis on facial expression, even though Helck's tools are different:

> I can't remember what it looked like when the surgeon removed my bandages for the first time – in my memory, I'm watching myself from across the room. So with chemo, I wanted to make sure that didn't happen. It started out just being about the hair loss and regrowth, but my body continued to change drastically too. I kind of wear my heart on my sleeve, so what's going on emotionally is visible on my face. (quoted in Krumboltz 2013)

Helck's blog (2013) resembles some of the breast cancer narratives considered earlier despite the differences in terms of the range of texts, images and cultural resources that she puts together. Citing Lorde's *The Cancer Journals*, she criticises the social pressure to use prosthesis and expresses her anger over pharmaceutical companies that treat breast cancer while producing carcinogenic products at the same time. Narrative performances such as this interrogate the view that social media – most notably Facebook – encourage only positive representations through the opportunities they give to their users to hide or dissociate from certain images and fashion the kinds of identities they wish to project. Social media and digital tools make such processes of selectivity easier, of course, given that images can be endlessly manipulated, but these operations do not only serve a single purpose.[8] Clarissa Jacob and Amy Tobin's comparison of Spence's use of the traditional family album as a mode of therapeutic self-analysis with Facebook's virtual archive is interesting in this respect (2013: 30). As they are right to argue, 'Spence's phototherapeutic restaging of the family album and studio portrait still applies to our desire to self-represent.' But, as they also point out, 'the question is whether a photographer could gain enough distance to undergo phototherapy when the image is so pervasive today' (32). In light of this, 'illness as many narratives' risks becoming reduced to a quantitative idea in the era of media convergence.

The need to gain enough distance from the flood of images circulating in contemporary culture brings up the issue of having the space and time to process and reflect on experience, which the increased use of mobile technologies that favour shorter and more frequent communication does not particularly encourage. Sara Maitland's argument that due to the obsession with narrative and noise, especially in contemporary Western culture, 'too much silence' is seen to be 'either "mad" (depressive, escapist, weird) or "bad" (selfish, antisocial)' (2008: 25) seems to be more true than ever in the age of social media. Even when narrative is replaced by visual media, visibility becomes as pervasive or conservative as narrative in its normativity. Is the solution to venture beyond language – or, instead, to reclaim the lost art of 'storytelling', to echo Walter Benjamin (2002: 143)? Kathleen Woodward chooses the second approach. In contrast to frequent accusations against the memoir as 'singing the same song' (Berlant 2001: 55), she defends this genre, and specifically the illness memoir, for promising, though not always delivering, 'intimate voices' drawing us into 'the nuanced sphere of subjectivity, where experience is not diminished to a sentence or two but elaborated and embedded in the uninflected language of information-prose' (Woodward 2009: 191). When located within a wider context of a media constellation of life narratives rather than juxtaposed against literature and its aesthetic criteria, it seems that the illness memoir can provide an antidote to what Woodward calls 'mock feelings' and 'affect bites'.[9]

Woodward's critique is not targeted at social media per se but encompasses a range of aspects of contemporary culture, from the 'consumer culture of manufactured and simulated excitement' to 'ever expanding channels of mass-mediated information, exploding networks of digital communication and new and multiple forms of visual entertainment' (25). Discussing a news article, she elaborates:

> [The writer's] words, plucked as they are to fit the compact and condensed frame of a news piece, necessarily lack the sense of a vital connection to a unique life, to a voice that articulates the tone and tenor of a particular experience. In these stories the depth of form given shape by an individual voice has been flattened; experience has been downgraded to a dulling sameness. For the logic of the genre of the information-story is additive, not the intensification of complexity. Easily absorbed information-language is just as easily forgotten. I find myself longing for the contours of individual voices reflecting on their own experience and speaking, so it seems, directly to me and not in words mediated by the Web site content provider or the news writer. I find myself longing for the unpredictability and color of adjectives and adverbs, for sentences that stretch beyond the boundaries of sound bites, for entire paragraphs and chapters that meditate on time and meaning, for something I could never imagine. (173)

This 'longing' is not a form of nostalgia like the one felt by those who lament the demise of literature due to the rise of the memoir.[10] Instead, it is a plea for the cultural politics and poetics of the emotions that are distinct from 'intensities or short-lived feelings' thanks to their 'analytical' and 'cognitive edge' (Woodward 2009: 26).

Woodward's statement that 'the large-scale narrative has been compressed to an image fragment' – *'affect bites* ... that attach us not to *people* but rather suture us to the task' (26) – has interesting resonances with recent debates about Twitter, particularly when it intersects with questions of illness, mourning and death. A well-documented case which has sparked conversations about the ability of Twitter to forge new affective communities is that of American journalist Scott Simon. Simon posted the following tweet to his 1.2 million followers on July 23, 2013: 'I just want to say that ICU nurses are remarkable people. Thank you for what you do for our loved ones.'[11] More tweets followed during the next few days about the last moments of his dying mother.

Simon's tweets from the ICU went 'viral' and elicited different kinds of responses by readers: from the headline by blog-related media company GigaOM, 'NPR host's live-tweeting of his mother's last moments shows the power of 140 characters' (Ingram 2013) to one commentator's following statement on a *Wall Street Journal* post: 'Now death itself in real time is the subject of internet sponsored chatter. If the dying moments of your mother can now be the subject of 140 characters publicly disseminated sound bites, then any regard for privacy, and any sense of awe of life's end, has been seriously anesthetized' (quoted in Bielanko 2013). Those who adopted a more measured view commented on the ways live-tweeting allowed Simon to express his grieving, and others to experience his mother's passing through his eyes, in real time, which would not have been possible before Twitter. Monica Hesse (2013) called this presentation 'a rough draft of [Simon's] own mourning', which he could have filtered, polished or reconsidered in a grief memoir, and noted the abrupt shifts in affect – some of the tweets 'were earnest tributes' and others 'were like giggling in church'. (We can imagine that these shifts were heightened for his followers, stumbling upon Simon's intimate tweets amidst a range of other, certainly jarring, updates.)

Other participants in this conversation clarified that what they found unsettling was the act of tweeting rather than the content of the messages. Tending to the dying and writing do not occur simultaneously; we encountered in Chapter 4 Wenders' uneasiness about being more concerned with making a film rather than being with his friend. Similarly, Lizzy Miles, a hospice social worker in Ohio who has helped popularise Death Cafes, informal coffee-shop-style meetings to discuss issues related to death, notes, 'I don't think one can be fully present in the moment and tweet at the same time' (quoted in Kaleem 2013). Another reader could not help but notice how 'even in 30 minutes after his mother's death, Simon sent 3 tweets'. If a camera can get between two people in ways that are ethically fraught, as seen in relation to *Lightning over Water*, it could be argued that the camera is still facing, and in this way bearing witness (albeit in a mediated fashion) to the person who is in front of it and his/her experience. On the contrary, the act of tweeting becomes 'an obligation *to others*' that removes us from the people who are physically around us (Paul 2013). The fact that messages transmitted through this medium address everyone and no one in particular complicates further the ways users relate to each other.

Twitter's brevity raises the question, as we have seen from readers' responses, whether a 140-character sentence could be as expressive, with all the implications this term has, as a more extended narrative. In this book I have considered mixed-media forms such as artists' books and short animated films that, despite not following larger temporal structures, are able to communicate illness experiences in complex and intensified ways. The criteria according to which we may judge tweets as failing to do the same are contested, given Twitter's recent invention.[12] In Simon's case, the use of Twitter was also scrutinised in terms of the particular mode of witnessing that it facilitates or occludes. While some commentators posited that the kind of temporality associated with this medium creates a visceral and more authentic way of witnessing an event, others pointed to the medium's inability to provide more than a peek.[13] A related objection that also relates to issues of consent is that the tweets moved attention away from the person who was dying to the person tweeting her death. This is not to suggest that the mourner's story is not legitimate, but simply to be aware of the voices that may get silenced in the process of telling one story (as we also saw in Chapter 5).

This well-publicised case would likely not have been as controversial and divisive if Simon had posted what he wrote in his tweets in a blog after the event. It was the fact that his commentary was live – and updates were being provided regularly – that unsettled many of the readers, thus drawing attention to the need to examine ethics in relation to genre/medium, as opposed to simply an individual's ethical disposition. But this controversy also raises larger questions about what we are to make of the proliferation and incessant circulation of illness and trauma stories online. Hesse (2013) writes that 'reading about a grown man crumbling over the bed of his dying mother … penetrated the hard shell of the Internet. It was reminding people what it meant to feel.' Referring to Adams' posts about her metastatic cancer amidst 'the buoyant mundanity' of the rest of her Twitter feed, Meghan O'Rourke (2014) makes a similar point about 'the disjunctiveness of posts like hers, which pop the bubble of the social-media surfaces that we slide along, as if our time here were a never-ending river rather than a journey that has a distinct end'. We encountered a similar clash in Chapter 4: that of Wenders counteracting the distance of his film images through video segments that capture a sense of embodied immediacy and biological decay, even as this risks undermining cinema's 'life-preserving' function. Not everyone, though, is persuaded by the potential of such moments to substitute emotion for daily short-lived feelings. In an acerbic piece, Roisin Kiberd (2014), for instance, rejects the phenomenon of illness becoming a 'personal hashtag' and describes illness narratives through these media as offering 'a momentarily "real" twinge of pain felt from the unreal act of clicking'. Implicating readers/viewers as opposed to only their authors, she adds that 'our fascination with pain and suffering make them natural clickbait, a new kind of online "wound culture"'. Such a view is, however, oblivious to the fact that even virtual communities are made of people with physical bodies, typing on their keyboards and mobile devices from a certain physical location, and responding to what they read/view in embodied ways that confirm their embeddedness in a material – that is, real – world.

Returning to Simon's tweets, the only aspect about which there was more consensus among readers was that this case confirmed the 'hunger on the part of Americans for a way to integrate death and mourning into [their] lives – a hunger that is being met by social media'. Considering the recent privatisation of death, according to O' Rourke (2013), Simon's Twitter feed, instead of necessarily becoming synonymous with a kind of 'gruesome exhibitionism', could be approached as 'a modern version of what has always existed: a platform for shared grief where the immediate loss suffered by one member of a community becomes an opportunity for communal reckoning and mourning'. Perhaps it is far-fetched to compare Facebook announcements of people having died (which are increasingly more common) to church bells ringing in the town square, as the author of this article does, but it is important to acknowledge the ways digital and social network media are increasingly shaping individual and collective narratives of death, mourning and bereavement.

While media such as Twitter undoubtedly present novel challenges for those who write, read and interpret illness representations, the fields of illness narratives and the critical medical humanities should pay more careful attention to the kind of work they do in contemporary culture, including their limitations. Only then can we challenge assumptions that they are merely personal, or promote ideas of individual authenticity. By bringing together chapters on photography, artists' books, performance art, film, theatre and animation, and examining a range of methods (aesthetic, ethical, pedagogical, political as well as collaborative) *Illness as Many Narratives* has shown the importance of amplifying rather than reducing the notion of narrative to verbal and written forms, across a wide variety of arts and media, both 'high' and 'low'. It has further demonstrated the importance of attending closely to their formal and generic complexity and the productive collisions they stage, thus suggesting that formal issues are as deeply critical and political as the contexts of these works' production and reception. Resisting full absorption by either artistic or medical concerns, and, in the context of this Afterword, digital technology, the many narrative performances I have considered in the case studies invite the kind of critical interloping through which cross-disciplinary dialogue can be forged. As such, they enlarge the goals and scope of the fields with which they come in contact and open spaces for a more critically engaged medical humanities, grounded in the radical intellectual and creative potential of the arts and humanities.

When carrying out the research for this book I began to see myself as a kind of interloper too. I became more and more interested in the relationship between medicine/health and different art forms and media, even though my academic background in literary studies does not provide me with strict expertise in these areas. While my grounding in the humanities allows me to assert that medical humanities is an important research field for both medicine *and* the humanities – to echo Shafer (2009: 3), therein lies the delight, rather than dilemma, of the medical humanities for me – I hope that my critical distance and approach has allowed me to pursue the conversations across disciplinary divides in a way that encourages more 'interlopers from distant disciplines' to affiliate themselves with this dynamic and important field.

Notes

1. Emma Keller's article has been removed from the *Guardian*'s website 'pending investigation'.
2. The nature of this narrative is not straightforward; Adams' individual circumstances are not taken into consideration when Keller (2014) compares her experience with his father-in-law's 'calm death', which leads to a discussion of the lost art of a 'humane and honorable' death.
3. See Strawson's account of the differences between narrative and non-narrative (or episodic) people in 'Against Narrativity' (2004), and n. 10 in this book's Introduction.
4. Despite not being characterised by the editorial distancing typical of published narratives, these accounts are also mediated, and it would be wrong to approach them as necessarily more authentic or closer to lived experience. See Sosnowy 2013.

5. The Web 2.0 concept is most often applied to the rise of blogging, photo, video and music file sharing, collaborative writing/editing, and social network media in the first decade of the twenty-first century (Meikle and Young 2011: 65–6). See also Jenkins 2006. On the use of social media in medicine and the relationship between media convergence and medical humanities, see Boateng and Black 2012, Meskó 2013 and the conference 'Medical Power & Ethics – Mediality and Media Convergence', 12–14 February 2014, Johannes Gutenberg-Universität Mainz, <http://www.medienkonvergenz.uni-mainz.de/2014/01/20/2014-02-medical-power-ethics-mediality-and-media-convergence/> (last accessed 27 July 2015).
6. The clinical files were in a closed, proprietary format, thus Iaconesi could not open them using his computer or send them in this format to all the people who could have helped him find a solution. In Italy, four deputies of the Democratic Party presented Iaconesi's initiative to the Ministry of Health, asking them to consider the possibility of releasing all Italian citizens' clinical data in a fully open format (Torgovnick 2012).
7. Iaconesi's website is available at: <http://opensourcecureforcancer.com/> (last accessed 27 July 2015).
8. See the case of a grieving father who asked strangers to digitally retouch a picture of his newly born baby (who had died) so that the hospital tubes could be removed, as it was the only photograph he had. The response from readers was overwhelming (Moir 2014).
9. It would be interesting to juxtapose this with Faith McLellan's exploration of the 'full of affect' language of blogs, including 'silly abbreviations <imho>< rotfl>, smiley faces :), Xs and Os' (1997: 101).
10. See Diedrich 2009 on this, specifically her introductory chapter.
11. His tweet can be seen here: <https://twitter.com/nprscottsimon/status/359724425093988352> (last accessed 27 July 2015).
12. For various forms of digital fiction, see Bell, Ensslin and Rustad 2013.
13. See O'Rourke and Paul 2013.

Bibliography

Aaron, Michele (2007), *Spectatorship: The Power of Looking On*, London: Wallflower.
Aaron, Michele (2014), *Death and the Moving Image: Ideology, Iconography and I*, Edinburgh: Edinburgh University Press.
ABIM Foundation, ACP-ASIM Foundation and European Federation of Internal Medicine (2002), 'Medical Professionalism in the New Millennium: A Physician Charter', *Annals of Internal Medicine*, 136, 243–6.
Adams, Rachel (2001), *Sideshow USA: Freaks and the American Cultural Imagination*, Chicago: Chicago University Press.
Ahmed, Sara (2000), *Strange Encounters: Embodied Others in Post-Coloniality*, London: Routledge.
Alarcón, Wilson Astudillo, and Carmen Mendinueta Aguirre (2007), 'The Cinema in the Teaching of Medicine: Palliative Care and Bioethics', *Journal of Medicine and Movies*, 1, 32–41.
Alter, Nora M. (1997), 'Documentary as Simulacrum; *Tokyo-Ga*', in Roger F. Cool and Gerd Gemünden (eds), *The Cinema of Wim Wenders: Image, Narrative and the Postmodern Condition*, Detroit: Wayne State University Press, 1997, pp. 136–62.
Animated Minds (2014), Mosaic Films, <http://animatedminds.com/the_concept/> (last accessed 27 July 2015).
Anzaldúa, Gloria (1999), *Borderlands/La Frontera: The New Mestiza*, San Francisco: Aunt Lute.
Arthurs, Deborah (2012), 'Cancer Survivor's Inspirational Mastectomy Photos BANNED by Facebook for Being "Pornographic"', *Daily Mail* online, <http://www.dailymail.co.uk/femail/article-2148029/Cancer-survivors-mastectomy-photos-BANNED-Facebook-pornographic.html> (last accessed 27 July 2015).
Atkinson, Paul (2009), 'Illness Narrative Revisited: The Failure of Narrative Reductionism', *Sociological Research Online*, 14: 5, <http://www.socresonline.org.uk/14/5/16.html> (last accessed 27 July 2015).
Atkinson, Sarah, Bethan Evans, Angela Woods and Robin Kearns (2015), '"The Medical" and "Health" in a Critical Medical Humanities', *Journal of Medical Humanities*, 36, 71–81.

Auton, Emilie (2013), '"Playing Doctor": Learning about Intimate Examinations in Medical School', Global Medical Humanities, Association for Medical Humanities Annual Conference, 8–10 July 2013, Aberdeen.

Bailes, Sara Jane (2011), *Performance Theatre and the Poetics of Failure: Forced Entertainment, Goat Island, Elevator Repair Service*, Abingdon: Routledge.

Bazin, André (2005), *What Is Cinema? Essays Selected and Translated by Hugh Gray*, Vol. 1, Berkeley: University of California Press.

Bell, Alice, Astrid Ensslin and Hans Rustad (eds) (2013), *Analyzing Digital Fiction*, London: Routledge.

Belling, Catherine (2012), 'A Happy Doctor's Escape from Narrative: Reflection in *Saturday*', *Medical Humanities*, 38, 2–6.

Benjamin, Walter (2002), 'The Storyteller', in Howard Eiland and Michael W. Jennings (eds), *Walter Benjamin: Selected Writing, Vol. 3 1935–1938*, Cambridge, MA: Harvard University Press, pp. 143–66.

Berlant, Lauren (2001), 'Trauma and Ineloquence', *Cultural Values*, 5: 1, 41–58.

Berlant, Lauren (2007), 'On the Case', *Critical Inquiry*, 33: 4, 663–72.

Best, Clare (2011), *Excisions*, Hove: Waterloo Press.

Best, Clare (2013), 'Attentive Writers': Healthcare, Authorship, and Authority, University of Glasgow, 23–5 August 2013, <http://selfportraitwithoutbreasts.wordpress.com/2013/08/28/attentive-writers-healthcare-authorship-and-authority/> (last accessed 27 July 2015).

Best, Clare (2014), 'Part 2: On Scars and Memories', guest post, *BMJ Medical Humanities* blog, 21 April 2014, <http://blogs.bmj.com/medical-humanities/2014/04/21/guest-blog-post-by-poet-and-writer-clare-best-part-2-on-scars-and-memories/> (last accessed 27 July 2015).

Bielanko, Monica (2013), 'Life, Death, Love and Loss in 140 Characters: It's Time to Look at Twitter in a New Light', <http://www.babble.com/mom/life-death-love-and-loss-in-140-characters-its-time-to-look-at-twitter-in-a-new-light/> (last accessed 27 July 2015).

Blanchot, Maurice (1995), *The Writing of the Disaster*, trans. Ann Smock, Lincoln, NE: University of Nebraska Press.

Bleakley, Alan (2013), 'Transitions in Health Humanities – Towards a "Critical" Health Humanities that Embraces Beauty', in Lianne McTavish and Pamela Brett MacLean (eds), *Insight 2: Engaging the Health Humanities*, Alberta: University of Alberta, pp. 10–14.

Bleakley, Alan (2014a), 'Towards A "Critical Medical Humanities"', in Victoria Bates, Alan Bleakley and Sam Goodman (eds), *Medicine, Health and the Arts: Approaches to the Medical Humanities*, London: Routledge, pp. 17–26.

Bleakley, Alan (2014b), 'The Medical Humanities in Medical Education', in Therese Jones, Delese Wear and Lester D. Friedman (eds), *Health Humanities Reader*, New Brunswick, NJ: Rutgers University Press, pp. 501–10.

Bleakley, Alan (2015), *Medical Humanities and Medical Education: How the Medical Humanities Can Shape Better Doctors*, London: Routledge.
Bleakley, Alan, Robert Marshall and Rainer Brömer (2006), 'Toward an Aesthetic Medicine: Developing a Core Medical Humanities Undergraduate Curriculum', *Journal of Medical Humanities*, 27, 197–213.
Bleakley, Alan, and Robert J. Marshall (2012), 'The Embodiment of Lyricism in Medicine and Homer', *Medical Humanities*, 38: 1, 50–4.
Boateng, Beatrice A., and Erik Black (2012), *Social Media in Medicine: The Impact of Online Social Networks on Contemporary Medicine*, Stillwater, OK: New Forums Press.
Bolaki, Stella (2011a), 'Challenging Invisibility, Making Connections: Illness, Survival, and Black Struggles in Audre Lorde's Work', in Christopher M. Bell (ed.), *Blackness and Disability: Critical Examinations and Cultural Interventions*, Münster: Lit Verlag, pp. 47–74.
Bolaki, Stella (2011b), *Unsettling the Bildungsroman: Reading Contemporary Ethnic American Women's Fiction*, Amsterdam: Rodopi.
Bolaki, Stella (2013), 'Illness and Transatlantic Sisterhoods in Audre Lorde's "A Burst of Light: Living with Cancer"', *Symbiosis: a Journal of Anglo-American Literary Relations*, 17: 1, 3–20.
Bolaki, Stella (2014), Skype interview with Andy Glynne, 7 February 2014, unpublished.
Bordo, Susan (1993), *Unbearable Weight: Feminism, Western Culture, and the Body*, Berkeley: University of California Press.
Bost, Suzanne (2010), *Encarnación: Illness and Body Politics in Chicana Feminist Literature*, New York: Fordham University Press.
Bouldin, Joanna (2000), 'Bodacious Bodies and the Voluptuous Gaze: A Phenomenology of Animation Spectatorship', *Animation Journal*, 8, 56–67.
Bouldin, Joanna (2004), 'Cadaver of the Real: Animation, Rotoscoping and the Politics of the Body', *Animation Journal*, 12, 7–31.
Bow, Leslie (2001), *Betrayal and Other Acts of Subversion: Feminism, Sexual Politics, Asian American Women's Literature*, Princeton: Princeton University Press.
Bracken, Patrick, and Philip Thomas (2005), *Postpsychiatry: Mental Health in a Postmodern World*, Oxford: Oxford University Press.
Brody, Howard (2002), *Stories of Sickness*, Oxford: Oxford University Press.
Brody, Howard (2011), 'Defining the Medical Humanities: Three Conceptions and Three Narratives', *Journal of Medical Humanities*, 32, 1–7.
Brodzinski, Emma (2010), *Theatre in Health and Care*, Basingstoke: Palgrave.
Brodzinski, Emma (2014), 'Performance Anxiety', in Victoria Bates, Alan Bleakley and Sam Goodman (eds), *Medicine, Health and the Arts: Approaches to the Medical Humanities*, London: Routledge, pp. 166–85.
Bronfen, Elizabeth (1992), *Over Her Dead Body: Death, Femininity and the Aesthetic*, Manchester: Manchester University Press.

Brown, Kate H., and Diane Gillespie (1997), ' "We Become Brave by Doing Brave Acts": Teaching Moral Courage through the Theater of the Oppressed', *Literature and Medicine*, 16: 1, 108–20.

Broyard, Anatole (1992), 'The Patient Examines the Doctor', in *Intoxicated by My Illness and Other Writings on Life and Death*, New York: Fawcett Columbine, pp. 31–58.

Bruzzi, Stella (2006), *New Documentary: A Critical Introduction*, New York: Routledge.

Buckman, Robert, and Tereza Whittaker (2000), *What You Really Need to Know about Breast Cancer*, New York: Lebhar-Friedman.

Burgin, Victor (ed.) (1982), *Thinking Photography*, London: Macmillan.

Burnett, Ron (1981), 'Wim Wenders, Nicholas Ray and *Lightning over Water*', *Ciné-Tracts: A Journal of Film and Cultural Studies*, 14, 11–14, <http://library.brown.edu/cds/cinetracts/CT14–15.pdf> (last accessed 27 July 2015).

Bury, Stephen (1995), *Artists' Books: The Book as a Work of Art, 1963–1995*, Aldershot: Scolar Press.

Campo, Rafael (1996), *What the Body Told*, Durham, NC: Duke University Press.

Campo, Rafael (1997), *The Desire to Heal: A Doctor's Education in Empathy, Identity, and Poetry*, New York: Norton.

Carel, Havi (2008), *Illness: The Cry of the Flesh*, Stocksfield: Acumen.

Carel, Havi, and Rachel Cooper (eds) (2012), *Health, Illness and Disease: Philosophical Essays*, Durham: Acumen.

Carnell, Simon (2010), *Hare*, London: Reaktion.

Cartwright, Lisa (1995), *Screening the Body: Tracing Medicine's Visual Culture*, Minneapolis: University of Minnesota Press.

Cartwright, Lisa (2000), 'Community and the Public Body in Breast Cancer Media Activism', in Janine Marchessault and Kim Sawchuk (eds), *Wild Science: Reading Feminism, Medicine, and the Media*, London: Routledge, pp. 120–38.

Caruth, Cathy (ed.) (1995), *Trauma: Explorations in Memory*, Baltimore: Johns Hopkins University Press.

Casilli, Antonio (2012), 'Open Cure: When Digital Humanities Meet Medical Humanities', BodySpaceSociety, A Blog for Recovering Social Scientists, 2 October 2012, <http://www.bodyspacesociety.eu/2012/10/02/open-cure/> (last accessed 27 July 2015).

Centre for Medical Humanities, Durham University (2011), 'Medical Humanities as Disruptive Teenager – A Response to Brody', 23 February 2011, Centre for Medical Humanities Blog, <http://centreformedicalhumanities.org/medical-humanities-as-disruptive-teenager-a-response-to-brody/> (last accessed 27 July 2015).

Chabram-Dernersesian, Angie, and Adela de la Torre (eds) (2008), *Speaking from the Body: Latinas on Health and Culture*, Tuscon: University of Arizona Press.

Chanter, Tina (ed.) (2001), *Feminist Interpretations of Emmanuel Levinas*, University Park: Pennsylvania State University Press.
Charon, Rita (2006), *Narrative Medicine: Honoring the Stories of Illness*, New York: Oxford University Press.
Chion, Michel (1999), *The Voice in Cinema*, ed. and trans. Claudia Gorbman, New York: Columbia University Press.
Chopra, Arun K., and Gillian Doody (2007), 'Schizophrenia, an Illness and a Metaphor: Analysis of the Use of the Term "Schizophrenia" in the UK National Newspapers', *Journal of the Royal Society of Medicine*, 100: 9, 423–6.
Clark, Mary Marshall (2005), 'Holocaust Video Testimony, Oral History, and Narrative Medicine: The Struggle against Indifference', *Literature and Medicine*, 24: 2, 266–82.
Cohen, Jordan J. (2007), 'Linking Professionalism to Humanism: What It Means, Why It Matters', *Academic Medicine*, 82: 11, 1029–32.
Conway, Kathlyn (2007), *Beyond Words: Illness and the Limits of Expression*, Albuquerque: University of New Mexico Press.
Cool, Roger F., and Gerd Gemünden (eds) (1997), *The Cinema of Wim Wenders: Image, Narrative and the Postmodern Condition*, Detroit: Wayne State University Press.
Corrigan, Timothy (1985), 'Cinematic Snuff: German Friends and Narrative Murders', *Cinema Journal*, 24: 2, 9–18.
Costa, Lucy, Jijian Voronka, Danielle Landry, Jenna Reid, Becky Mcfarlane, David Reville and Kathryn Church (2012), 'Recovering Our Stories: A Small Act of Resistance', *Studies in Social Justice*, 6: 1, 85–101.
Coulehan, Jack (2007), 'Written Role Models in Professionalism Education', *Medical Humanities*, 33: 2, 106–9.
Couser, Thomas G. (1997), *Recovering Bodies: Illness, Disability, and Life-Writing*, Madison: University of Wisconsin Press.
Couser, Thomas G. (1998), 'Making, Taking, and Faking Lives: The Ethics of Collaborative Life Writing', *Style*, 32: 2, 334–50.
Couser, Thomas G. (2004), *Vulnerable Subjects: Ethics and Life Writing*, Ithaca, NY: Cornell University Press.
Couser, Thomas G. (2009), *Signifying Bodies: Disability in Contemporary Life Writing*, Ann Arbor: University of Michigan Press.
Couser, Thomas G. (2012), *Memoir: An Introduction*, Oxford: Oxford University Press.
Crawford, Paul, Brian Brown, Charley Baker, Victoria Tischler and Brian Adams (2015), *Health Humanities*, Basingstoke: Palgrave Macmillan.
Croce, Arlene (1994/5), 'Discussing the Undiscussable', *The New Yorker*, 26 December – 2 January 1994/5, 54–60.
Cvetkovich, Ann (2012), *Depression*, Durham, NC: Duke University Press.
Darbyshire, Daniel, and Paul Baker (2012), 'A Systematic Review and Thematic Analysis of Cinema in Medical Education', *Medical Humanities*, 38, 28–33.

de Bloois, Joost (2008), 'On Autohagiography: Sam Taylor-Wood's "Self Portrait as a Tree,"' *Image and Narrative*, 9: 22, <http://dare.uva.nl/document/137674> (last accessed 27 July 2015).

Debney, Patricia (2011), 'Waving and Drowning: Writing, Our Family and Type 1 Diabetes', blog, <http://wavingdrowning.wordpress.com/> (last accessed 27 July 2015).

Deloney, Linda, and James Graham (2003), '*Wit*: Using Drama to Teach First-year Medical Students about Empathy and Compassion', *Teaching and Learning Medicine*, 15: 4, 247–51.

Derrida, Jacques (1977), 'Signature Event Context', in *Limited Inc*, Evanston, IL: Northwestern University Press, pp. 1–24.

DeShazer, Mary K. (2013), *Mammographies: The Cultural Discourses of Breast Cancer Narratives*, Ann Arbor: The University of Michigan Press.

Diedrich, Lisa (2007), *Treatments: Language, Politics, and the Culture of Illness*, Minneapolis: University of Minnesota Press.

Dillon, Sarah (2005), 'Reinscribing De Quincey's Palimpsest: The Significance of the Palimpsest in Contemporary Literary and Cultural Studies', *Textual Practice*, 19: 3, 243–63.

Dillon, Sarah (2007), *The Palimpsest: Literature, Criticism, Theory*, London: Bloomsbury.

Dooks, Chris (2013), 'The M.E.thodologies of the Fragmented Filmmaker', conference paper, Exhaustion, University of Kent, Canterbury, 25 October 2013.

Drucker, Johanna (1994), 'Artists' Books and the Cultural Status of the Book', *Journal of Communication*, 44: 1, 12–42.

Drucker, Johanna (1998), *Figuring the Word: Essays on Books, Writing and Visual Poetics*, New York: Granary Books.

Drucker, Johanna (2004), *The Century of Artists' Books*, New York: Granary Books.

Drucker, Johanna (2011), 'Intimate Authority: Women, Books, and the Public–Private Paradox', in Krystyna Wasserman (ed.), *The Book as Art: Artists' Books from the National Museum of Women in the Arts*, New York: Princeton Architectural Press, pp. 14–17.

Dubriwny, Tasha N. (2013), *The Vulnerable Empowered Woman: Feminism, Postfeminism, and Women's Health*, New Brunswick, NJ: Rutgers University Press.

Eakin, Paul (1999), *How Our Lives Become Stories: Making Selves*, Ithaca, NY: Cornell University Press.

Egan, Susanna (1999), *Mirror Talk: Genres of Crisis in Contemporary Autobiography*, Chapel Hill: University of North Carolina Press.

Ehrenreich, Barbara (2001), 'Welcome to Cancerland', *Harper's Magazine*, 1 November 2001, pp. 43–53.

Ehrlich, Nea (2011), 'Animated Documentaries as Masking', *Animation Studies Online Journal*, 6, <http://journal.animationstudies.org/nea-ehrlich-animated-documentaries-as-masking/> (last accessed 27 July 2015).

Elsey, Judy (1992), 'The Rhetoric of the NAMES Project AIDS Quilt: Reading the Text(ile)', in Emmanuel S. Nelson (ed.), *AIDS: The Literary Perspective*, New York: Twayne, pp. 187–96.
Epstein, Ronald M. (1999), 'Mindful Practice', *Journal of the American Medical Association*, 282: 9, 833–9.
Evans, Jessica (2000), 'Photography', in Fiona Carson and Claire Pajaczkowska (eds), *Feminist Visual Culture*, Edinburgh: Edinburgh University Press, pp. 105–22.
Farmer, Paul (2005), *Pathologies of Power: Health, Human Rights, and the New War on the Poor*, Berkeley: University of California Press.
Farmer, Paul (2013), *To Repair the World: Paul Farmer Speaks to the Next Generation*, Berkeley: University of California Press.
Felman, Shoshana, and Dori Laub (1992), *Testimony: Crisis of Witnessing in Literature, Psychoanalysis, and History*, New York: Routledge.
Felski, Rita (2008), *Uses of Literature*, Malden: Blackwell.
Fennell, Dana, and Ana S. Q. Libera (2007), 'Learning to Live with OCD: Labeling, the Self, and Stigma', *Deviant Behavior*, 28: 4, 305–31.
Fernández-Morales, Marta (2012), '"We Are Not the Same Person": (Auto) Biography, (Self)Representation, and Brechtian Performativity in Lisa Kron's *Well*', *Revista de Estudios Norteamericanos*, 16, 45–62.
Foucault, Michel [1977] (1995), *Discipline and Punish: The Birth of the Prison*, trans. Alan Sheridan, New York: Vintage.
Foucault, Michel (1989), *The Birth of the Clinic: An Archaeology of Medical Perception*, trans. A. M. Sheridan, Abingdon: Routledge.
Foucault, Michel (1998), 'Technologies of the Self', in Luther H. Martin, Huck Gutman and Patrick H. Hutton (eds), *Technologies of the Self: A Seminar with Michel Foucault*, Amherst: University of Massachusetts Press, pp. 16–49.
Frank, Arthur (1995), *The Wounded Storyteller: Body, Illness, and Ethics*, Chicago: University of Chicago Press.
Frank, Arthur (1997), 'Enacting Illness Stories: When, What and Why', in Hilde Lindemann Nelson (ed.), *Stories and Their Limits: Narrative Approaches to Bioethics*, London: Routledge, pp. 31–49.
Frank, Arthur (2004), *The Renewal of Generosity: Illness, Medicine, and How to Live*, Chicago: University of Chicago Press.
Frank, Arthur (2007), Review of Rita Charon, *Narrative Medicine: Honoring the Stories of Illness*, *Literature and Medicine*, 26: 2, 408–12.
Frank, Arthur (2013), 'Afterword: Endangered Storytelling', in *The Wounded Storyteller: Body, Illness, and Ethics*, second edition, Chicago: University of Chicago Press, pp. 187–221.
Freeman, Mark (2008), 'Beyond Narrative: Dementia's Tragic Promise', in Lars-Christer Hydén and Jens Brockmeier (eds), *Health, Illness and Culture: Broken Narratives*, New York: Routledge, pp. 169–84.
Freud, Sigmund [1919] (2003), *The Uncanny*, trans. David McLintock, London: Penguin.

Friedman, Lester D. (1995), 'See Me, Hear Me: Using Film in Health-Care Classes', *Journal of Medical Humanities*, 16: 4, 223–8.

Friedman, Richard A. (2005), 'Learning Words They Rarely Teach in Medical School: "I'm Sorry"', *The New York Times*, 26 July 2005, <http://www.nytimes.com/2005/07/26/science/26essa.html> (last accessed 27 July 2015).

Fusco, Coco (2001), *The Bodies That Were Not Ours and Other Writings*, London: Routledge.

Garden, Rebecca (2007), 'The Problem of Empathy: Medicine and the Humanities', *New Literary History*, 38 (2007): 551–67.

Gardner, Lyn (2009), 'Well', *Guardian*, 6 January 2009, <http://www.theguardian.com/stage/2009/jan/06/theatre-review-well> (last accessed 27 July 2015).

Garland-Thomson, Rosemarie (1997), *Extraordinary Bodies: Figuring Physical Disability in American Culture and Literature*, New York: Columbia University Press.

Garland-Thomson, Rosemarie (2009), *Staring: How We Look*, Oxford: Oxford University Press.

Gawande, Atul (2014), *Being Mortal: Illness, Medicine and What Matters in the End*, London: Profile Books.

Geist, Kathe (1981–2), 'Review of *Lightning over Water*', *Film Quarterly*, 35: 2, 46–51.

Geller, Matthew (1981), *Difficulty Swallowing: A Medical Chronicle*, New York: Works Press.

Gilman, Sander L. (1988), *Disease and Representation: Images of Illness from Madness to AIDS*, Ithaca, NY: Cornell University Press.

Giroux, Henry A. (2011), *On Critical Pedagogy*, New York: Continuum.

Glynne, Andy (2013), 'Drawn from Life: The Animated Documentary', in Brian Winston (ed.), *The Documentary Film Book*, Basingstoke: Palgrave, BFI, pp. 73–5.

Gómez-Peña, Guillermo (2001), 'Chicano Interneta: The Search for Intelligent Life in Cyberspace', *Hopscotch: A Cultural Review*, 2: 2, 80–91.

Gómez-Peña, Guillermo (2005), *Ethno-Techno: Writings on Performance, Activism, and Pedagogy*, New York: Routledge.

Gómez-Peña, Guillermo (2011), *Conversations across Borders*, ed. Laura Levin, London: Seagull Books.

Gómez-Peña, Guillermo (2014), 'Gómez-Peña on Illness, the Human Body, Performance and Quantum Physics: A Psychomagic Script for a Hard Recovery', *TDR: The Drama Review*, 58: 2, 149–62.

Green, Jesse (2004), 'Theater: A One-Woman Show Learns to Share', *The New York Times*, 21 March 2004, <http://www.nytimes.com/2004/03/21/arts/theater-a-one-woman-show-learns-to-share.html> (last accessed 27 July 2015).

Green, Michael J., and Kimberly R. Myers (2010), 'Graphic Medicine: Use of Comics in Medical Education and Patient Care', *British Medical Journal*, 340, 574–7.

Grigsby, Darcy Grimaldo (1991), 'Dilemmas of Visibility: Contemporary Women Artists' Representations of Female Bodies', in Laurence Goldstein (ed.), *The Female Body: Figures, Styles, Speculations*, Ann Arbor: University of Michigan Press, pp. 83–102.

Gurdon, Meghan Cox (2011), 'Darkness Too Visible', *The Wall Street Journal*, 4 June 2011, <http://online.wsj.com/news/articles/SB10001424052702303 657404576357622592697038> (last accessed 27 July 2015).

Hall, Lynda (2000), 'Passion(ate) Plays "Wherever We Found Space": Lorde and Gomez Queer(y)ing Boundaries and Acting In', *Callaloo*, 23: 1, 394–421.

Hall, Martha A. (2003), *Holding In, Holding On*, exhibition catalogue, Mortimer Rare Book Room, Smith College, Northampton, MA: Smith College/Herlin Press.

Hall, Martha A. (2004), *I Make Books*, film, dir. Hollis Haywood and Kari Wagner, Martha A. Hall Collection, Maine Women Writers Collection, Portland, ME: University of New England.

Hallas, Roger (2007), 'Sound, Image and the Corporeal Implication of Witnessing in Derek Jarman's *Blue*', in Frances Guerin and Roger Hallas (eds), *The Image and the Witness: Trauma, Memory and Visual Culture*, London: Wallflower Press, pp. 37–51.

Hallas, Roger (2009), *Reframing Bodies: AIDS, Bearing Witness, and the Queer Moving Image*, Durham, NC: Duke University Press.

Hamilton, Rachel Segal (2012), 'Mosaic Films' Andy Glynne: Making Animated Documentaries', 18 June 2012, <http://www.ideastap.com/ideasmag/the-knowledge/mosaic-films-andy-glynne> (last accessed 27 July 2015).

Hawkins, Anne Hunsaker (1999), *Reconstructing Illness: Studies in Pathography*, West Lafayette, IN: Purdue University Press.

Hawkins, Katy (2006), 'Woven Spaces: Eve Kosofsky Sedgwick's *Dialogue On Love*', *Women & Performance: A Journal of Feminist Theory*, 16: 2, 251–67.

Heddon, Deirdre (2008), *Autobiography and Performance*, Houndmills: Palgrave Macmillan.

Helck, Emily (2013), 'Just Girls', *The Real*, blog, 9 September 2013, <http://rtonj.blogspot.co.uk/search?updated-min=2013-01-01T00:00:00-05:00&updated-max=2014-01-01T00:00:00-05:00&max-results=50> (last accessed 27 July 2015).

Herman, David (ed.) (2007), *The Cambridge Companion to Narrative*, Cambridge: Cambridge University Press.

Herndl, Diane Price (2002), 'Reconstructing the Posthuman Feminist Body Twenty Years after Audre Lorde's *Cancer Journals*', in Rosemarie Garland-Thomson, Brenda Brueggeman and Sharon Snyder (eds), *Enabling the Humanities: A Sourcebook for Disability Studies in Language and Literature*, New York: MLA, pp. 144–55.

Hesse, Monica (2013), 'NPR's Scott Simon takes Twitter to a New Frontier: His Mother's Hospital Bed', *The Washington Post*, 29 July 2013, <http://www.washingtonpost.com/lifestyle/style/nprs-scott-simon-takes-twitter-to-a-new-frontier-his-mothers-hospital-bed/2013/07/29/44cc67ea-f86f-11e2-8e84-c56731a202fb_story.html> (last accessed 27 July 2015).

Hirsch, Marianne (1997), *Family Frames: Photography, Narrative, and Postmemory*, Cambridge, MA: Harvard University Press.

Hooker, Claire, and Estelle Noonan (2011), 'Medical Humanities as Expressive of Western Culture', *Medical Humanities*, 37, 79–84.

Höttges, Bärbel (2009), 'Blogging the Pain: Grief in the Time of the Internet', *Gender Forum*, 26, <http://www.genderforum.org/issues/literature-and-medicine-ii/blogging-the-pain/> (last accessed 27 July 2015).

Hubert, Renée Riese, and Judd D. Hubert (1999), *The Cutting Edge of Reading: Artists' Books*, New York: Granary Books.

Hughley, Matty (2010), 'Theater Review: Lisa Kron's *Well*', *The Oregonian*, 6 March 2010 <http://www.oregonlive.com/performance/index.ssf/2010/03/theater_review_lisa_krons_well.html> (last accessed 27 July 2015).

Hydén, Lars-Christer (2011), 'Broken and Vicarious Voices in Narratives', in Lars-Christer Hydén and Jens Brockmeier (eds), *Health, Illness and Culture: Broken Narratives*, New York: Routledge, pp. 36–53.

Hydén, Lars-Christer, and Jens Brockmeier (eds) (2011), *Health, Illness and Culture: Broken Narratives*, New York: Routledge.

Iaconesi, Salvatore (2012), 'Hacker Diagnosed with Breast Cancer ...', Zone-H, <http://zone-h.org/news/id/4743> (last accessed 27 July 2015).

Ingram, Mathew (2013), 'NPR Host's Live-Tweeting of His Mother's Last Moments Shows the Power of 140 Characters', Gigaom, 29 July 2013, <http://gigaom.com/2013/07/29/npr-hosts-live-tweeting-of-his-mothers-last-moments-shows-the-power-of-140-characters/> (last accessed 27 July 2015).

Jacob, Clarissa, and Amy Tobin (2013), 'Considering Her Final Project', in Louisa Lee (ed.), *Jo Spence: The Final Project*, Manchester: Riding House, pp. 29–37.

Jacobsen, Torild, Anders Baerheim, Margret Rose Lepp and Edvin Schei (2006), 'Analysis of Role-Play in Medical Communication Training Using a Theatrical Device The Fourth Wall', *BMC Medical Education*, 6: 51, <http://www.biomedcentral.com/1472-6920/6/51> (last accessed 27 July 2015).

Jenkins, Henry (2006), 'Welcome to Convergence Culture', blog, <http://henryjenkins.org/2006/06/welcome_to_convergence_culture.html> (last accessed 27 July 2015).

Jodorowsky, Alejandro (2010), *Psychomagic: The Transformative Power of Shamanic Psychotherapy*, Rochester, VT: Inner Traditions.

Jones, Therese, Delese Wear and Lester D. Friedman (eds) (2014), *Health Humanities Reader*, New Brunswick, NJ: Rutgers University Press.

Jordanova, Ludmilla (2000), *Defining Features: Scientific and Medical Portraits 1660–2000*, London: Reaktion.

Jordanova, Ludmilla (2014), 'Medicine and the Visual Arts', in Victoria Bates, Alan Bleakley and Sam Goodman (eds), *Medicine, Health and the Arts: Approaches to the Medical Humanities*, London: Routledge, pp. 41–63.

Jost, Jon (1981), 'Wrong Move', *Sight and Sound*, 50: 2, 94–6.

Jurecic, Ann (2012), *Illness as Narrative*, Pittsburgh: University of Pittsburgh Press.

Kaleem, Jaweed (2013), 'Scott Simon's Tweets about Dying Mother Spur Conversation on Public Grief, Death on Social Media', *Huffington Post*, 15 August 2013, <http://www.huffingtonpost.com/2013/08/09/scott-simon-tweets_n_3721527.html> (last accessed 27 July 2015).

Kaplan, Ann (2005), *Trauma Culture: The Politics of Terror and Loss in Media and Literature*, Piscataway, NJ: Rutgers University Press.

Keating, AnaLouise (ed.) (2009), *The Gloria Anzaldúa Reader*, Durham, NC: Duke University Press.

Keller, Bill (2014), 'Heroic Measures', *The New York Times*, 12 January 2014, <http://www.nytimes.com/2014/01/13/opinion/keller-heroic-measures.html?hpw&rref=opinion&_r=2> (last accessed 27 July 2015).

Keller, Emma G. (2014), 'Forget Funeral Selfies: What Are the Ethics of Tweeting a Terminal Illness?' *Guardian*, 8 January 2014.

Kiberd, Roisin (2014), 'The Internet of Pain: When Suffering Goes Viral', Motherboard, 26 June 2014, <http://motherboard.vice.com/en_au/read/the-internet-of-pain-when-suffering-goes-viral> (last accessed 27 July 2015).

Kilby, Jane (2001), 'Carved in Skin: Bearing Witness to Self-Harm', in Sara Ahmed and Jackie Stacey (eds), *Thinking through the Skin*, London: Routledge, pp. 124–42.

King, Susan E. (1993), *Treading the Maze: An Artist's Journey through Breast Cancer*, San Francisco: Chronicle Books.

Kirmayer, Laurence J. (2000), 'Broken Narratives: Clinical Encounters and the Poetics of Illness Experience', in Cheryl Mattingly and Linda C. Garro (eds), *Narrative and the Cultural Construction of Illness and Healing*, Berkeley: University of California Press, pp. 153–80.

Klawiter, Maren (2008), *The Biopolitics of Breast Cancer: Changing Cultures of Disease and Activism*, Minneapolis: University of Minnesota Press.

Kleinman, Arthur (1988), *The Illness Narratives: Suffering, Healing, and the Human Condition*, New York: Basic Books.

Kleinman, Arthur, and Peter Benson (2006), 'Anthropology in the Clinic: The Problem of Cultural Competency and How to Fix It', *PLOS Medicine*, 3: 10, 1673–6.

Klima, Stefan (1998), *Artists Books: A Critical Survey of the Literature*, New York: Granary Books.

Kouba, Petr (2014), *The Phenomenon of Mental Disorder: Perspectives of Heidegger's Thought in Psychopathology*, London: Springer.

Kraut, Alan M. (1995), *Silent Travelers: Germs, Genes, and the Immigrant Menace*, Baltimore: Johns Hopkins University Press.

Kritsky, Gene, and Ron Cherrie (2000), *Insect Mythology*, Lincoln, NE: Writers Club Press.

Kron, Lisa (2001), *2.5 Million Ride* and *101 Humiliating Stories*, New York: Theatre Communications Group.

Kron, Lisa (2006a), *Well*, New York: Theatre Communications Group.
Kron, Lisa (2006b), 'The Importance of Being Lisa Kron: An Interview by Wendy Weisman', *Theatre Communications Group*, <http://www.tcg.org/publications/at/mar06/sheik.cfm> (last accessed 27 July 2015).
Krumboltz, Mike (2013), 'Breast Cancer Survivor Posts Time-Lapse Video of Treatment', Yahoo News, <http://news.yahoo.com/cancer-survivor-posts-time-lapse-video-of-treatment–204001044.html> (last accessed 27 July 2015).
Kuppers, Petra (2001), 'Deconstructing Images: Performing Disability', *Contemporary Theatre Review*, 11: 3/4, 25–40.
Kuppers, Petra (2003), *Disability and Contemporary Performance: Bodies on Edge*, London: Routledge.
Kuppers, Petra (2007), *The Scar of Visibility: Medical Performances and Contemporary Art*, Minneapolis: University of Minnesota Press.
LaCapra, Dominick (1994), *Representing the Holocaust: History, Theory, Trauma*, Ithaca, NY: Cornell University Press.
Langellier, Kristin M. (2001), '"You're Marked": Breast Cancer, Tattoo, and the Narrative Performance of Identity', in Jens Brockmeier and Donal Carbaugh (eds), *Narrative and Identity: Studies in Autobiography, Self, and Culture*, Amsterdam: John Benjamins, pp. 145–84.
Langellier, Kristin M. (2009), 'Performing Narrative Medicine', *Journal of Applied Communication Research*, 37: 2, 151–8.
Lauf, Cornelia, and Clive Phillpot (1998), *Artist/Author: Contemporary Artists' Books*, New York: The American Federation of Arts.
Leibovitz, Annie (2006), *A Photographer's Life, 1990–2005*, New York: Random House.
Lester, Rebecca J. (1997), 'The (Dis)Embodied Self in Anorexia Nervosa', *Social Science & Medicine*, 44: 4, 479–89.
Levinas, Emmanuel [1969] (2007), *Totality and Infinity: An Essay on Exteriority*, trans. Alphonso Lingis, Pittsburgh: Duquesne University Press.
Levinas, Emmanuel (1996), *Basic Philosophical Writings*, ed. Adriaan T. Peperzak, Simon Critchley and Robert Bernasconi, Bloomington: Indiana University Press.
Levinas, Emmanuel (1998), 'Philosophy and the Idea of Infinity', in *Collected Philosophical Papers*, trans. Alphonso Lingis, Pittsburgh: Duquesne University Press, pp. 47–59.
Linton, Simi (2006), *My Body Politic: A Memoir*, Ann Arbor: University of Michigan Press.
López, Marva (2003), 'A Critical Analysis of Guillermo Gómez-Peña's Performance Art: A Study in the Cultural Borderlands with Implication for Art Education', Florida State University, *Electronic Theses, Treatises and Dissertations*, Paper 1064, <http://diginole.lib.fsu.edu/cgi/viewcontent.cgi?article=3169&context=etd> (last accessed 27 July 2015).
Lorde, Audre (1996), *The Audre Lorde Compendium: Essays, Speeches and Journals*, London: Pandora.

Lorenz, Karl, Jillisa Steckart and Kenneth Rosenfeld (2004), 'End-of-life Education Using the Dramatic Arts: The Wit Educational Initiative', *Academic Medicine*, 79: 5, 481–6.
Loughrey, Felicity (2006), 'Sam I Am', *Australian Vogue Magazine*, 1 April 2006, FPC Magazines, p. 91.
Lovejoy, Margot (1994), *The Book of Plagues*, Purchase, NY: State University of New York Visual Arts Division.
Ludmerer, Kenneth M. (1999), 'Instilling Professionalism in Medical Education', *Journal of the American Medical Association*, 282: 9, 881–2.
Lupton, Deborah (2012), *Medicine as Culture: Illness, Disease and the Body*, London: Sage.
Lyons, Joan (1989), *The Gynecologist*, Rochester, NY: Visual Studies Workshop Press.
Macneill, Paul Ulhas (2011), 'The Arts and Medicine: A Challenging Relationship', *Medical Humanitities*, 37, 85–90.
McCarney, Scott L. (1988), *Memory Loss*, Rochester, NY: Visual Studies Workshop Press.
McCartney, Mary (2008), 'Contributors', *Harper's Bazaar*, 1 January 2008, p. 20.
McCloud, Scott (1993), *Understanding Comics: The Invisible Art*, Northampton, MA: Kitchen Sink Press.
McCormick, Gail (2001), *Living with Multiple Chemical Sensitivity: Narratives of Coping*, Jefferson, NC: McFarland.
McKechnie, Claire Charlotte (2014), 'Anxieties of Communication: The Limits of Narrative in the Medical Humanities', *Medical Humanities* (published online first), 28 May 2014, 1–6, <http://mh.bmj.com/content/early/2014/05/28/medhum–2013–010466.full> (last accessed 27 July 2015).
McLane, Janice (1996), 'The Voice on the Skin: Self-Mutilation and Merleau-Ponty's Theory of Language', *Hypatia*, 11: 4, 107–19.
McLellan, Faith (1997), ' "A Whole Other Story": The Electronic Narrative of Illness', *Literature and Medicine*, 16: 1, 88–107.
Maitland, Sara (2008), *A Book of Silence*, London: Granta.
Margulies, Ivone (1993), 'Delaying the Cut: The Space of Performance in *Lightning Over Water*', *Screen*, 34: 1, 54–68.
Marks, Laura U. (2002), *Touch: Sensuous Theory and Multisensory Media*, Minneapolis: University of Minnesota Press.
Martin, Rosy (2013), 'Inhabiting the Image: Photography, Therapy and Re-enactment Phototherapy', in Del Loewenthal (ed.), *Phototherapy and Therapeutic Photography in a Digital Age*, London: Routledge, pp. 69–81.
Mason, Helen Rachel (2009), 'Dare to Dream: The Use of Animation in Occupational Therapy', *Mental Health Occupational Therapy*, 14: 3, 111–15.
Mattingly, Cheryl (2000), 'Emergent Narratives', in Cheryl Mattingly and Linda C. Garro (eds), *Narrative and the Cultural Construction of Illness and Healing*, Berkeley: University of California Press, pp. 181–211.

Mattingly, Cheryl, and Linda C. Garro (eds) (2000), *Narrative and the Cultural Construction of Illness and Healing*, Berkeley: University of California Press.

Matuschka (1992), 'The Body Positive: Got to Get This off My Chest', *On the Issues*, 25, 30–7.

Meikle, Graham, and Sherman Young (2011), *Media Convergence: Networked Digital Media in Everyday Life*, Houndmills: Palgrave Macmillan.

Meskó, Bertalan (2013), *Social Media in Clinical Practice*, London: Springer.

Mienczakowski, Jim (1997), 'Theater of Change', *Research in Drama Education*, 2: 2, 159–72.

Miller, J. Hillis (2008), 'Touching Derrida Touching Nancy: The Main Traits of Derrida's Hand', *Derrida Today*, 1: 2, 145–66.

Miller, Nancy K. (2000), *Bequest and Betrayal: Memoirs of a Parent's Death*, Bloomington: Indiana University Press.

Mills, Letha E. (2003), 'Martha Hall's Books', in *Holding In, Holding On*, exhibition catalogue, Mortimer Rare Book Room, Smith College, Northampton, MA: Smith College/Herlin Press, pp. 4–9.

Minich, Julie Avril (2014), *Accessible Citizenships: Disability, Nation, and the Cultural Politics of Greater Mexico*, Philadelphia: Temple University Press.

Mitchell, Breon (1996), 'The Secret Life of the Book: The Livre d'Artiste and the Act of Reading', in Laurie Edson (ed.), *Conjunctions: Verbal-Visual Relations*, San Diego: San Diego University Press, pp. 161–7.

Mitchell, David T., and Sharon L. Snyder (2000), *Narrative Prosthesis: Disability and the Dependencies of Discourse*, Ann Arbor: University of Michigan Press.

Moir, Sophia (2014), 'Man Asks Strangers to Photoshop a Picture of His Baby Daughter after She Passes Away in Hospital', Yahoo, <https://uk.lifestyle.yahoo.com/man-asks-strangers-to-photoshop-a-picture-of-his-baby-daughter-after-she-passes-away-in-hospital–095125195.html#nt> (last accessed 27 July 2015).

Montgomery, Hunter K. (2006), *How Doctors Think: Clinical Judgement and the Practice of Medicine*, Oxford: Oxford University Press.

Moore, Samantha (2010), 'The Truth of Illusion: Animated Documentary and Theory', 11 November 2010, <http://www.apengine.org/2010/11/the-truth-of-illusion-animated-documentary-and-theory-by-samantha-moore/> (last accessed 27 July 2015).

Moore, Samantha (2011), '"Does this Look Right?" Working inside the Collaborative Frame', conference paper, Animated Realities: Animation, Documentary and the Moving Image, University of Edinburgh, Edinburgh College of Art and the Edinburgh International Film Festival, 23–4 June 2011.

Morgan, Michael L. (2011), *The Cambridge Introduction to Emmanuel Levinas*, Cambridge: Cambridge University Press.

Morris, David B. (1998), *Illness and Culture in the Postmodern Age*, Berkeley: University of California Press.

Mulvey, Laura (1975), 'Visual Pleasure and Narrative Cinema', *Screen*, 16: 3, 6–18.
Mulvey, Laura (2006), *Death 24x a Second: Stillness and the Moving Image*, London: Reaktion.
'My Body the Battleground: Sam Taylor-Wood Bares All after Cancer and Two Births', (2007) *Daily Mail Online*, 13 December 2007, <http://www.dailymail.co.uk/femail/article-501216/My-body-battleground-Sam-Taylor-Wood-bares-cancer-births.html> (last accessed 27 July 2015).
Neri, Louise (2006), 'Theatre of the Selves: Sam Taylor-Wood's Portraiture', essay in exhibition brochure *Sam Taylor-Wood*, Sydney: Museum of Contemporary Art.
Nichols, Bill (1993), ' "Getting to Know You ...": Knowledge, Power and the Body', in Michael Renov (ed.), *Theorizing Documentary*, New York: Routledge, pp. 174–92.
Nichols, Bill (2001), *Introduction to Documentary*, Bloomington: Indiana University Press.
Novoa, Mónica (2014), 'Chicago Hospital Deports Quadriplegic Man, Hate Speech Cheers', *Colorlines*, 14 February 2011, <http://colorlines.com/archives/2011/02/chicago_hospital_deports_quadriplegic_man_hate_speech_cheers.html> (last accessed 27 July 2015).
Oliver, Kelly (2001), *Witnessing: Beyond Recognition*, Minneapolis: University of Minnesota Press.
O'Rourke, Meghan (2013), 'Tweeting Death', *The New Yorker*, 31 July 2013, <http://www.newyorker.com/culture/culture-desk/tweeting-death> (last accessed 27 July 2015).
O'Rourke, Meghan (2014), 'Tweeting Cancer', *The New Yorker*, 13 January 2014, <http://www.newyorker.com/culture/culture-desk/tweeting-cancer> (last accessed 27 July 2015).
Pattison, Stephen (2003), 'Medical Humanities: A Vision and Some Cautionary Notes', *Medical Humanities*, 29, 33–6.
Paul, Trisha (2013), 'Tweeting and Grieving', Investigating Illness Narratives, blog, <http://illnessnarratives.com/2013/08/02/tweeting-and-grieving/> (last accessed 27 July 2015).
Payer, Lynn (1996), *Medicine and Culture*, New York: Henry Holt.
Paz, Octavio (1961), *The Labyrinth of Solitude: Life and Thought in Mexico*, trans. Lysander Kemp, New York: Grove Press.
Perreault, Jeanne (1995), *Writing Selves: Contemporary Feminist Autography*, Minneapolis: University of Minnesota Press.
Power, Simon, Rachel Kent, Justine McLisky and Jasmin Stephens (2006), *Sam Taylor-Wood*, Education kit, Sydney: Museum of Contemporary Art, 28 pages <http://citygallery.org.nz/assets/New-Site/Education/Education-Resources/Sam%20Taylor-Wood%20Resource%20Kit.pdf> (last accessed 27 July 2015).
Prendergast, Catherine (2008), 'The Unexceptional Schizophrenic: A Post-Postmodern Introduction', *Journal of Literary Disability*, 2: 1, 56–62.

Prince, Muriel (2008), 'Women and Books', *The Bonefolder: an e-journal for the bookbinder and book artist*, 4: 2, 3–10, <http://www.philobiblon.com/bonefolder/BonefolderVol4No2.pdf> (last accessed 27 July 2015).

Radetsky, Peter (1997), *Allergic to the Twentieth Century: The Explosion in Environmental Allergies – From Sick Buildings to Multiple Chemical Sensitivity*, London: Little, Brown.

Radley, Alan (2009), *Works of Illness: Narrative, Picturing, and the Social Response to Serious Disease*, Ashby-de-la-Zouch: InkerMen Press.

Radley, Alan, and Susan E. Bell (2007), 'Artworks, Collective Experience and Claims for Social Justice: The Case of Women Living with Breast Cancer', *Sociology of Health & Illness*, 29: 3, 366–90.

Randolph, Theron G., and Ralph W. Moss (1980), *An Alternative Approach to Allergies: The New Field of Clinical Ecology Unravels the Environmental Causes of Mental and Physical Ills*, New York: Lippincott & Crowell.

Raoul, Valerie, Connie Canam, Angela D. Henderson and Carla Paterson (eds) (2007), *Unfitting Stories: Narrative Approaches to Disease, Disability and Trauma*, Waterloo, ON: Wilfrid Laurier University Press.

Ratcliffe, Matthew (2014), *Experiences of Depression: A Study in Phenomenology*, Oxford: Oxford University Press.

Ray, Nicholas (1993), 'The Attitude toward Today . . .', in Susan Ray (ed.), *I Was Interrupted: Nicholas Ray on Making Movies*, Berkeley: University of California Press, pp. 157–68.

Ray, Nicholas, Wim Wenders, Gerry Bamman and Susan Ray (1993), '*Lightning over Water*', in Susan Ray (ed.), *I Was Interrupted: Nicholas Ray on Making Movies*, Berkeley: University of California Press, pp. 205–13.

Reagan, Leslie J., Nancy Tomes and Paula A. Treichler (eds) (2007), *Medicine's Moving Pictures: Medicine, Health, and Bodies in American Film and Television*, Rochester, NY: University of Rochester Press.

Reid, Katharine J., Meshak Kgakololo, Ruth M. Sutherland, Susan L. Elliott and Agnes E. Dodds (2012), 'First-year Medical Students' Willingness to Participate in Peer Physical Examination', *Teaching and Learning in Medicine*, 24: 1, 55–62.

Reiheld, Alison (2010), 'Patient Complains of . . . How Medicalization Mediates Power and Justice', *International Journal of Feminist Approaches to Bioethics*, 3: 1, 72–98.

Renov, Michael (1999), 'Domestic Ethnography and the Construction of the "Other" Self', in Jane M. Gaines and Michael Renov (eds), *Collecting Visible Evidence*, Minneapolis: University of Minnesota Press, pp. 140–55.

Richardson, Ruth (2000), 'A Necessary Inhumanity?' *Medical Humanities*, 26: 2, 104–6.

Rimmon-Kenan, Shlomith (2006), 'What Can Narrative Theory Learn from Illness Narratives?', *Literature and Medicine*, 25: 2, 241–54.

Roe, Annabelle Honess (2009), *Animating Documentary*, PhD dissertation, University of Southern California, <http://digitallibrary.usc.edu/cdm/ref/collection/p15799coll127/id/257788> (last accessed 27 July 2015).
Roe, Annabelle Honess (2013), *Animated Documentary*, Houndmills: Palgrave Macmillan.
Román, David (2005), *Performance in America: Contemporary US Culture and the Performing Arts*, Durham, NC: Duke University Press.
Rosenbaum, Jonathan (2014), 'Looking for Nicholas Ray', in Steven Rybin and Will Scheibel (eds), *Lonely Places, Dangerous Ground: Nicholas Ray in American Cinema*, Albany, NY: State University of New York Press, pp. 9–18.
Rossiter, Kate (2012), 'Bearing Response-Ability: Theater, Ethics and Medical Education', *Journal of Medical Humanities*, 33, 1–14.
Rossiter, Kate, Pia Kontos, Angela Colantonio, Julie Gilbert, Julia Gray and Michelle Keightley (2008), 'Staging Data: Theater as a Tool for Analysis and Knowledge Transfer in Health Research', *Social Science & Medicine*, 66: 1, 130.
Russell, Catherine (1995), *Narrative Mortality: Death, Closure, and New Wave Cinemas*, Minneapolis: University of Minnesota Press.
Sartwell, Crispin (2000), *End of Story: Toward an Annihilation of Language and History*, Albany, NY: State University of New York Press.
Sawday, Jonathan (2006), 'The Paradoxes of Interiority', in Andrew Patrizio and Dawn Kemp (eds), *Anatomy Acts: How We Come to Know Ourselves*, Edinburgh: Birlinn, pp. 1–15.
Saywell, Cherise, Lesley Henderson and Liza Beattie (eds) (2000), 'Sexualized Illness: The Newsworthy Body in Media Representations of Breast Cancer', in *Ideologies of Breast Cancer: Feminist Perspectives*, New York: St Martin's, pp. 37–62.
Scannell, Kate (1999), *Death of the Good Doctor: Lessons from the Heart of the AIDS Epidemic*, San Francisco: Cleis.
Scheibler, Susan (1993), 'Constantly Performing the Documentary: The Seductive Promise of *Lightning Over Water*', in Michael Renov (ed.), *Theorizing Documentary*, New York: Routledge, pp. 135–50.
Schweitzer, Mary (1997), 'Chronic Fatigue Syndrome and the Cynics: A Review of Elaine Showalter's *Hystories: Hysterical Epidemics and Modern Media*', Essays about ME/CFS, <http://www.cfids-me.org/marys/elaine.html> (last accessed 27 July 2015).
Sculpture in the Close (2005), exhibition featuring Sam Taylor-Wood, Jesus College, University of Cambridge, <http://www.cam.ac.uk/news/sculpture-in-the-close> (last accessed 27 July 2015).
Sedgwick, Eve Kosofky (1994), *Tendencies*, London: Routledge.
Sedgwick, Eve Kosofsky (1999), 'In the Bardo', screed distributed at the installation *Floating Columns/In the Bardo*, City University of New York.
Sedgwick, Eve Kosofsky (2003), *Touching Feeling: Affect, Pedagogy, Performativity*, Durham, NC: Duke University Press.

Self, Donnie J, and DeWitt C. Baldwin (1990), 'Teaching Medical Humanities through Film Discussions', *Journal of Medical Humanities*, 11: 1, 23–9.
Serlin, David (ed.) (2010), *Imagining Illness: Public Health and Visual Culture*, Minneapolis: University of Minnesota Press.
Shafer, Audrey (2009), 'Medical Humanities: Demarcations, Dilemmas and Delights', *Medical Humanities*, 35: 3–4.
Shapiro, Johanna (2007), 'Using Literature and Arts to Develop Empathy in Medical Students', in Tom F. D. Farrow and Peter W. R. Woodruff (eds), *Empathy in Mental Illness and Health*, Cambridge: Cambridge University Press, pp. 473–94.
Shapiro, Johanna (2008), 'Walking a Mile in their Patients' Shoes: Empathy and Othering in Medical Students' Education', *Philosophy, Ethics, & Humanities in Medicine*, 3, 10.
Shapiro, Johanna (2012), 'Whither (Whether) Medical Humanities? The Future of Humanities and Arts in Medical Education', *Journal for Learning through the Arts*, 8: 1, <https://escholarship.org/uc/item/3x2898ww> (last accessed 27 July 2015).
Shapiro, Johanna, and Linda Hunt (2003), 'All the World's a Stage: The Use of Theatrical Performance in Medical Education', *Medical Education*, 37, 922–7.
Shapiro, Johanna, Jack Coulehan, Delese Wear and Martha Montello (2009), 'Medical Humanities and Their Discontents: Definitions, Critiques, and Implications', *Academic Medicine*, 84: 2, 192–8.
Shorter, Edward (1992), *From Paralysis to Fatigue: A History of Psychosomatic Illness in the Modern Era*, New York: The Free Press.
Showalter, Elaine (1997), *Hystories: Hysterical Epidemics and Modern Culture*, London: Picador.
Skoller, Jeffrey (2011), 'Making It (Un)real: Contemporary Theories and Practices in Documentary Animation', *Animation: An Interdisciplinary Journal*, 6: 3, 207–14.
Smajdor, Anna, Andrea Stöckl and Charlotte Salter (2011), 'The Limits of Empathy: Problems in Medical Education and Practice', *Journal of Medical Ethics*, 37, 380–3.
Sobchack, Vivian (2004), *Carnal Thoughts: Embodiment and Moving Image Culture*, Berkeley: University of California Press.
Sontag, Susan (1979), *On Photography*, London: Penguin.
Sontag, Susan (1991), *Illness as Metaphor and AIDS and Its Metaphors*, London: Penguin.
Sontag, Susan (2004), *Regarding the Pain of Others*, London: Penguin.
Sosnowy, Collette (2013), *Blogging Chronic Illness and Negotiating Patienthood: Online Narratives of Women with MS*, PhD dissertation, City University of New York, <http://gradworks.umi.com/35/61/3561642.html> (last accessed 27 July 2015).
Spence, Jo (1986), *Putting Myself in the Picture: A Political, Personal and Photographic Autobiography*, London: Camden.

Spence, Jo (1990), 'No I Can't Do That, My Consultant Wouldn't Like It', in *Silent Health: Women, Health, and Representation*, London: Camerawork, pp. 75–87.
Spence, Jo (1995), *Cultural Sniping: The Art of Transgression*, London: Routledge.
Spence, Jo (2013), *Jo Spence: The Final Project*, ed. Louisa Lee, Manchester: Riding House.
Squier, Susan M. (2007), 'Beyond Nescience: The Intersectional Insights of Health Humanities', *Perspectives in Biology and Medicine*, 50: 3, 334–47.
Squier, Susan M., and Anne Hunsaker Hawkins (2004), 'Medical Humanities and Cultural Studies: Lessons Learned from an NEH Institute', *Journal of Medical Humanities*, 25: 4, 243–53.
Strawson, Galen (2004), 'Against Narrativity', *Ratio*, 17, 428–52.
Svenaeus, Fredrik (2000), *The Hermeneutics of Medicine and the Phenomenology of Health*, Dordrecht: Kluwer Academic.
Svenaeus, Fredrik (2011), 'Illness as Unhomelike Being-in-the-World: Heidegger and the Phenomenology of Medicine', *Medicine, Health Care and Philosophy*, 14, 323–31.
Swick, Herbert M., Philip Szenas, Deborah Danoff and Michael E. Whitcomb (1999), 'Teaching Professionalism in Undergraduate Medical Education', *Journal of the American Medical Association*, 282: 9, 830–2.
Sykäri, Venla (2009), 'Dialogues in Rhyme: The Performative Contexts of Cretan *Mantinádes*', *Oral Tradition*, 24: 1, 89–123.
Tanner, Laura E. (2006), *Lost Bodies: Inhabiting the Borders of Life and Death*, Ithaca, NY: Cornell University Press.
Taylor, Alice (2008), 'Maximum Exposure', *Harper's Bazaar*, 1 January 2008, pp. 100–5.
Taylor-Wood, Sam, Michael Bracewell, Jeremy Millar and Clare Carolin (2002), *Sam Taylor-Wood*, Göttingen: Steidl for the Hayward Gallery.
Toombs, S. Kay (1992), *The Meaning of Illness: A Phenomenological Account of the Different Perspectives of Physician and Patient*, Dordrecht: Kluwer Academic Publishers.
Torgovnick, Kate May (2012), 'How Salvatore Iaconesi Has Started a Movement for Open-Source Medical Files', TED blog, <http://blog.ted.com/2012/10/02/how-salvatore-iaconesi-has-started-a-movement-for-open-source-medical-files/> (last accessed 27 July 2015).
Torgovnick, Kate May (2013), 'Why I Open-Sourced Cures to My Cancer: Salvatore Iaconesi at TEDGlobal 2013', TED blog, <http://blog.ted.com/2013/06/14/why-i-opensourced-cures-for-my-cancer-salvatore-iaconesi-at-tedglobal–2013/> (last accessed 27 July 2015).
Townsend, Molly Smith (2011), 'Guillermo Gómez-Peña, Francis Alÿs, and the Situationist International', MA thesis, Faculty of San Diego State University, <http://sdsu-dspace.calstate.edu/bitstream/handle/10211.10/1204/Townsend_Molly.pdf?sequence=1 http://www.urbandictionary.com/define.php?term=brownout> (last accessed 27July 2015).

Tuttle, Jennifer (2003), personal email correspondence with Martha Hall, 19 March 2003.
Underhill, Linn (1981), *Thirty Five Years/One Week*, Rochester, NY: Visual Studies Workshop Press.
Vaccarella, Maria (2013), 'Exploring Graphic Pathographies in the Medical Humanities', *Medical Humanities*, 39, 70–1.
Veracity, Dani (2006), 'Human Medical Experimentation in Modern Times: How Immigrants, Poor People, Minorities and Children Are Modern-Day Guinea Pigs for Big Pharma', 7 March 2006, *Natural News*, <http://www.naturalnews.com/019193_drug_Big_Pharma_guinea_pigs.html> (last accessed 27 July 2015).
Verghese, Abraham (1994), *My Own Country: A Doctor's Story of a Town and Its People in the Age of AIDS*, New York: Simon and Schuster.
Waddington, Keir, and Martin Willis (2013), 'Introduction: Rethinking Illness Narratives', *Journal of Literature & Science*, 6: 1, iv–v.
Wald, Priscilla (2008), *Contagious: Cultures, Carriers, and the Outbreak Narrative*, Durham, NC: Duke University Press.
Walton, Judith May (2010), *By Hand and Eye: Dance in the Space of the Artist's Book*, PhD dissertation, School of Communication and the Arts, Faculty of Arts, Education, and Human Development, Victoria University, <http://vuir.vu.edu.au/16100/1/Judith_Walton_PhD.pdf> (last accessed 27 July 2015).
Ward, Paul (2005), *Documentary: The Margins of Reality*, London: Wallflower.
Wasserman, Krystyna (ed.) (2011), *The Book as Art: Artists' Books from the National Museum of Women in the Arts*, New York: Princeton Architectural Press.
Wear, Delese, and Joseph Zarconi (2007), 'Can Compassion Be Taught? Let's Ask Our Students', *Journal of General Internal Medicine*, 23, 948–53.
Wells, Paul (1998), *Understanding Animation*, Abingdon: Routledge.
Wells, Paul (2011), ' "Never Mind the Bollackers": Repositories, Sites and Archives in Animated Non-Fiction', keynote paper, Animated Realities: Animation, Documentary and the Moving Image, University of Edinburgh, Edinburgh College of Art and the Edinburgh International Film Festival, 22–4 June 2011.
Wenders, Wim (2001), *On Film: Essays and Conversations*, London: Faber and Faber.
Wenders, Wim (2008a), 'Interview with Wim Wenders' by Ian Haydn Smith, September 2008, inside booklet of *Wim Wenders' Documentaries* DVD, London: Axiom, 2008, pp. 1–4. Interview transcript also available online, <http://www.axiomfilms.co.uk/discover/interviews/interview-with-wim-wenders-on-the-documentaries.html> (last accessed 27 July 2015).
Wenders, Wim (2008b), 'In Memory of Nick', inside booklet of *Wim Wenders' Documentaries* DVD, London: Axiom, 2008.
Weston, Heather (2000), *Binding Analysis: Double Bind*, London: Bookery.

Whitehead, Anne (2014), 'The Medical Humanities: A Literary Perspective', in Victoria Bates, Alan Bleakley and Sam Goodman (eds), *Medicine, Health and the Arts: Approaches to the Medical Humanities*, London: Routledge, pp. 107–27.

Widdowson, Alex (2013), Review of *Caldera* by Evan Viera, 11 May 2013, <https://animateddocs.wordpress.com/tag/mental-health/> (last accessed 27 July 2015).

Wikan, Unni (2000), 'With Life in One's Lap: The Story of an Eye/I', in Cheryl Mattingly and Linda C. Garro (eds), *Narrative and the Cultural Construction of Illness and Healing*, Berkeley: University of California Press, pp. 212–36.

Williams, Ian C. M. (2014), 'Graphic Medicine: The Portrayal of Illness in Underground and Autobiographical Comics', in Victoria Bates, Alan Bleakley and Sam Goodman (eds), *Medicine, Health and the Arts: Approaches to the Medical Humanities*, London: Routledge, pp. 64–84.

Willis, Martin, Keir Waddington and Richard Marsden (2013), 'Imaginary Investments: Illness Narratives Beyond the Gaze', *Journal of Literature & Science*, 6: 1, 55–73.

Woods, Angela (2011a), 'The Limits of Narrative: Provocations for the Medical Humanities', *Medical Humanities*, 37, 73–8.

Woods, Angela (2011b), *The Sublime Object of Psychiatry: Schizophrenia in Clinical and Cultural Theory*, Oxford: Oxford University Press.

Woods, Angela (2012), 'Beyond the Wounded Storyteller: Rethinking Narrativity, Illness and Embodied Self-Experience', in Havi Carel and Rachel Cooper (eds), *Health, Illness and Disease: Philosophical Essays*, Durham: Acumen, pp. 113–28.

Woods, Angela (2013), 'Rethinking "Patient Testimony" in the Medical Humanities: The Case of Schizophrenia Bulletin's First Person Accounts', *Journal of Literature and Science*, 6: 1, 38–54.

Woodward, Kathleen (2009), *Statistical Panic: Cultural Politics and Poetics of the Emotions*, Durham, NC: Duke University Press.

Zagarell, Sandra A. (1998), 'Narrative of Community: The Identification of a Genre', *Signs*, 13: 3, 498–527.

Zubeil, Francine (1993), *Panique Générale*, Marseille: Editions de l' Observatoire.

Index

Notes: 'n' denotes references to chapter notes; *italics* indicate illustrations.

Aaron, Michele, 128
Adams, Lisa Bonchek, 211, 212, 219
Adams, Rachel, 99
Ahmed, Sara, 84
AIDS, 10–11, 81, 133, 150n, 192–3, 209n
  memorial quilt, 59–60
allergies, 165–8, 172, 176n
alternative medicine, 30, 49n, 89, 122n, 134
animated documentary, and mental health, 177–80, 208n
  'excess' and bearing witness, 194–9, 206–7
  testimonies, reception and influence, 199–207
  voice in, 191–5, 209n
  workings/function, 181–91
  see also *Animated Minds* (short film series; Glynne)
Animated Minds (short film series; Mosaic Films; Glynne), 21–2, 178–207, 208n
  An Alien in the Playground, 185, 187, 190, *191*

Becoming Invisible, 185, 188, 190–1, 192, 201, 203–4
Dimensions, 184, 200, 204
Fish on a Hook, 187, 188–9, *189*, 198, 202
The Light Bulb Thing, 188, 192, 198
My Blood is My Tears, 187, 188, 189–90, 197, 201, 202, 203, 205–6
Obsessively Compulsive, 185–6, *186*, 194, 197
Over and Over (and Over) Again, 186, 192, 205
  see also animated documentary, and mental health
Antonetti, Martin, 72
Anzaldúa, Gloria, 116, 124n
Aristotle, 50n
artists' books, 51–5, 85n
  and breast cancer treatment, 63–75, 87n
  and doctor-patient relationships, 75–85
  within the medical humanities, 55–8

physical form, and sense of touch, 58–63, 81, 83, 84–5, 86n
and witnessing, 196
authorship, and 'relational' narratives, 156, 161–2
autism, 178, 195, 208n, 209n
autobiography, 8, 37, 56–7, 154–8, 174, 180

Bailes, Sara Jane, 127, 161, 162, 175n
Bataille, Georges, 42
Bazin, André, 139, 140
Bell, Susan E., 60–1
Belling, Catherine, 83
Benjamin, Walter, 216
Benson, Peter, 94–5
Berlant, Lauren, 160
Best, Clare, 51–2
Beuys, Joseph, 41–2
Bleakley, Alan, 8, 82, 93, 164
blogs/blogging, 212–13, 214–16, 221n, 222n
body
　animated, purpose and effect, 186–90, *189*, *191*
　association with books and paper, 51, 58–9, 84, 189–90, 206
　clothing and ornaments, 68
　and the face, 194, 209n
　female, 27, 32, 43–5, 46–7, 49, 50n, 55–6
　and performance art, spectacle and extreme, 95–105, *98*, *100*, 214–15
　sense of touch, and artists' books, 58–63, 81, 83, 84–5, 86n

　and voice, 192–3, 194
　see also death; palimpsest
Bolaki, Stella, father's story, 1–3
book-making, 51–2, 53, 72, 75; *see also* Hall, Martha A., and artists' books
books, artists' *see* artists' books
Bouldin, Joanna, 187
Bracken, Patrick, 202
breast cancer
　and online documentation, 211, 215–16
　treatment culture, and artists' books, 63–75, 87n
　see also photography, and breast cancer
Brecht, Bertolt, 128, 161
Brody, Howard, 8, 9
Brodzinski, Emma, 162–3
Bronfen, Elizabeth, 130
Brown, Allison Cooke, 87n
Broyard, Anatole, 66–7, 78, 134, 212
Bruzzi, Stella, 149n
Burgin, Victor, 7
Burnett, Ron, 151n

Campo, Rafael, 51, 66, 133
cancer *see* breast cancer; photography, and breast cancer; liver cancer
Cancer Journals, The (Lorde) *see* Lorde, Audre, *The Cancer Journals*: and readings on photography
Carel, Havi, 71–2
Carnell, Simon, 41, 42
Carolin, Clare, 29
Cartwright, Lisa, 33
Chardin, Jean-Baptiste-Siméon, 42
Charon, Rita, 9, 76–7, 82–3

Chion, Michel, 192
chronic fatigue syndrome (CFS), 166–7, 175n
collaboration
　and animated documentary, 181–2, 197–8
　online, and peer-to-peer, 213, 222n
collaborative film, as terminal care, 125–8, 150n
　editing, 128–31
　and ethics, 129–30, 131–7, 142–3, 146–7, 149n
　on video and cinema, 137–43
　and writing *vs.* visual image, 143–9
concealment *see* visibility/concealment
Conway, Kathlyn, 181
Corrigan, Timothy, 133
Costa, Lucy, 207
Couser, Thomas G., 4, 9, 131, 149n
Crimp, Douglas, 11
Croce, Arlene, 10–11
cures
　La Mia Cura Open Source (Open Source Cure), 213, 222n
　personal notion of, 147–8

Daily Mail, The (newspaper), 46
de Bloois, Joost, 29, 37
death
　and readings on collaborative film, 125–8, 134–5, 136, 138–40, 146
　and readings on digital narratives, 218, 219, 220
　and readings on performance art, 103–4, 109–10, 122n, 123n
　and readings on photography, 42, 44, 46
Debney, Patricia, 214
Dennett, Terry, 30, 31, 32, 46
Derrida, Jacques, 60
diagnosis, and mental health problems, 204–5
diary entries, 143–5, 151n
　and artists' books, 56
Diedrich, Lisa
　on breast cancer culture, 28, 49n
　on failure in medicine, 80, 127
　and illness narratives, 10, 12, 57, 116, 133, 142–3
digital era, and artists' books, 53, 85n
digital narratives, 23, 211–21, 221n, 222n
Dillon, Sarah, 108
dissection, 102, 123n
doctor-patient relationships, 30–1, 33–4, 54–5, 66–8, 72–3, 75–85, 86n
documentary *see* animated documentary, and mental health; collaborative film, as terminal care; theatre, and expert knowledge
Dooks, Chris, 124n
Drucker, Johanna, 53, 54, 55, 57, 64, 78
Dubriwny, Tasha N., 38, 50n

Eakin, Paul, 156
eating disorders, 203–4
Edson, Margaret, 152–3, 158, 159, 175n
Egan, Susanna, 9, 135–6
Ehrenreich, Barbara, 38, 67, 73, 74

Elsey, Judy, 59–60
endings, of illness narratives, 173–4
Ensler, Eve, 172
environmental medicine, 167, 176n
Estrada, Maria Alejandra, *100*
ethics
   of collaboration and filmmaking, 129–30, 131–7, 142–3, 146–7, 149n, 182
   live tweeting, and death, 218–19, 220
   and touch, 58–63
ethnography, 94–5, 99, 103, 122n
expert knowledge *see* theatre, and expert knowledge

Facebook (website), 214, 215, 216, 220
Fadiman, Anne, 24n, 122n
failure, artistic and medical, 80, 127–8, 162–3
Farmer, Paul, 104–5
Felski, Rita, 10
feminist responses to illness, 4, 15, 16
   and artists' books, 55–6, 74–5
   and breast cancer, 33–4, 38, 39, 40–1, 43, 47, 48–9, 50n
   and eating disorders, 203–4
   and the female body, 27, 32, 43–5, 46–7, 49, 50n, 55–6
   and theatre, 172
Fennell, Dana, 205
Fernández-Morales, Marta, 172
film *see* animated documentary, and mental health; collaborative film, as terminal care

Foucault, Michel, 168
Frank, Arthur, 4, 5, 9, 24n, 77, 78, 101, 201, 210n, 212
Freud, Sigmund, 187–8, 209n
Fusco, Coco, 99–100, 122n

Gardner, Lyn, 174
Garland-Thomson, Rosemarie, 99, 146–7
Gawande, Atul, 127, 136
Geller, Matthew, 56
Gilman, Sander L., 183
Glynne, Andy, and animated documentary, 188, 197, 199, 201; *see also Animated Minds* (short film series; Mosaic Films; Glynne)
Gómez-Peña, Guillermo, and performance art, 17–18, 88–90
   and the body, 90–105, *98*, *100*
   personal illness, and palimpsest, 105–15, 124n
   practice of, and personal illness, 115–19
   provocation and the political, 119–21
   and radical pedagogy, 90–5, 122n
   Brownout 2, 104, 105–15, 124n
   Califas 2000, 123n
   El Cuerpo Diferente, 115
   Ethno-Techno, 88, 89, 90, 93, 99, 101, 122n
   'Gómez-Peña on Illness, the Human Body, Performance and Quantum Physics', 115, 118–19
   Guatinaui World Tour, The (and Fusco), 99–100

Gómez-Peña (*Cont.*)
  'In Defense of Performance',
    88, 113
  Mapa/Corpo, 100, 100–1, 103
  *The New Barbarians
    Collection*, 99
  No Portraits, 97, 98
Grigsby, Darcy Grimaldo, 45
Grover, Jan Zita, 11
Guardian, The (newspaper),
  211, 221n
Gurdon, Meghan Cox, 200–1

Hall, Martha A.
  and artists' books, 16–17,
    51–8, 85n, 119, 196, 197
  books, physical form, 58–9,
    60–3, 61, 64, 69 86n
  and the doctor-patient
    relationship, 75–85, 80, 87n
  and medical culture, 63–75,
    81, 86n
  Anxiety (to Martin Antonetti),
    72
  Black Box, 64, 65
  Ghost Friends, 87n
  I Make Books (documentary),
    72, 74, 75, 79, 84, 119
  It's Nothing, 80–1
  Jane, with Wings, 60–3,
    61, 66
  Just to Know, 65–6, 67, 73
  Legacy, 76, 78, 79, 86n
  Paper Passages (Hall and
    Brown), 87n
  Playing with Fire, 68, 86n
  Prescriptions, 69–71
  Rest of My Life, The, 68–9,
    72, 196, 197
  Rest of My Life II, The,
    69, 70
  Small Rooms, 67–8
  Tattoo, 77
  Tell Me, 84
  Test Day, 66, 67, 73, 74, 81
  Voices: Five Doctors Speak,
    76–8, 79–80, 80, 86n
  *What You Don't Want To
    Know*, 64–5
Hallas, Roger, 192, 193, 194,
  209n, 214
Hammid, Hella, 31–3, 35, 37,
  38, 39, 51, 54
Hawkins, Anne Hunsaker, 4, 9,
  14–15
health
  and healing and recovery,
    116–18
  within illness, 71–2
  and personal responsibility,
    111–12
  see also illness; wellness
Health 2.0, 23, 212–14, 222n
Heddon, Deirdre, 155–6
Helck, Emily, 215–16
Herndl, Diane Price, and
  readings on photography,
    15, 16, 26–7, 28–9, 38
  and failure, 127
  and masking, 183
  and medical technology,
    66, 97
  and politics of visibility,
    39–40, 41, 43–4, 45, 47, 48,
    49, 81, 106
Hesse, Monica, 218, 219
Hogarth, William, 102
Hooker, Claire, 95
Höttges, Bärbel, 212
Hubert, Renée Riese and Judd
  D., 55–6, 86n
Hunter, William, 103

Iaconesi, Salvatore, 213–14, 222n
illness
  and artistic practice, 115–19, 124n
  as basis for art, 125–7, 138
  and terminology, 164–5
  works on *vs.* works about, 197–9
illness narratives, 1–3, 24n
  case studies, 12–23
  and the critical medical humanities, 3–12, 24n, 25n
  features, 67
  on 'illness as many narratives', 3, 12, 14, 23
  role, 57–8
illustration, and illness, 183
immigration/migrants, 17, 99–104, 108–9, 110–11, 112–14, 171
infantilisation, women patients', 30–1, 33–4, 73–4, 76
interloping, critical, 12–15, 28, 57, 88, 131, 153, 177, 195, 221

Jacob, Clarissa, 216
Jansen, Peter W., 127
Jarman, Derek, 192–3, 194, 209n
Jodorowsky, Alejandro, 117
Jones, Bill T., 10–11
Jordanova, Ludmilla, 89
Jost, Jon, 125, 130
Jurecic, Ann, 10, 12, 24n, 122n

Keller, Bill, 211, 221n
Keller, Emma, 221n
Kiberd, Roisin, 220

Kilby, Jane, 206
King, Susan E., 68, 86n
Kirmayer, Laurence J., 175n
Klawiter, Maren, 33, 49
Kleinman, Arthur, 3–4, 94–5, 165
Kolgen, Claudia, 87n
Kron, Lisa, *Well* and theatre, 20–1, 152–5, 174n
  life and messiness *vs.* coherence, 170–4
  and professional structures, 158–64
  as solo show *vs.* 'relational' narrative, 155–8, 182
  and wellness *vs.* illness, 164–70
  2.5 Minute Ride, 152, 155, 161
  Facing Life's Problems, 173
Kuppers, Petra, 96, 106

La Mia Cura Open Source (Open Source Cure), 213, 222n
Langellier, Kristin M., 31, 34, 82
Leibovitz, Annie, 125–6
Levinas, Emmanuel, 60, 85, 86n, 92, 147, 194, 209n
Libera, Ana S. Q., 205
lifestyle, and controlling health, 50n, 111–12, 170–4
Lightning over Water (Wenders) *see* Wenders, Wim, film and *Lightning over Water*
liver cancer, 34, 64
liver disease, 3, 18, 107, 112, 115

Lorde, Audre, *The Cancer Journals*
  and readings on animated documentary, 22, 202
  and readings on artists' books, 71
  and readings on digital narratives, 215, 216
  and readings on performance art, 112, 115, 117
  and readings on photography, 15–16, 26–9, 33–4, 38, 39–40, 43, 44–5, 47, 48, 49n
  and readings on theatre, 172
  A Burst of Light, 33–4, 71, 117
Lovejoy, Margot, 86n
Lyons, Joan, 55

McCarney, Scott L., 86n
McCartney, Mary, 46
McCloud, Scott, 193, 194, 209n
McLane, Janice, 206
McLellan, Faith, 217, 222n
Macneill, Paul Ulhas, 90, 97
Maitland, Sara, 216
mantináda, 2, 23n
Margolles, Teresa, 123n
Marks, Laura, 141–2
Marshall, Robert, 164
Martin, Rosy, 30, 73
Martinez, Ursula, 174
masks, and animation, 190–1
Mattingly, Cheryl, 6–7
Matuschka, 34–5, 36, 37, 38, 39
MCS (multiple chemical sensitivity), 166–7, 175n

ME (myalgic encephalomyelitis), 166–7, 175n
Medfest 2012 (film festival), 178–9, 208n
medical animation, 180, 209n
medical care, right to, 103, 104–5
medical humanities, 3–12, 24n, 25n
  and artists' books, 55–8
  case studies and, 12–23
  and digital humanities, 213, 222n
  and health humanities, 21, 24n, 178, 207
  instrumental *vs.* critical, 3–12, 15, 23, 24n, 25n, 57–8, 91, 220–1
  phenomenological approaches to illness, 181, 196, 209n
  see also performance art, and medical humanities
medical pedagogy, 8–9, 25n, 88
  and animated documentary, 208n
  and artists' books, 54–5, 77, 83
  and performance art, 88, 89, 93–5, 103, 122n
  theatre as, 152–3, 159–60, 162–3, 175n
medical profession
  expert knowledge, and theatre, 155, 157–64, 166
  and failure, 127–8, 149n
medical records, hacking into, 213, 222n
medicalisation, of the body, 33–4, 102, 167
medication, 69–71
medicine, alternative, 30, 49n, 89, 122n, 134

memoir, 10, 57, 129, 149n, 216–17
mental health *see* animated documentary, and mental health
metaphor, 7, 41–3, 44, 50n, 188–91, 196–7
Metzger, Deena, 31–3, 35, 37, 38, 39, 51, 54
Miles, Lizzy, 218
Millar, Jeremy, 36–7
Miller, Susan, 172
Mills, Letha, 78–9
Minich, Julie Avril, 104, 113
Mitchell, Breon, 58, 63
Montgomery, Kathryn, 127–8
Moore, Samantha, 179, 180, 182
Mulvey, Laura, 139
Murphy, Robert, 123n

narratives, illness *see* illness narratives
National Cancer Institute, 64
New York Times, The (newspaper), 211
New York Times Magazine, The (magazine), 35
New Yorker, The (magazine), 10–11
Nichols, Bill, 182
Nick's Film - Lightning over Water (Wenders) *see* Wenders, Wim, film and *Lightning over Water*
Nixon, Nicholas, 11
Noonan, Estelle, 95

Observer, The (newspaper), 35
Obsessive Compulsive Disorder (OCD), 205
Obsessively Compulsive (short film; Glynne), 185–6, *186*, 194, 197
Over and Over (and Over) Again (short film; Glynne), 186, 192, 205
Oliver, Kelly, 63, 85, 87n
online *see* digital narratives
Open Source Cure (La Mia Cura Open Source), 213, 222n
Orlan, 89, 90, 95–6, 97
O'Rourke, Meghan, 219, 220

palimpsest
 and breast cancer representations, 31, 33, 43, 44, 64
 and performance art, 104, 105–15, 214–15
patients, within the medical community, 94–5, 103, 122n, 202
 doctor-patient relationships, 30–1, 33–4, 54–5, 66–8, 72–3, 75–85, 86n
 testimonies, reception and influence, 199–207
Pattison, Stephen, 153
Payer, Lynn, 71
Paz, Octavio, 109, 116
pedagogy *see* medical pedagogy
performance art
 artistic practice and illness, 115–19, 124n
 and the body, extreme and spectacle, 95–105, *98*, *100*
 and medical humanities, 82–3, 88–90
 and palimpsest, 104, 105–15, 214–15

performance art (*Cont.*)
  and provocation, 90–1, 119–21
  and radical pedagogy, 90–5
  spectacle, extreme bodies and invisible surgeries, 95–105, 214–15
  vs. theatre, 94, 122n
  see also theatre, and expert knowledge
photography
  and death, 125–6
  and narrative, 7, 29
  of people and illness, 11
photography, and breast cancer, 26–9
  breast cancer photography (Spence; Taylor-Wood), 29–39, *32*, *36*
  politics of voice and/or visible self, 33–5, 39–49, 124n
Pirandello, Luigi, 157, 175n
political, the
  and animated documentary, 182–3
  and artists' books, 56, 57, 74–5
  and performance art, 90–5, 97–104, 99, *100*, 111–13, 122n
  and photography, 33–5, 39–49
  and theatre, 168–71
postmodern/postmodernism, 4, 28, 40, 105, 179
Prendergast, Catherine, 203

Radley, Alan, 10–11, 60–1, 79, 195–6, 197, 198
Randolph, Dr Theron G., 167, 176n

Ray, Nicholas, 20, 56, 125, 131, *141*, 148–9, 151n
  cure, notion of, 147–8
  and ethics of filming illness, 129–30, 131–7, 142–3, 146–7, 149n
  as filmmaker's subject, 126–7, 128–9, 130, 131
  handwritten diary, 143–5, 151n
  and video images of, 137–43
reading, and artists' books, 62–3, 83
Reiheld, Alison, 167
Rembrandt van Rijn, 102
Renov, Michael, 136
Rimmon-Kenan, Shlomith, 62–3
Roberts, David, 46
Roe, Annabelle Honess, 184, 194, 195
romanticising illness, and animation, 200–2, 209n
Rossiter, Kate, 147
Russell, Catherine, 142

Sabiston, Bob, 209n
Sawday, Jonathan, 102
schizophrenia, 86n, 200, 201, 203, 204
Schweitzer, Mary, 175n
Sedgwick, Eve Kosofsky, 45, 106, 111
self-harm, 190, 205–6
SEMEFO (art group), 123n
Shafer, Audrey, 12–13, 221
Shapiro, Johanna, 25n, 159
Shaw, Peggy, 124n
Sheard, Tim, 31
Shorter, Edward, 168
Showalter, Elaine, 175n

Sifuentes, Roberto, 101, 107
Silverman, Leigh, 152
Simon, Scott, 217–19, 220
skin *see* body
Sobchack, Vivian, 105–6, 126, 136–7, 143
social media, 211–21, 221n, 222n
Sontag, Susan, 125–6, 147, 167
soul, 66–7
Spence, Jo
  photography, and breast cancer, 26, 27–8, 29–40, 44–6, 47–8, 49, 49n, 50n, 124n
  and readings on animated documentary, 21
  and readings on artists' books, 64, 65, 73, 74
  and readings on digital narratives, 215, 216
  and readings on performance art, 96, 101, 121, 124n
  works, within the medical community, 13–14
  Beyond the Family Album, 29–30
  Cancer Project, The (exhibition), 31
  The Final Project, 46, 50n
  Infantilization (Spence; Martin), 30, 31
  Marked Up for Amputation (Spence; Dennett), 31
  Narratives of Dis-ease (Excised, Exiled, Expected, Expunged, Included, undated) (Spence; Sheard), 31
  The Picture of Health? (exhibition), 26, 27–8, 31, 49n, 73–4

  Property of Jo Spence? (Spence; Dennett), 31–9, 32, 46, 49
  Putting Myself in the Picture (autobiography), 33
Squier, Susan Merrill, 9, 14–15
Stelarc, 96–7
Strawson, Galen, 221n
Svenaeus, Fredrik, 187

Tanner, Laura, 59, 60
Taylor-Wood, Sam (*later* Taylor-Johnson)
  photography, and breast cancer, 26, 27–8, 35–9, 36, 41–7, 50n, 81
  work as case study, 15–16
  Ascension, 44
  Bound Ram, 37
  Five Revolutionary Seconds, 41
  Fuck/Suck/Spank/Wank, 37, 38
  Harper's Bazaar portrait (McCartney), 46–7, 50n
  A Little Death, 42, 43
  Mute, 41
  Poor Cow, 37
  Self Portrait as a Tree, 37, 42
  Self Portrait in a Single Breasted Suit with Hare, 26, 35–9, 36, 40, 41–7, 49, 50n
  Self Portrait Suspended (photo series), 43
  Slut, 37
  Strings, 41
technology
  and the body, in performance art, 96–7
  and body reconstruction, 43–4

technology (*Cont.*)
  and filmmaking, impact, 132, 137–43, 150n
  medical, and artists' books, 66–7, 81–2
  see also digital narratives
testimonies, reception and influence, 199–207
theatre, and expert knowledge, 152–5
  autobiographical and 'relational' narratives, 155–8
  control/messiness, wellness *vs.* sickness, 170–4
  illness and wellness, in the individual and community, 164–70
  professional structures and expert knowledge, 155, 157–64, 166
  see also performance art, and medical humanities
Thomas, Philip, 202
time, as theme in artists' books, 68–9, 72
Tobin, Amy, 216
touch, sense of, and artists' books, 58–63, 81, 83, 84–5, 86n
tuberculosis, 147–8, 168
Tuttle, Jennifer, 83
Twitter (website), 118, 211, 212, 217–19, 220, 222n

Underhill, Linn, 56

verbatim theatre, 156, 197
Verghese, Abraham, 81, 133
Viera, Evan, 209n

visibility/concealment
  and breast cancer, 33–5, 37–8, 39–49
  of illness, politics of, 182–3
  masks, and animation, 190–1
  see also witnessing, implications of
voice
  in animated documentary, 191–5, 209n
  and censorship, 215
  vs. speech, 192

Waddington, Keir, 8–9
Wall Street Journal (newspaper), 218
Walton, Judith May, 87n
Ward, Paul, 194
wellness
  lifestyle choices, and control, 170–4
  as term, 164–5
Wells, Paul, 180, 184
Wenders, Wim, film and *Lightning over Water*, 20, 125–8, 137, 148–9, 150n
  and documenting dying, 218, 219–20
  editing history of, 128–31
  ethics, illness and collaboration, 129–30, 131–7, 142–3, 146–7, 149n
  language, written *vs.* cinematic, 143–5, 150n
  and readings on animated documentary, 193–4, 196, 209n
  and readings on artists' books, 56–7

and readings on theatre, 21, 152, 153, 156, 158, 159, 161, 162, 170, 173, 174, 175n
truth and video, 137–43, *141*
The American Friend, 134, 150n
Back to Room 666 (Spolidoro), 138, 150n
Hammett, 143
'Impossible Stories' (talk/essay), 143
Notebook on Cities and Clothes, 130, 139, 150n
Weston, Heather, 86n
Whitehead, Anne, 8, 9, 127–8

Wikan, Unni, 202
Willis, Martin, 8–9
witnessing, implications of, 128, 138, 146–7, 155, 194–9, 206–7, 218, 219–20; *see also* visibility/concealment
Woods, Angela, 5–6, 7, 8, 24n, 207
Woodward, Kathleen, 216–17
writing, 170, 218–19

X-rays, 71, 81

Zubeil, Francine, 86n

EU representative:
Easy Access System Europe
Mustamäe tee 50, 10621 Tallinn, Estonia
Gpsr.requests@easproject.com

www.ingramcontent.com/pod-product-compliance
Lightning Source LLC
Chambersburg PA
CBHW061710300426
44115CB00014B/2630